Protest Movements in 1960s
West Germany

Protest Movements in 1960s West Germany

A Social History of Dissent and Democracy

Nick Thomas

Oxford • New York

First published in 2003 by
Berg
Editorial offices:
150 Cowley Road, Oxford, OX4 1JJ, UK
838 Broadway, Third Floor, New York, NY 10003–4812, USA

Berg is an imprint of Oxford International Publishers Ltd.

Library of Congress Cataloging-in-Publication Data
Thomas, Nick, 1970-
    Protest movements in 1960s West Germany : a social history of
dissent and democracy / Nick Thomas.
        p. cm.
Includes bibliographical references and index.
        ISBN 1-85973-645-9 (cloth) — ISBN 1-85973-650-5 (pbk.)
    1. Social movements—Germany (West)—History—20th century.
2. Protest movements—Germany (West)—History—20th century. I.
Title.
        HN445.5 .T476 2003
        303.48'4'0943—dc21

                                                                2002151465

British Library Cataloguing-in-Publication Data
A catalogue record for this book is available from the British Library.

ISBN   1 85973 645 9 (Cloth)
        1 85973 650 5 (Paper)

Typeset by JS Typesetting Ltd, Wellingborough, Northants.
Printed in the United Kingdom by Biddles Ltd, Guildford and King's Lynn.

For Gaby

Contents

Contents

Acknowledgements

In the English-speaking world Germans have a reputation for being cold, arrogant, humourless authoritarians, applying rules and regulations unquestioningly while working themselves into the ground. Germans protest at this image of themselves with complete justification. Throughout the research for this book I have consistently experienced hospitality, generosity, and warmth of spirit wherever I have gone and have regularly been taken aback by the almost complete absence of rules in many archives, to an extent that would make most British archivists weep.

I must first acknowledge the debt of gratitude I owe to the Arts Faculty Research Committee and the Research Development Committee of the Open University for providing me with the necessary funds to make my research possible. My colleagues in the Department of History at the Open University, especially the members of the Sixties Research Group, have been a constant source of support and advice. The regular day-conferences held by the Sixties Research Group have also been an invaluable forum for testing some of the ideas put forward in this book. I have been particularly lucky in finding such welcoming colleagues at Nottingham University, where this book was finished.

Archives across Germany have been consulted, and my task has been made easier by a number of people who deserve special mention. At the Bundesarchiv Koblenz, Dr Koops and the capable Reading Room staff deserve thanks for pointing me in some useful directions. Dorothee Ledig and Jürgen Bacia at the Archiv für Alternatives Schrifftum in NRW, Duisburg, were patient beyond the call of duty in one of the most unusually situated archives (in a converted school) I've ever come across. Staff at the Institut für Zeitgeschichte in München and the Landesarchiv Berlin were unfailingly generous with their time. Also in Berlin, the Archiv 'APO und soziale Bewegungen', Fachbereich Politische Wissenschaft der Freien Universität Berlin (ehem. ZI 6) is perhaps the most eccentrically organized archive I've ever used, as well as one of the richest. I am grateful to Siegeward Lönnendonker for allowing me almost completely unsupervised access to this vast collection. Special mention, however, is reserved for Barbara Brohmeyer at the Dokumentationsstelle für unkonventionelle

Acknowledgements

Literatur, Bibliothek für Zeitgeschichte, Stuttgart, and for Reinhart Schwarz at the Hamburger Institut für Sozialforschung. Both preside over archival treasure houses with professionalism, patience and humour.

Accommodation in Germany was a particularly difficult issue, and I was lucky enough to rent rooms from several people during their absence from Germany. My thanks go to Sharno Willy in Stuttgart, Alexandra Surer in Schwabing, Munich and Svenja Blanke in Schöneberg, Berlin. I also need to express my heartfelt gratitude to my parents-in-law, Erwin and Anna Neher, and to Marcus, Uwe, Armin and Robin Neher, for their support while I was in Germany. My sister-in-law, Conny Neher, deserves a special note of thanks for all her hard work in sorting out my accommodation in Munich and for her hospitality throughout my visit.

In Britain, Richard Temple at the Modern Records Centre of the University of Warwick has been, as ever, a fount of information and sage advice, while the German Historical Institute in London has provided an excellent working environment. The theories, and the mistakes, included here are my own, but I must acknowledge the useful new insights I have been given by a number of fellow historians, including Holger Nehring, Gerry Carlin, Mark Jones, Niek Pas, Axel Schildt, Detlef Siegfried, Wilfried Mausbach, Klaus Weinhauer and the late Hans Righart. At Berg Joanne Hutt, Samantha Jackson, Kathryn Earle and Kathleen May, have been unwavering in their patience, efficiency, and enthusiasm. Thanks also to the anonymous reader, and to George Pitcher for his sterling work as copy-editor.

My warmest thanks are reserved for my wife, Gaby Thomas-Neher, who has put up with my long absences in Germany, and much else besides, without complaint. Her boundless energy and her composure in the face of demands from all quarters are inspirational. Completing this project without her assistance, and especially her advice on all things German, would have been impossible.

Preface

I came to this project in April 1998 after completing my PhD on student protest in Britain in the 1960s. The project had been set up before my arrival within the Sixties Research Group of the History Department at the Open University and was originally intended as a continuation of the work begun by Arthur Marwick in his book, *The Sixties*. This was published shortly after I arrived in the Department. Upon starting the research as a full-time Research Fellow I soon realized that the original remit, on youth in 1960s Germany, was impossibly ambitious and so I narrowed the parameters to include only the protest movements of the 1960s. This was a major deviation from the original plan that made it possible for me to explore some of the themes and interests I had developed during my doctoral research. I therefore came to the project as a 1960s historian rather than as a German historian, a difference that may be lost on some, but which will no doubt cause indignation for others.

This does not mean that I came to the project with a fixed set of ideas about either the 1960s or post-war Germany. My acceptance of the generational model, albeit modified by the application of other ideas, has entailed a reversal of the position I held during my doctoral work. This rethink was prompted by the convincing arguments presented by James Hinton and John Stevenson, the internal and external examiners for my PhD. Above all, the sources have dictated the theory, rather than the other way around, since much previous work has presented a picture of the decade that is unrecognizable from the original sources.

Nick Thomas,
University of Nottingham

List of Abbreviations

AFAS   Archiv für Alternatives Schrifftum in Nordrhein Westfalia, Duisburg (Archive for Alternative Literature in North Rhein Westphalia, Duisburg).

APO   *Außerparlamentarische Opposition* (Extra-Parliamentary Opposition).

APOusB   *Archiv 'APO und soziale Bewegungen', Fachbereich Politische Wissenschaft der Freien Universität Berlin (ehem. ZI 6)* (Archive 'APO and Social Movements', School of Political Science of the Free University Berlin, formerly ZI 6).

AstA   *Allgemeiner Studentenausschuß* (General Student Committee).

BfZS   *Dokumentationstelle für unkonventionelle Literatur, Bibliothek für Zeitgeschichte, Stuttgart* (Document Store for Unconventional Literature, Library for Contemporary History, Stuttgart).

BK   *Bundesarchiv Koblenz* (Federal Archive, Koblenz).

BRD   *Bundesrepublik Deutschland* (Federal Republic of Germany).

CDU   *Christlich-Demokratische Union* (Christian-Democratic Union).

CSU   *Christlich-Soziale Union* (Christian-Social Union).

DDR   *Deutsche Demokratische Republik* (German Democratic Republic).

DGB   *Deutscher Gewerkschaftsbund* (German Trade Union Federation).

FDJ   *Freie Deutsche Jugend* (Free German Youth).

FDP   *Freie Demokratische Partei* (Free Democratic Party).

FU   *Freie Universität, Berlin* (Free University, Berlin).

GASt   *Gewerkschaftlicher Arbeitskreis der Studenten* (Student Trade Union Working Group).

GSG 9   *Grenzschutz Gruppe 9* (Border Security Group 9).

HifS   *Hamburger Institut für Sozialforschung* (Hamburg Institute for Social Research).

HSU   *Humanistische Studentenunion* (Humanist Student Union).

IdK   *Internationale der Kriegdienstgegner* (International of the Opponents of War).

List of Abbreviations

IfZM	*Institut für Zeitgeschichte, München* (Institute for Contemporary History, Munich).
KdA	*Kampf dem Atomtod* (Fight Nuclear Death).
KfA	*Kampagne für Abrüstung* (Campaign for Disarmament).
KfDA	*Kampagne für Demokratie und Abrüstung* (Campaign for Democracy and Disarmament).
KOM	*Kriminalobermeister* (Detective, roughly equivalent of Sergeant).
KPD	*Kommunistische Partei Deutschlands* (Communist Party of Germany).
KU	*Kritische Universität* (Critical University).
LB	*Landesarchiv Berlin* (Berlin State Archive).
LSD	*Liberaler Studentenbund Deutschlands* (Liberal Student Federation of Germany).
NHB	*Nationaldemokratischer Hochschulbund* (National Democratic University Federation).
NPD	*Nationaldemokratische Partei Deutschlands* (National Democratic Party of Germany).
NRW	Nordrhein-Westfalia (North Rhein Westphalia).
OMGUS	Occupation Military Government, United States.
POM	*Polizeiobermeister* (Police Officer, roughly equivalent of Sergeant).
RAF	*Rote Armee Fraktion* (Red Army Faction).
RC	*Republikanischer Club* (Republican Club).
RCDS	*Ring Christlich-Demokratischer Studenten* (Circle of Christian-Democratic Students).
SDS	*Sozialistische Deutsche Studentenbund* (Socialist German Student Federation).
SED	*Sozialistische Einheitspartei Deutschlands* (Socialist Unity Party of Germany).
SEW	*Sozialistische Einheitspartei Westberlins* (Socialist Unity Party of West Berlin).
SHB	*Sozialdemokratischer Hochschulbund* (Social Democratic University Federation).
SJD	*Sozialistische Jugend Deutschlands–Die Falken* (Socialist Youth of Germany–The Falcons).
SNCC	Student Nonviolent Coordinating Committee (From 1960 to Summer 1967. After this, Student National Coordinating Committee).
SPD	*Sozialdemokratische Partei Deutschlands* (Social Democratic Party of Germany).

List of Abbreviations

SRP	*Sozialistische Reichspartei* (Socialist Reich Party).
TU	*Technische Universität* (Technical University).
VDS	*Verband Deutscher Studentenschaften* (Union of German Student Societies).
WRK	*Westdeutsche Rektorenkonferenz* (West German Rector's Conference).

Introduction

The 1960s usually provoke extreme reactions and until recently taking a
balanced view of the 1960s has been rare. It has either been seen as the
best of times or the worst of times, with little option for the middle ground
between the two.[1] Yet the easy categories in which the 1960s are often
placed are not readily applicable to West Germany's 1960s. For West
Germany, the 1960s were complex years of change in the wake of military
defeat, when the *Bundesrepublik* (Federal Republic) suffered intense
shocks and growing pains on the road to political maturity. Central to that
process were the protest movements that were front-page news throughout
the period. These events are undoubtedly controversial, but to utilize
historical analysis to produce a panegyric to, or denunciation of, the 1960s
would be to produce a distorted picture that fails to appreciate the importance of the decade for German society, whether for good or for ill. Instead
I intend to produce a detailed and rounded picture of events, in the context
of social change and wider international events. This allows for new
interpretations not just of the protests, but also of their impact on Germany
in subsequent decades.

Looking at the often contradictory ways in which protests were viewed
by contemporaries raises important questions about the meaning and
nature of 'democracy' in West Germany in the 1960s, and will be central
to the discussion throughout. Germany's unique recent past, especially the
twelve years of Nazi rule and the Cold War division of Germany, played
a key role in forming opinions about 1960s protests. People with a wide
range of viewpoints could claim to be defending democracy, and it is important to understand this in the light of fears brought about by Germany's
past. For instance, for many participants, protests were a method of introducing reform to a state and society that was perceived as authoritarian,
conservative and traditionalist. Protests strengthened the new democratic
credentials of the young *Bundesrepublik* by encouraging a greater popular
participation in the political process, the development of individual critical
thought and a popular sense of political responsibility. This could, for

1. Perhaps Bloom, A., *The Closing of the American Mind* and Collier, P. and Horowitz,
D., *Destructive Generation* are the most well known anti-1960s texts.

some, also have been a means of encouraging popular identity with the emergent Republic in contrast to the widespread apathy to Weimar democracy and the subsequent descent into Nazism.

In contrast, many members of the general public, or those in authority, viewed protests as a challenge to the democratic order. They were a repetition of the conflict and instability of the Weimar years, and threatened to plunge West Germany into another period of dictatorship, this time under communists, just as it was regaining its economic and political place in the world. This broad view could encompass a wide variety of attitudes, from the liberal to the extreme, that highlighted the legacy of the past and resultant fears for the future. Many comments by the public indicate attitudes to democracy that owed much to the experience of Nazi rule, including anti-communist attitudes that continued through to the Cold War. The *Bundesrepublik*, a democracy, was seen as the best hope for peace, prosperity and international acceptance. Support for the *Bundesrepublik* therefore meant support for democracy, while criticism of the *Bundesrepublik* was a threat to both stability and, by definition, democracy. In these circumstances loyalty to 'democracy' could be seen as compatible with attitudes that were fundamentally undemocratic. One member of the public responded to a 1967 Hamburg survey on attitudes to student protests by saying, 'the Police have done the right thing in being so strict with these [students]. They all belong in Forced Labour Camps. The insolent kids should know that democracy does not exist so that everyone can do what they want.'[2]

A similar survey in Berlin made it clear that many people blamed students for creating a dangerous atmosphere of conflict. One person told the students carrying out the survey 'you allow Easterners [communists], through provocateurs, to travel with you and to incite. The general populace of Berlin is against student riots'. An 'old Berliner' claimed 'we Berliners distance ourselves from Rowdies who behave like the last Mob [the Nazis]', while another demanded 'Students get out! When do you actually study! Rowdies!!! You should all be killed! The Police are still too humane.'[3] Many of these comments are undoubtedly extreme,

---

2. Schübel, R., 'Rowdies, Gammler und Schmarotzer: Reaktion der Bevölkerung auf studentische Demonstrationen', *Auditorium*, July 1967, no. 48, pp. 9–10, ZA 745, Hamburger Institut für Sozialforschung (henceforth HIfS). This was the student newspaper at Hamburg University.

3. 'Sonderinformation des Komitee für Öffentlichkeitsarbeit', B/166/1322, Bundesarchiv Koblenz (henceforth BK). The Free University (FU) Berlin AStA carried out this survey.

and necessarily give only a limited picture of public opinion in the 1960s, but they provide striking evidence that a number of issues from Germany's past remained unresolved. Indeed, the far left argued that the *Bundesrepublik* was essentially fascistic and undemocratic. It therefore had to be overthrown and replaced by a socialist model, initially through the employment of popular protest to undermine and destabilize the existing regime. Later, when this failed, some turned to the use of terrorism. Yet these are just some of the myriad ways in which the protests could be seen by contemporaries.

This picture of polarization is confirmed by the details of the protests themselves. The state response in particular highlighted an inability to countenance the variety of viewpoints that is essential to democracy. Heavy-handed police tactics included the use of baton charges and water cannon, and in the latter half of the decade several protesters were fatally wounded in clashes with police. On 2 June 1967 the student Benno Ohnesorg was even shot by a plain-clothes police officer during a particularly violent demonstration in Berlin. The officer was later acquitted of any criminal wrongdoing, thereby undermining faith in the justice system and raising suspicions of Establishment collusion. These concerns were further strengthened by the prosecution of protesters, often in dubious circumstances, and the suspension of constitutional guarantees, such as the banning of demonstrations in Berlin after Ohnesorg's death. A Grand Coalition of all parties was created in December 1966, removing effective parliamentary opposition and allowing the introduction of *Notstandsgesetze* (Emergency Laws) in May 1968, aimed at curtailing civil liberties in times of national crisis. Throughout the decade these events were reported to the German public by a predominantly right-wing press, dominated by Axel Springer's publishing empire, whose newspapers attacked demonstrators in rabid terms as fascists or Soviet-backed communists. When student leader Rudi Dutschke was shot by a right-wing fanatic in Berlin in April 1968, those who took part in the subsequent wave of protests blamed the vicious attacks on Dutschke in the Springer press for creating the atmosphere of hatred in which such an assassination attempt could take place.

A situation of action and reaction quickly became a vicious circle of self-fulfilling prophecies for both sides, in which all parties could claim to be defending democracy from extremism. As the decade proceeded, protesters responded to the actions of the state with increasing militancy, thereby confirming the worst fears of those in authority, and prompting even more extreme actions against protesters. Although most participants on both sides stayed within the boundaries of the law and the spirit of the existing parliamentary democracy, there can be little doubt that this democracy was challenged by the actions of groups on both sides. Withdrawing the right to demonstrate in Berlin, the West's showpiece frontier town in the heart of Communist East Germany, may have been an attempt to defend the state against forces that were perceived as undemocratic, but at the same time it removed basic democratic rights for Berliners. Similarly, the terrorism of the *Rote Armee Fraktion* (RAF) may have been an attempt to defend the Left against the oppression of state forces that were seen as undemocratic, and to overthrow those forces in the name of a more democratic alternative. Yet it undermined democratic rights in Germany, both inherently and by provoking a harsh and authoritarian response from the state. Nonetheless, post-war West Germany was essentially democratic in nature, and it will be a key argument of this book that the events of the 1960s, including the protest movements, were crucial in augmenting the foundations of its democracy. A country that was previously a stranger to parliamentary democracy embraced personal political involvement and the right and duty of citizens to question those in authority.

This took place in a context of wider social and cultural change in which social mores were undermined, traditions were challenged, institutions and relationships were fundamentally altered and new lifestyles were forged. The protests were both reflections of, and factors in, this social change. As a result of sustained post-war prosperity, opportunities for personal expression and experimentation were created and grasped. Established relationships, particularly attitudes to authority, were reassessed. This took place in parallel with similar developments throughout the Western world. The 1960s have often been blamed as the point of origin for the decline in 'social cohesion' that has supposedly marked Western societies since, and which governments of all political viewpoints have sought to address. It will be argued here that by misunderstanding the nature of the changes that took place in the 1960s, and particularly their origins, the complex social problems of subsequent decades have also been misunderstood.

This analysis is an addition to, and progression from, current debates on the German protest movements of the 1960s. Despite a profusion of titles on post-war German politics and foreign policy, literature in English on German social history, and especially on the protest movements, is rare. Yet there have been some useful critical studies that have created the foundations for balanced analysis of the period. The small volume *Protest and Democracy in West Germany* by Rob Burns and Wilfred van der Will is the only work devoted solely to the subject. There are also a small number of chapters in collected works, most notably in Carole Fink,

Philipp Gassert and Detlef Junker's excellent *1968: The World Transformed*, three chapters in Gerard DeGroot's *Student Protest*, and the limited attention given to 1968 in Mark Roseman's *Generations in Revolt*. Ronald Fraser's *1968: A Student Generation in Revolt* is an invaluable source of oral history testimony, but repeats a common problem with 1960s research by concentrating mainly upon high-profile student activists who were not representative of 'ordinary' protesters. Unfortunately, none of these titles can claim to provide a comprehensive and detailed survey of events in Germany. While carrying out research at the Dokumentationstelle für unkonventionelle Literatur in the Bibliothek für Zeitgeschichte in Stuttgart, one Australian historian told me that he 'didn't know Germany had had a Vietnam Campaign'. This says a lot about the absence of literature on the subject in English.

In German the period has been given more attention, though once again there is no single comprehensive survey. The importance attached to the events of the 1960s in Germany is attested to by the constant stream of books being published on the period: some bookshops even have shelves marked '1968 bewegung' within their History sections. Many of these books have filled specific gaps, such as Gerd Langguth's exhaustive study of the post-1968 Left in Germany, or Stefan Aust's definitive account of the *Rote Armee Fraktion*.[4] Others provide the perspective of different academic approaches, such as the sociological study of student protest in Berlin in the 1960s by Heinz Bude and Martin Kohli in their *Radikalisierte Aufklärung*. The more philosophical and abstract consideration of the meaning of 1968 is covered by a plethora of titles, among them Rainer Bieling's *Die Tränen der Revolution*, Oskar Negt's *Achtundsechzig*, and Wolfgang Kraushaar's *1968 als Mythos, Chiffre und Zäsur*.[5] There have even been collections of essays, most notably Ingrid Gilcher-Holtey's edited volume *1968*. Yet these titles are limited to individual aspects of the protest movements, or particular time periods. This also applies to the few historical analyses of the subject. Wolfgang Kraushaar's exhaustive three-volume study, *Frankfurter Schule und Studentenbewegung*, although definitive in its field, is limited to the student movement, and covers the whole period from 1946 to 1995.[6] The history of the student movement by Gerhard Bauß is the only thorough historical treatment of this subject

---

4. Langguth, G., *Protestbewegung*; Aust, S., *Der Baader-Meinhof Komplex*.

5. Other heavily theoretical works include Juchler, I., *Die Studentenbewegung in den Vereinigten Staaten und der Bundesrepublik Deutschland der sechziger Jahre*, Baier, L. et al., *Die Früchte der Revolte*, and Rolke, L., *Protestbewegung in der Bundesrepublik*.

6. Kraushaar W. (ed.), *Frankfurter Schule und Studentenbewegung*.

in German, but even this only starts in 1965.[7] This is one of the few books to make use of archive sources but, excellent though this book undoubtedly is, it was written as long ago as 1977 and the archive sources are almost entirely from one personal archive in Marburg. The other major work to make significant use of original source material, Karl A. Otto's study of the Extra-Parliamentary Opposition, provides an invaluable glimpse at the archival sources, but cannot be described as a historical analysis.[8]

Besides this singular lack of historical literature on the subject, there are a number of other problems. As with the study of 1960s protest movements in other countries, the available literature has been predominantly produced by participants themselves. Many of these works have been written by, and often also about, members of protest movements, with attendant biases and limitations.[9] Many previous titles have been dominated by the recollections of people who were high-profile members of political organizations, and who are not representative of ordinary protesters, or the 'poor bloody infantry' of protest movements. It cannot be denied that this has added to our knowledge of the period, but much work is informed by a limited Marxist discussion that continues the appropriation of the period for political purposes that has been a feature of the treatment of the 1960s by both Right and Left throughout the Western world.[10] There has been a resultant distortion of the picture, especially as regards the importance of 1968 as the key date and high point of the protests in Germany, and the voices of ordinary protesters have been all but lost.[11] Above all, there has been an almost total lack of analysis within a wider historical context, seeking to understand the protests as part of the enormous social and cultural changes taking place in Germany in the 1960s.[12]

7. Bauß, G., *Die Studentenbewegung der sechziger Jahre*. Kleßman, C., *Zwei Staaten, eine Nation*, pp. 256–98 is a brief account of the APO using original, mostly published, source material, with a good account of the crisis in higher education in the mid-1960s.

8. Otto, K.A., *Die außerparlamentarische Opposition in Quellen und Dokumenten 1960–1970*.

9. See for instance Landgrebe, C. and Plath, J. (eds), *'68 und die Folgen*; Cohn-Bendit, D. and Mohr, R., *1968*; and Mosler, P., *Was wir wollten, was wir wurden*.

10. Hermand, J., *Die Kultur der Bundesrepublik Deutschland 1965–1985* is a Marxist interpretation, while Wolfschlag, C.M. (ed.), *Bye-bye '68* is a series of essays from a Marxist perspective.

11. Besides the titles concentrating on 1968 already named, see François, E. et al. (eds), *1968*; Heinemann, K.H. and Jaitner, T, *Ein langer Marsch*; Uesseler, R., *Die 68er*; and Voigt, L., *Aktivismus und moralischer Rigorismus*.

12. An important exception has been Ruppert, W. (ed.), *Um 1968*.

There are therefore still a number of important gaps in the current literature that remain to be filled. Those seeking here for a history of post-war West German politics or society, or a comparative study of events in East and West Germany, a discussion of the dynamics of the crowd, or analyses of voting patterns, the role of religion in German politics and society, or the labour movement, will be disappointed. While some of these issues will be touched upon, they do not represent the central themes of this book. Similarly, although some attention will be given to the theoretical models that informed the far left of the 1960s, including the ideas of the Frankfurt School, this book is not intended as a history of post-war Marxism, nor an abstract philosophical discussion of Marxist theory. There is nevertheless a need for a survey of the whole period, which considers the whole range of protest movements within the wider context of social and cultural change, and which makes detailed use of archival research. This book sets out to perform these functions. Perhaps most importantly, there has been an emphasis upon historical method in the construction of a historical account of these events in English for the first time. This has meant extensive reference to archive sources from all over Germany, including research at archives in Koblenz, Duisburg, Hamburg, Stuttgart, Munich and Berlin. This has provided an invaluable overview of events in Germany as a whole, making it possible to produce a detailed history of protests throughout the country and throughout the period. The experiences of ordinary participants in protests can be included along with the historical analysis of events and trends so that human voices can be added to the account. Detailed information on individual events has also been uncovered that allows for previously impossible reconstructions of important events. The more rounded picture this produces, when placed in the wider context of the parallel events and changes in German society, makes it clear why 1967, and the Ohnesorg shooting in particular, was the turning point for protesters, 'the year that changed everything', rather than 1968.[13]

In terms of the subject matter discussed, an inclusive approach has been necessary. The term 'protest' has been taken to mean all forms of public demonstration of support or opposition, for or against policies, decisions or activities, by those in authority. This wide view means that actions ranging from the RAF bombing campaigns to marches to the satire and custard bombs of *Kommune I* are all deemed to be acts of protest. This also reflects the wide-ranging nature of the protests of the *außerparlament-arische Opposition* (APO). The APO was not a central organization, but

13. Kraushaar, W., *1968: Das Jahr, das alles verändert hat.*

was rather a collective term for a number of campaigns, by a variety of organizations, throughout the decade, making it difficult to define. Hans Karl Rupp notes that the term has often been mistakenly limited to the activities of groups centred on the SDS (*Sozialistische Deutsche Student-enbund* or Socialist German Student Federation) in attacking the 'Establishment'. He also argues that to concentrate solely upon political groups or organizations is to mistake the meaning of the APO, and suggests that when discussing the APO one is referring to 'Extra-parliamentary actions'. By this he means an all-inclusive definition, encompassing 'every attempt to mobilize the Mass media and (or) all contactable citizens for or against a *definite* political position'.[14] Karl A. Otto makes it clear not only that the term has been used interchangeably with 'student movement' and 'youth protest', but also that such narrow definitions fail to express the broad nature of the issues addressed by groups who can be identified as part of the APO. He suggests that the Peace Movement was the origin and natural centre of the APO from which the other movements sprang.[15]

The definition used here will be a critical interpretation of Rupp's and Otto's perspectives. Rupp's definition allows for the inclusion of oppositional activity by individuals as well as critical thought, writing and activity. It nonetheless also allows, because of its breadth, the potential inclusion of right-wing political activities by neo-Nazis who were also opposed to the *Bundesrepublik*. This would not be an accurate representation of the meaning of the term in the 1950s and 1960s, or provide a useful tool for the historian. Otto's definition, on the other hand, only deals with organizations. A middle ground will be followed here, including all liberal, left-liberal, social democratic, or socialist organizations, coalitions and individuals engaged in oppositional activity outside the parliamentary process that took a critical stance toward the parliamentary system, parliamentary parties, or government policy. This includes protests throughout Germany by a sometimes bewildering variety of organizations and individuals on a number of different issues including nuclear weapons, the *Notstandsgesetze*, the Vietnam War, university reform and women's rights, among others. This definition of the APO does not, however, include such terrorist activities as the bombing campaigns by the RAF. While these were undoubtedly acts of protest, and they did evolve from the experiences of protesters in APO campaigns, they were attempts to destroy a political system through violence, rather than to institute reform or to generate a revolution through political means and popular opposition. This

---

14. Rupp, H.K., *Außerparlamentarische Opposition in der Ära Adenauer*, p. 20.
15. Otto, *Die außerparlamentarische Opposition*, p. 23.

is not to deny that the RAF and other terrorist organizations acted, from their perspective at least, to defend or pursue democracy, as they understood it. Their viewpoint adds yet another valuable dimension to the varied ways in which democracy could be interpreted in post-war Germany.

The protests were of much greater length, intensity and scale than is suggested by a concentration solely upon 1968, so that the whole period after 1945 must be considered when looking at the events of the 1960s. Post-war reconstruction, the Nazi legacy, and the difficulties of adjusting to life in a democracy, and the Cold War, all played their part. This book will not discuss the whole post-war period in detail, although the first chapter will give background information on post-war German society. The main body of the discussion will concentrate mainly on the period from the late 1950s to the mid-1970s. This covers the foundations of the Peace Movements and the origins of the APO, through the 1960s, to the disintegration of the various campaigns in the 1970s. Despite this concentration upon the detail of the protest movements, it is the key aim of this book to highlight the relationship between these protests and changes in German society as a whole. These protests were products of, and factors in, fundamental changes in both political and personal attitudes in the 1960s that had a lasting impact upon the social history of Germany in subsequent decades.

Part I
1945–1964

Post-war Reconstruction and the APO

Bertold Brecht's 1928 comment 'first comes the full stomach, then come the morals' is a particularly prescient description of attitudes that informed life in Germany immediately following the end of the Second World War.[1] Rather than examining the Nazi past, West Germans concentrated upon economic recovery, social reconciliation, and rebuilding Germany's international standing. The resultant attitudes to denazification, the Nazi past, and democracy are all central, along with the economic recovery itself, to understanding the nature of the protest movements that emerged in the 1960s.[2] The presence of former Nazis in positions of authority, the failure to address the issues raised by the Nazi period, and an authoritarian, consensus-based democracy allowed protesters to ask whether the new Federal Republic was a restoration or a new beginning. The experience of Nazism created particularly strong generational divisions in West Germany, while the prosperity provided for by the economic boom created qualitative differences in generational experiences, and the concomitant contrast in expectations and norms of behaviour that fuelled generational conflict.

The post-war economic boom was the motor for much of the rapid social change that took place in the 1960s, and contrasts starkly with the experiences of West Germans in 1945. In his history of the post-war German family, Robert G. Moeller quotes a woman as saying that 'after '45 no one thought about confronting the past. Everyone thought about how they were going to put something in the pot, so that their children could eat something, and about how to start rebuilding and clearing away the rubble'.[3] The statistics for the period make for grim reading: Hermann Glaser states that

---

1. The comment comes from Brecht's *Threepenny Opera*, Act two, Scene six.
2. Jamison, A. and Eyerman, R., *Seeds of the Sixties* is a detailed discussion of the ways in which many of the themes of 1960s America had their origins in the 1950s. Marwick, A., *The Sixties* also uses 'the Long Sixties', running from 1958 to 1974, as one of its central premises.
3. Moeller, R.G., *Protecting Motherhood*, p. 13.

In Europe 19.6 million soldiers were dead or missing, of whom 3.7 million were German; 14.7 million civilians had been killed (of whom 3,640,000 Germans were victims of bombing and around 2 million were victims of expulsion) . . . 12 million Germans were in flight as refugees, 6 to 7 million German soldiers were prisoners of war. Around 2 million soldiers and civilians were among the war injured. 3 million people were homeless; 2.25 million apartments were completely destroyed, and 2.5 million were damaged. The piles of rubble created by the warfare covered around 400 million cubic metres.[4]

By July 1945 the average intake of calories in the British zone was only between 950 and 1,150 calories per day.[5] In his *Memoirs*, Konrad Adenauer stated that only 300 houses in Cologne had survived intact and that at the time of the Nazi surrender 'there was no gas, no water, no electric current, and no means of transport'. With a population of only 32,000 compared to its pre-war figure of 760,000, Cologne was 'a ghost town'.[6] In the Bavarian town of Fürth 40 per cent of the children had no winter clothing, while in Kassel 7.5 per cent had no shoes. In Mannheim 70 per cent said their parents had nothing with which to heat their accommodation.[7] Shortages of food, fuel, housing and clothing featured in the stories of all 498 Berlin families who participated in the survey carried out by Hilda Thurnwald in 1946 and 1947.[8]

Despite these desperate circumstances, the potential for a rapid economic recovery was great. Alan Kramer has noted that there was so much spare capacity in the economy that no new factories were required for the first six years after the War, and machine tools were often intact under the rubble of bombed factories: at the Junkers factory, producing diesel engines, 10 per cent of buildings were damaged, compared to just 1 per cent of the machinery.[9] There were undoubtedly impediments in the way of recovery: Werner Abelhauser lists problems ranging from Allied dismantling of industrial plant to Allied export restrictions, but adds 'once Germany had independent control of her own resources and the foreign trade situation became favourable, rapid economic growth should have

4. Glaser, H., *Kleine Kulturgeschichte*, p. 13.

5. Berghahn, V. R., *Modern Germany*, p. 180. Abelhauser, W., *Die Langen Fünfziger Jahre* remains the classic text on post-war economic reconstruction, and provides an exhaustively detailed account of the process described all too briefly here.

6. Adenauer, K., *Memoirs 1945–53*, p. 21.

7. Glaser, *Kleine Kulturgschichte*, pp. 72–3.

8. See for instance Family A, Thurnwald, H., *Gegenwartsprobleme Berliner Familien*, pp. 232–5.

9. Kramer, A, *The West German Economy, 1945–1955*, pp. 2 and 25.

been expected', and this began as early as 1947 to 1948.[10] The Marshall Plan (European Recovery Programme) announced by US Secretary of State George Marshall in June 1947, therefore, came at exactly the right time. Between 1948 and 1952 1.5 billion dollars were given to West Germany under the Plan.[11] Whether or not Germany would have recovered without this aid, the West German economy experienced an economic miracle (*Wirtschaftswunder*) in the 1950s. The statistics are impressive: In 1951 the German economy grew by 10.4 per cent, and by 8.9 per cent in the following year. This spectacular growth rate was maintained well past the initial phase of reconstruction, so in 1959 the economy grew 7.3 per cent, and then by 9 per cent in 1960.[12] In 1949 there were 214,000 apartments and houses constructed, the following year 362,000 were built, with a further 433,000 in 1951.[13] Again, the pace was maintained throughout the decade, with 591,000 built in 1956.[14] Unemployment fell from 1,538,000 in 1949 to just 187,000 in 1959.[15] This was matched by a rapid rise in income, so that wages nearly doubled in value in real terms in the period from 1950 to 1962. By 1957 expenditure of disposable income on items such as cars, furniture and leisure activities represented an average of 33.6 per cent of total income for the average German household.[16] By 1964 ten million households in Germany had access to a television, thirty million had a radio, 6.7 million had a washing machine and 9.6 million had a refrigerator.[17] In 1956 only 0.2 million DM (*Deutschmarks*) had been spent on televisions, but this had already risen to 12 million DM in 1958. Just two years later 132 million DM were spent on televisions and by 1964 this had nearly tripled to 374 million DM.[18] In 1946 Germans owned only 192,438 automobiles (excluding Berlin and the Saarland), but by 1953 they already owned more than a million, and by 1961 the total had risen to more than five million.[19] In 1965 36 per cent of households had a car, and this rose to include half of all households just four years

10. Abelhauser, W., 'American Aid and West German Economic Recovery: A Macroeconomic Perspective', in C.S. Maier (ed.), *The Marshall Plan and Germany*, 378–81.

11. Quoted in Benz, W., *Die Gründung der Bundesrepublik*, p. 94.

12. Berghahn, *Modern Germany*, p. 262, table 12.

13. Statistisches Bundesamt Wiesbaden (ed.), *Statistisches Jahrbuch, 1953*, p. 23.

14. Statistisches Bundesamt Wiesbaden (ed.), *Statistisches Jahrbuch, 1960*, p. 25.

15. *Statistisches Jahrbuch, 1953*, p. 21 and *Statistisches Jahrbuch, 1960*, p. 21.

16. Berghahn, *Modern Germany*, pp. 273–4, tables 26 and 29.

17. 'Sowjet-Union: Plannung, Versuch mit Nöspl', *Der Spiegel*, 10 February 1965, p. 69.

18. 'Fernsehen: Springer, "Bild" im Bildscherm', *Der Spiegel*, 3 February 1965, p. 50.

19. Glaser, *Kleine Kulturgeschichte*, p. 215.

later.[20] It was therefore perhaps only in the 1960s, when economic and political stability was assured, that German society was in a position to debate the issues raised by the Nazi past. Moreover, the formative experiences of the younger generation had taken place amid economic security and material wealth that was in stark contrast to those of their parents.

It was this post-war generation that usually formed the majority group within the protest movements of the 1960s and the economic boom was crucial in creating qualitative differences in expectations between them and older generations. It will be seen that members of older generations did take part in protests on various issues, most notably rearmament, but the young generally dominated protests in Germany in the 1960s, as they did in every Western country throughout the decade. Interpretations of the protests have often suffered from a lack of differentiation between those in Western capitalist economies, and movements in Africa, South America, communist Eastern Europe, and so on, which had very different origins, intentions, and circumstances. In this sense, Eric Hobsbawm's description of the protests as 'the last hurrah of the old world revolution', or Immanuel Wallerstein's view that their 'origins, consequences, and lessons cannot be analysed correctly by appealing to the particular circumstances of the local manifestations of this global phenomenon', do little to further our understanding of these events.[21] A more discerning approach is needed, concentrating on protest movements that shared characteristics, for a more meaningful analysis; although the Western protest movements undoubtedly reflected complex local conditions and issues, they often shared striking similarities. Almost all Western countries experienced a combination of all or some of the following stages of protest: peace or civil rights campaigns, usually in the late 1950s and early 1960s, then student revolts in the mid- to late 1960s, and then terrorism, feminism and environmentalism in the 1970s. Of course the application of this model needs to be sufficiently flexible to allow for varying degrees of emphasis and important differences in detail, but it would summarize the protest movements in almost every Western country. The United States, Britain and Germany, for instance, all fit the model perfectly. Common issues such as the Vietnam War, university reform, race relations, police violence, democratic representation, norms of behaviour, and attitudes to authority

20. Maase, K., 'Freizeit', in W. Benz (ed.), *Die Geschichte der Bundesrepublik Deutschland: Band 3*, p. 359.

21. Hobsbawm, E., *Age of Extremes*, p. 446 and Wallerstein, I., '1968, Revolution in the World System: Theses and Queries', *Theory and Society*, No. 18, July 1989, p. 431. See also François, E., 'Annäherungsversuche an ein außergewöhnliches Jahr', in E. François, et al., *1968*, pp. 11–12.

ran throughout the protest campaigns of every country in the West. These protests were carried out mainly by the young and usually took the form of marches, sit-ins, sit-downs, and mass meetings, often with the intention of provoking a response from those in authority. Although their political character and outlooks differed, they were usually informed to a greater or lesser extent by some variant of the New Left critique of Western capitalism that distanced itself equally from Soviet totalitarianism.[22] They were marked by only limited, or at most temporary, involvement by the traditional organizations of the labour movement. All of these countries also shared in the economic boom of the post-war period, and it is this that holds the key to understanding the international nature of the protests as well as many of the generational differences that informed them.

Wealth creates social mobility, higher expectations, a weakening of traditional social structures and dependencies, and a reduction in deference. It allows for challenges to established privileges and norms of behaviour, and for the previously disenfranchised (in this case the young) it creates the desire for inclusion in decision-making. This is what 1960s protests were about, whether seeking to influence government policy on Vietnam, or attempting to gain student representation within university governments. Robert V. Daniels, in his history of protests in 1968, has given a succinct summary of this theory. For Daniels, 'revolution is most likely to occur not when a society is in a state of hopelessness, but when it is developing dynamically and enjoying rising expectations. It then experiences frustration and outrage as social and economic advance encounters obstinacy and entrenched government or custom'.[23] The protests, then, were both reflections of, and factors in, social change. Former SDS activist Bernd Rabehl has acknowledged that although the anti-authoritarian wing of SDS 'fought American imperialism in Vietnam . . . at the same time they prepared the way for American civilization and its life-style' by challenging norms of behaviour, even though he subscribed to Herbert Marcuse's view that modern capitalism had succeeded in neutralizing working-class opposition through the creation and fulfilment of imaginary material needs.[24] Participation in protests was a challenge to previous attitudes to authority, just as new attitudes to sex, new lifestyles, and much new popular culture were challenges to established codes of

22. For a useful, if partisan, history of the New Left around the world in the 1960s see Katsiaficas, G., *The Imagination of the New Left*, although Katsiaficas fails to differentiate between Western protest movements and those elsewhere in the world.

23. Daniels, R.V., *Year of the Heroic Guerrilla*, p. 11. See also Fraser, *1968*, p. 354–5.

24. Rabehl, B., *Am Ende der Utopie*, p. 246 and Marcuse, M., *One-Dimensional Man*.

behaviour. Post-war prosperity was the key factor in creating the conditions for an international wave of protests, even if local conditions and local issues shaped these campaigns in unique ways. The importance of new technologies in allowing for the rapid dissemination of news and information is regularly presented as a central factor in creating international protest movements and international youth cultures. That this is an important consideration is beyond question, yet without the money to pay for televisions, radios, newspapers, glossy magazines, records, and so on, these new technologies would merely have been the preserve of the rich few.

A vibrant youth culture developed in the *Bundesrepublik* from the early 1950s, on the back of the rapid increase in disposable income available to a broad spectrum of society. As with youth cultures elsewhere in the West the emphasis on free time was dominated by the influence of the nascent youth culture in America, particularly rock n' roll.[25] The politicizing effect of this youth culture can be overemphasized. The *Halbstarke* (half strong) riots that took place in cities throughout West Germany in the mid- to late 1950s were not overtly political in motivation, but mainly involved sometimes violent disturbances predominantly by adolescent working-class males. They focused in particular upon cinemas during or following showings of films like 'Blackboard Jungle', 'Rock Around the Clock', and 'Don't Knock the Rock'.[26] The direct comparisons made by Martina Fischer-Kowalski between the *Halbstarke* and the student protests

25. The debate on the extent of American influence in Germany rages on. See for instance Berghahn, V.R, *The Americanization of German Industry*, and Willett, R., *The Americanization of Germany*. Pommerin, R., (ed.), *The American Impact on Postwar Germany* contains useful sections on daily life and teenagers. All suggest American influence on various aspects of life in Germany to a greater or lesser extent, although Sywottek, A., 'The Americanization of Everyday Life? Early Trends in Consumer and Leisure-Time Behaviour', in M. Ermarth, (ed.), *America and the Shaping of German Society*, pp. 132–152 is an important corrective to Willetts' presentation of almost complete American cultural dominance. Also useful are Schildt, A., *Moderne Zeiten*, and Schildt, A. and Sywottek, A. (eds), *Modernisierung im Wiederaufbau*. Junker, D., *Die USA und Deutschland*, provides essays on almost every aspect of American influence.

26. Zinnecker, J., *Jugenkultur*, p. 125 estimates that around 50 of these riots, involving 50 or more people, took place in various German cities between 1956 and 1958, although they seem to have been occurring regularly since around 1953, often involving as many as 300 or 400 people. Grotum, T., *Die Halbstarken* is the most complete recent study of the *Halbstarke* phenomenon, while Fröhner, R., *Wie Starke sind die Halbstarke?* is a contemporary study that goes to some lengths to show the German public that the *Halbstarke* were few in number amid fears that they were a cover for East German infiltration.

of 1968 often stretch the point too far, indulging in unconvincing general-ization and doing nothing to explain any genuine relationship between the two.[27]

Uta Poiger has nevertheless presented a convincing case for consider-ing the youth culture of the 1950s, including the *Halbstarke riots* in which some women participated, as politically significant as liberating influences for young women. It allowed for a redefinition of gender roles meaning that 'public visibility became an option for women of all classes'. The concept of the 'teenager' 'ran counter to the traditional ideal image of the woman who exerted restraint in matters of consumption and sexuality'.[28] As a challenge to established norms of behaviour, particularly for women, the new youth culture prompted a national debate in the press and among politicians that encompassed a reassessment of gender relations that were informed by notions of the traditional family. For Poiger the 'raised expectations for individual expression and sexual openness among many young women' were eventually translated into political action in the late 1960s with the emergence of the feminist movement.[29] In looking at 'the personal as political' then, Poiger presents a direct challenge to Helmut Schelsky's model of a 'sceptical generation', wary of politics and inter-ested only in itself.[30] Poiger has also shown that the *Halbstarke* issue was further politicized by the government and media who viewed it as a threat to masculinity and therefore to national security. The supposedly mindless worship of American culture was equated with the worship of Nazism and the *Halbstarke* riots were presented as similar to SA acts of violence.[31] Young people of the 1950s may not have been politically active in a con-ventional sense, but Poiger describes an environment in which profound social changes took place that prepared the ground for the protest move-ments of the 1960s.

27 Fischer-Kowalski, M., 'Halbstarke 1958, Studenten 1968: Eine Generation und zwei Rebellionen', in U. Preuss-Lausitz, *Kriegskinder, Konsumkinder, Krisenkinder*, pp. 54–6. On the other hand, the politicizing influence can be underestimated, as in Maase, K., *Bravo Amerika*, which is an excellent account of the American influence on German youth culture, or Hermand, J., *Kultur im Wiederaufbau*, which gives a good overview of both high and popular culture with the Marxist interpretation that the new youth culture distracted people from true political rebellion.

28. Poiger, U.G., 'Rock n' Roll, Female Sexuality, and the Cold War Battle over German Identities', *Journal of Modern History*, 68 (September 1996), pp. 608–9.

29. Ibid., p. 615.

30. Schelsky, H., *Die skeptische Generation*.

31. 'Rebels with a Cause? American Popular Culture, the 1956 Youth Riots, and New Conceptions of Masculinity in East and West Germany', in R. Pommerin (ed.), *The American Impact on Postwar Germany*, pp. 108–13.

It is one of the great ironies of the 1960s that the economic prosperity the Left despised and the Right applauded should have been so instrumental in creating the conditions in which the protests of the 1960s, that were attacked by the Right and hailed by the Left, could flourish. This is particularly so in light of the ongoing condemnation of the decade by the Right for destroying the social cohesion and moral certainties of the preceding decades. In his sustained rant against the 1960s, Allan Bloom has made the incredible statement that 'whether it be Nuremberg or Woodstock, the principle is the same'.[32] He is supported in this view by Peter Collier and David Horowitz, two former radicals who have recanted their earlier beliefs, and who now peddle the view that 'in the inchoate attack against authority, we had weakened our culture's immune system, making it vulnerable to opportunistic diseases. The origins of metaphorical epidemics of crime and drugs could be traced to the Sixties, as could literal ones such as AIDS'.[33] The views of Thatcherite and Reaganite administrations in Britain and America have consistently endorsed these viewpoints. Conservative governments throughout the West, including Helmut Kohl's regime, have introduced family policies that sought unsuccessfully to challenge sexual permissiveness, rising numbers of working and single mothers, and soaring divorce rates in a bid to halt the destruction of the traditional family for which the 1960s are blamed.[34] The link between this apparent 'moral degeneration' and the unprecedented prosperity of the post-war period has been largely ignored. For the post-war generation this prosperity meant qualitative differences in experiences, attitudes and opportunities between them and older generations, creating lines of conflict represented both by youth culture and protests.

The post-war generation was also free of the taint of Nazism, and the emphasis on the integration of former Nazis into the new Federal Republic, while pragmatic, entailed a readiness to seek reconciliation rather than redress that created particularly strong generational divisions in West Germany. According to the April 1945 directive issued by the American Joint Chiefs of Staff, JCS 1067, 'the principal Allied objective is to prevent Germany from ever again becoming a threat to the peace of the world'. The 'elimination of Nazism and militarism in all their forms' were central to this aim, involving the removal of all former Nazis from 'public office

32. Bloom, A., *The Closing of the American Mind*, pp. 314 and 326.
33. Collier, P. and Horowitz, D., *Destructive Generation*, p. 16.
34. A particularly interesting analysis is given by Cockett, R., 'The New Right and the 1960s: The Dialectics of Liberation', in G. Andrews et al. (eds), *New Left, New Right and Beyond*, pp. 85–105. See also Brinkley, A., '1968 and the Unraveling of Liberal America', in Fink et al., *1968: The World Transformed*, pp. 219–36.

and from positions of importance in quasi-public and private enter-prises'.[35] As a result 200,000 former Nazis were interned by the Western Allies between 1945 and 1949, and 150,000 government personnel lost their jobs in the first half of 1946 alone, along with a further 73,000 people in industry.[36] Pursuing denazification was fraught with difficulties: Allied Control Council directives were often vague, open to interpretation, and subject to frequent change, and the policy was applied differently in each Zone according to different assumptions. According to Ian Turner the British occupation authorities assumed that Nazism was 'endemic to the German national character', rendering attempts at thorough root and branch denazification futile.[37] In contrast to the American Zone of occu-pation, where policies for the removal of former Nazis and sympathizers were strictly enforced, in the British Zone the emphasis was placed upon removing from positions of authority those who remained opposed to Allied aims. In consequence it was possible for former Nazis to travel from the American Zone to the British Zone in order to avoid the denazi-fication process.[38] The policy also created resentment: Konrad Adenauer, leader of the newly created Christian Democratic Union (CDU), consist-ently objected to the scope of the denazification process, saying in July 1946 that 'leading Nazis' were being ignored while 'poor devils were being hanged'. He followed this up in August by demanding 'now at last leave the followers in peace' and objected to the hardships being suffered by minor Nazis and their families.[39] Instead Adenauer wanted an inclus-ive settlement in which major Nazi criminals would be prosecuted and repentant former Nazis would play a full role in post-war West Germany. His emphasis was upon reconciliation in the creation of a strong new state, and those who maintained their loyalty to Nazism would be shunted to the margins of society.

The practical problems presented by excluding so many former Nazis from employment were particularly acute, and lent weight to Adenauer's calls for pragmatism and accommodation. While the great mass of former

35. 'Directive of the United States Joint Chiefs of Staff to the Commander-in-Chief of the United States Forces of Occupation Regarding the Military Government of Germany (JCS 1067), quoted in Oppen, B.R. von (ed.), *Documents on Germany under Occupation 1945–1954*, pp. 16–17.

36. Herf, J., *Divided Memory*, p. 204. On p. 202 Herf estimates that 8 million Germans had been members of the Nazi Party in May 1945.

37. Turner, I., 'Denazification in the British Zone' in I.D. Turner (ed.), *Reconstruction in Post-war Germany*, p. 242.

38. Ibid., p. 249.

39. Herf, *Divided Memory*, pp. 223.

party members remained banned from their professions, it was impossible to meet the shortfall in teachers, doctors, civil servants, lawyers, and so on. General Clay estimated that in one city in the American Zone 60 per cent of teachers had been Nazi party members.[40] Excluding these people from their posts meant that in 1945 there were only 12,849 teachers for 1.1 million pupils in the American Zone, representing a shortfall of 16,000 teachers.[41] Robert Birley has estimated that there was a similar shortfall of 16,000 teachers in the British Zone.[42] In the American Zone alone, 27 per cent of the population (3,669,239 persons) were chargeable as former members of the Nazi party, although it was realized that most had not been active, and 2,373,115 were pardoned in an amnesty introduced in August 1946, aimed at all those born after 1919 who had not been charged with major offences.[43] The denazification programme was scaled down, and then handed over to the newly created *Land* (state) governments in October 1947, with instructions to bring it to an end by 1 January 1948.[44] Former party members were allowed back into employment after they had been through a re-education programme, while only the major party members and perpetrators of atrocities were prosecuted. In the Nuremberg trials and the related prosecutions in different Western zones up to 1947, only 5,025 people were convicted of war crimes or crimes against humanity, with 806 death sentences, of which 486 were carried out.[45]

When responsibility for denazification was handed over to *Land* authorities the number of prosecutions dwindled. In 1949 there were 1,523 former Nazis sentenced, and this had already fallen to 809 in 1950, 123 in 1953, and a mere 44 in 1954.[46] Denazification has been interpreted variously as an unmitigated disaster that failed to bring Nazis to justice and allowed former Nazis and fellow travellers back into positions of authority and, alternatively, as a victory for pragmatism that allowed for the creation of an inclusive new democracy.[47] Whatever the case, rehabilitation and reconciliation in the late 1940s and through the 1950s did not allow for

40. Clay, *Decision in Germany*, p. 299.

41. Merritt, *Democracy Imposed*, p. 273.

42. Birley, R., 'British Policy in Retrospect' in A. Hearnden (ed.), *The British in Germany*, p. 52.

43. Quoted in Fitzgibbon, C., *Denazification*, p. 132.

44. 'British Military Government Ordnance No. 110: Transfer to the Länder Governments of Responsbility for Denazification', quoted in von Oppen, *Documents on Germany*, pp. 247–51.

45. Herf, *Divided Memory*, p. 206.

46. Quoted in Hoffmann, C., *Stunden Null?*, p. 115.

47. Turner, 'Denazification in the British Zone', pp. 240–1 gives a good summary of the various perspectives.

critical debate or a re-examination of the Nazi past in West Germany. Attempts have been made by some historians to suggest that a re-examination of the Nazi period did take place, but such attempts have had only limited success: Wiesen's work on attitudes among German industrialists challenges the notion of a conspiracy of silence, but his discussion is based upon examples of desperate attempts by business leaders to disassociate themselves from the Nazi past and absolve themselves from blame.[48] This was hardly indicative of a critical culture of self-examination and searching inquiry, and a significant body of work on the families of former Nazis supports the claim that the Nazi past was rarely, if ever, discussed.[49]

The impact on the political climate in West Germany was profound. Richard L. Merritt argues in his description of post-war German attitudes to democracy that the inability to deal with dissent was built into the denazification process instituted by the Allies. This 'punished those who . . . had harmed their fellow citizens and German society as a whole', while it also 'prevented access to power and influence by those who had not adapted rapidly and completely to the newly emerging German democratic order'. Merritt goes on to suggest that this latter aspect of the denazification process implicitly legitimized the use of the legal weaponry in the state's armoury in order to silence those who did not support, or were critical of, the *Bundesrepublik*.[50] This manifested itself most clearly in the banning of the tiny communist party, the *Kommunistische Partei Deutschlands* (KPD) in 1956 amid fears that it represented the advance guard for Soviet ambitions.[51] Gerhard Schröder, the Interior Minister at the time, argued in a *Bundestag* debate in April 1958 that far-right and far-left organizations should be treated as the same under the Basic Law provision that organizations that threatened to undermine democratic freedoms should be banned. In answer to objections to this he responded 'do you believe that I would stand before the German people, in order to introduce further measures against the right, while at the same time allowing a nature reserve for communists to exist?'.[52] Those who accepted the *Bundesrepublik*, including former Nazis, would therefore be accepted as reformed characters, while those who opposed or criticized the post-war settlement were to be seen as enemies.

---

48. Wiesen, S.J., *West German Industry*.

49. See Bar On, D., *Legacy of Silence*; Sicharovsky, P., *Born Guilty*; von Westernhagen, D., *Die Kinder der Täter*; and Lebert, S., *My Father's Keeper*.

50. Merritt, R.L., *Democracy Imposed*, p. 406.

51. Major, P., *The Death of the KPD* gives a detailed description of the anti-communist atmosphere of post-war German politics and of the banning of the KPD.

52. Quoted in Schröder, G., *Wir brauchen eine heile Welt*, p. 148.

Indeed, Adenauer's government after his election as the new Federal Republic's first Chancellor in 1949 was an embodiment of the spirit of inclusion and reconciliation. For Tom Bower, Adenauer's government made sure that 'the men who dedicated themselves to making sure the wheels of National Socialism turned smoothly and profitably would not be denied the chance to do the same for the new political dispensation'.[53] Perhaps most controversially, Dr Hans Globke, Adenauer's key advisor and head of his Chancellery staff from 1953, had worked alongside Wilhelm Stuckart in the preparation of the Nuremburg Racial Laws of 1935 which institutionalized the persecution of Jews. In May 1960 Theodor Oberländer, the Minister for Refugees, was forced to resign amid allegations that he had participated in a massacre in Lemberg in 1941. Although the allegations were later found to be false, he was an active Nazi who had been in Lemberg at the time. Herbert Blankenhorn, Adenauer's personal advisor, was also a former Nazi party member, as was Gerhard Schröder, the Interior Minister from 1953 who oversaw the banning of the KPD. One of Adenauer's biographers, the journalist Terence Prittie, has noted that when Adenauer ordered the creation of a group of staff in May 1950 as a preliminary to forming a Foreign Ministry, there were 14 former Nazis among the 31 executive staff. When the new Ministry was created it was found that 39 of the 49 senior members were former Nazi party members.[54] Charles Williams, in the most recent biography of Adenauer, has gone so far as to say that he was 'prepared to tolerate them [former Nazis] in the administration provided their membership of the party had been inactive or necessary for them to keep their job' but that 'if they stepped out of line – Adenauer's line – they could expect a case for denazification to be re-opened'.[55] The opportunity this presented as a tool for quashing dissent even at the heart of government is clear, necessarily strengthening Adenauer's authority, and that of his successors.

That authority was further strengthened by the consensus-based nature of post-war politics in West Germany. Eva Kolinsky has described the post-war political system as an attempt to avoid problems that had bedevilled the Weimar period, most notably the refusal of most parties to play a part in government, which made it possible for them to retain their fundamental opposition to the state itself and refrain from seeking compromise.[56] The post-war system sought to include all parties in *Bundestag* committees, as well as *Land* and city governments, so that 'all parties,

---

53. Bower, T., *The Pledge Betrayed*, p. 355. See also Teschke, J.P., *Hitler's Legacy*.
54. Prittie, T., *Konrad Adenauer*, p. 199.
55. Williams, C., *Adenauer*, pp. 390–1.
56. Kolinsky, E., *Parties, Opposition and Society in West Germany*, p. 1.

whether in government or in opposition, are actively involved in the legislative process'.[57] In consequence, compromise and consensus were at the heart of the West German political process, creating strong representative democracy, but also forcing parties to find common ground that made it more difficult for electorates to distinguish between them. The system's strengths were reinforced by the social market policies pursued by Ludwig Erhard, which combined a liberal market economy with an inclusive welfare system and created not simply economic recovery in the 1950s, but allowed prosperity to be enjoyed by a greater cross-section of society than ever before. Further, the creation of vested interests in the retention of liberal parliamentary democracy was particularly noticeable in policy toward the trade union movement. The introduction of the Collective Bargaining Law on industrial relations in April 1949, and the creation of systems between 1950 and 1952 allowing for the participation of workers in decision-making processes within firms through co-determination (*Mitbestimmung*) again encouraged consensus-based rather than confrontational politics.[58] Such inclusion, in stark contrast to the sectional divisions that dogged Weimar, prompted West German trade unions to take an active role in wider political life beyond their narrow interests, to the extent that Andrei S. Markovits insists 'the unions have from the Federal Republic's inception been among the staunchest defenders of the pluralist order'.[59] In this environment Adenauer was able to remain as Chancellor from 1949 to 1963, forming a series of coalitions with opportunist minority parties, notably the Free Democrat Party (FDP), and forging a strong 'Chancellor democracy', thereby giving West Germans the political stability they had long craved.

'Chancellor democracy', then, fulfilled a need for firm and inspirational leadership since, although Germans had moved on from the Nazi period and had embraced democracy, the desire for strong government remained, along with sympathy for the achievements of Nazism. Richard L. Merritt has made it clear that the majority of Germans embraced the new democratic institutions as their best hope of peace, prosperity and long-term stability. Surveys were carried out by OMGUS (Occupation Military Government, United States) from 1947 to 1950. These found that in August 1947 47 per cent of respondents, by far the largest group, described a democratic republic as the best form of government for the future of Germany, while 56 per cent described it as the preferred form of government. Only

57. Ibid., p. 7.
58. See Markovits, A.S., *The Politics of the West German Trade Unions*, pp. 39–43 on Collective Bargaining, and pp. 53–60 on Co-determination.
59. Ibid., p. 3.

one per cent described a communist government as the best, reflecting already existing fears of communism that clearly grew with the deepening of the Cold War, because less than half a per cent of respondents favoured this form of government in the 1950 survey. Of the other proposed forms of government, the 1947 survey found 8 per cent in favour of a monarchy, 5 per cent in favour of a dictatorship, and 9 per cent preferring a 'socialist' government.[60] Nonetheless, the *Bundesrepublik* was an immature new democracy, in which the multiplicity of opinions, the active participation, and the critical stance toward those in authority that is essential for a watchful and balanced democracy were often seen as dangerous. Merritt points to a 'concept of legitimized authority' that 'bedevilled Germans during the Nazi era – and Allied authorities afterward', and which 'linked authority inextricably to obedience'. He quotes a March 1946 survey in which two-fifths of respondents agreed with the proposition that 'the individual should always obey the orders of the state without question'.[61]

In the 1960s, therefore, the inflexible approach to dissent, and particularly extra-parliamentary dissent inherent in 'Chancellor democracy' and in the inclusion of former Nazis within West German society, led to a rapid escalation in the confrontation between protesters and authorities, particularly along generational lines. Andrei S. Markovits and Philip S. Gorski, for instance, have emphasized the ways in which differences in attitudes to the Nazi past led to a situation in which 'generational cleavages in the Federal Republic are more pronounced than in other comparable liberal democracies'.[62] In their survey of the Left in post-war West Germany they have highlighted the existence of a clear fault line in attitudes between the post-war generation and older Germans who had experienced Nazism. They present the older generation as having sublimated its guilt in contrast to the younger generation whose protests were both 'a critique of the complacency and accommodation of the Bonn republic's institutions and political culture vis-à-vis the Nazi regime' and 'the first time that massive protests erupted on German soil against Germany's Nazi period'. The post-war generation was undoubtedly able to take a moralistic stance: Heinz Bude has insisted that 'the "68 generation" is the last generation for which the experience of National Socialism created a common connection'.[63] A survey carried out in 1968 by the University of Mannheim found that when asked whether National Socialism had been a good idea badly

---

60. Merritt, *Democracy Imposed*, p. 338.

61. Ibid., p. 93.

62. Markovits, A.S. and Gorski, P.S., *The German Left*, pp. 21–2.

63. Bude, H., *Bilanz der Nachfolge*, p. 90. Bude, H., *Das Alten einer Generation* is a more detailed study of the "68 generation".

carried out 50 per cent of the general public agreed. In contrast 91 per cent of students disagreed. A further 68 per cent of the public supported the idea that the task of the Opposition was 'to support the government', but this position was opposed by 73 per cent of students.[64] The refusal by protesters to give uncritical endorsement to the post-war settlement, their questioning of the role of former Nazis in post-war West Germany, their interpretation of the Federal Republic as complicit in glossing over the issues raised by the Nazi past were equated by their opponents in government and among the general public as opposition to the inclusive assumptions upon which the Republic was based and, in turn, to the Republic itself.

In this context it is essential to acknowledge the extent to which the approval of Nazism, and support for Nazi attitudes, continued in the post-war period, since public opinion was by no means uniform. While some former Nazis refused to change their views, many made a full commitment to the *Bundesrepublik* as a democracy. The presence of numerous non-Nazis and anti-Nazis in the German population, including Adenauer himself, is a further qualification that must be acknowledged. Hilda Thurnwald's survey expresses these patterns clearly. The father of Family F was a former party member who even insisted that the family stand and give the Nazi salute when the national anthem or the *Horst Wessel Lied* were played on the radio. Thurnwald noted that 'recently husband and wife hope for a resurgence of National Socialism' and despite the evidence of their own desperate living conditions they 'think that under Hitler "everything would be much better"'.[65] Family G, described as 'supporters' of the Nazi party, tried to emphasize the 'good side of National Socialism', arguing that 'no one was hungry, no one was cold, and if Adolf returned now, then everything would quickly be back to normal'.[66] These were nonetheless extreme cases, and other families expressed disillusionment with the Nazis or claimed to have been long-standing opponents of the Nazi regime. In Family H, for instance, the father said he had been an 'outspoken Nazi opponent', while his wife's former social democratic leanings had transformed into support for the new CDU. Although Herr H 'didn't want to have any more to do with politics', he described Hitler as 'the Anti-Christ' and his wife professed to having hated Hitler 'from time immemorial'. Unlike the families of former party members, where

---

64. 'Bevölkerung und Jugendliche neigen eher zu Gewalt als die Studenten', *Abendzeitung*, 24. April 1968, file 'Zeitungen April 1968', HIfS.

65. Thurnwald, *Gegenwartsprobleme*, p. 258.

66. Ibid., pp. 267–8.

their treatment was universally condemned as too hard, Frau H took the view that some former Nazis were treated too harshly, others not harshly enough. She was particularly embittered by the release of former Propaganda Ministry official and broadcaster Hans Fritzsche.[67] Of course, these people could have been telling surveyors what they thought they wanted to hear, although clearly many former Nazis did not feel it was inappropriate to voice their support for the Nazi regime.

Surveys carried out by the occupying forces also suggested a mixed view of the Nazi past, with an enduring presence of Nazi attitudes. A series of surveys carried out by OMGUS from November 1945 to April 1947 found that 48 per cent of people felt Nazism was 'a good idea badly carried out'. This increased to 55 per cent in May 1947, and continued to increase in the following two years, while over the period from November 1945 to January 1949 the proportion who described Nazism as wholly bad dropped from more than 40 per cent to around 30 per cent. Even in the early 1950s, after the creation of the *Bundesrepublik*, 41 per cent of people surveyed said they felt there was more good than evil in National Socialism, and only 36 per cent took the opposite view. Although there was no support for the Nazi persecution of Jews, there was approval of many Nazi policies such as compulsory labour service. This positive image of Nazism was only slowly eroded over time. The proportion of people describing the Nazi regime as criminal rose from 54 per cent to 71 per cent from May 1964 to February 1979. Surveys carried out from 1975 to 1979 found that 36 per cent approved of Nazism apart from the persecution of the Jews and the War, while 42 per cent disapproved of Nazism.[68] This did not translate into support for parties espousing Nazi policies, however. Far-right parties such as the *Sozialistische Reichspartei* (SRP), which was banned in October 1952, only ever received tiny electoral support. It will be shown in subsequent chapters that although the *Nationaldemokratische Partei Deutschlands* (NPD) achieved some success in *Land* elections, it was never more than a marginal party in the 1960s, and caused considerable alarm, again illustrating disapproval of those who failed to conform or adapt to the political realities of the *Bundesrepublik*. Strikingly, a survey in 1951 found that only 3 per cent of Germans would actively support a Nazi seizure of power.[69] Although there was support for some Nazi policies, then, democracy – or perhaps what was understood as 'democracy' – represented by the post-war settlement as a whole enjoyed

67. Ibid., p. 278.
68. Merritt, *Democracy Imposed*, pp. 97–101.
69. Ibid., p. 102.

popular support as the most favoured form of government. The vast majority of the population approved of the *Bundesrepublik*, with only 7 per cent of people expressing dissatisfaction with it in a survey carried out in November 1949.[70]

Whatever the strengths of the political system of the Federal Republic, though, it was all too easy for protesters in the 1960s to portray it as unrepresentative, rigid, dominated by the authoritarian personality of the Chancellor, and frustratingly unresponsive to opposition by parliamentary means. The presence of so many former Nazis in government and positions of authority, along with enduring Nazi sympathies, a pervasive intolerance of dissent, and consensus politics, meant that for the left in the 1960s it was possible to equate 'Chancellor democracy' with a restoration of totalitarianism by stealth.

–2–

The Origins of the APO

By the late 1950s the tensions inherent in the post-war settlement began to manifest themselves in new protest movements, in a rebellious youth culture, and above all in a questioning of both traditional attitudes to authority and norms of behaviour. A new peace movement emerged as West Germany's first mass-protest movement of the post-war period amid fears of a revival of militarism and aggressive nationalist expansionism that prompted people from across the social spectrum to take part in the activities of a new *Außerparlamentarische* or Extra-parliamentary Opposition (APO). The inability to take a measured approach to these changes expressed itself in heavy-handed police tactics and a popular equation of dissent with communist infiltration. Government responses to the Schwabing Riots and the Spiegel Affair not only threatened democracy, but also played into the hands of those who questioned the very nature of the post-war settlement and started a spiral of mutual recrimination.

Adenauer's announcement in August 1950 of plans for a rearmament programme was met by widespread but ineffective opposition, from both the general public and the *Sozialdemokratische Partei Deutschlands* (Social Democratic Party of Germany or SPD).[1] The policy was certainly unpopular: a survey in December found that 70 per cent of West Germans were opposed to rearmament.[2] The *Ohne Mich* campaign (literally 'without me') in which young men refused to take part in military service was necessarily a passive campaign toward a policy that had not even been introduced. Support for it is therefore difficult to quantify: it failed to lay the foundations for a sustained protest movement, and ultimately it highlights the apathy toward political engagement prevailing in the West German electorate in the 1950s. In 1954, 57 per cent of young people had no interest in politics whatsoever, compared with just 36 per cent in 1964.[3]

1. See 'Adenauer für starke Verteidigungsgruppe', *Die Welt*, 19 August 1950, p. 1.
2. Drummond, G.D., *The German Social Democrats in Opposition, 1949–1960*, p. 54.
3. EMNID survey 'Der Verhältnis zur Politik', Bundesministerium für Familie und Jugend, B/153/001476, BK.

The SPD leader Kurt Schumacher, who had little sympathy for the *Ohne Mich* campaign, instead called for new Federal elections, insisting that the German public had been unable to vote on this new issue in the 1949 elections. Adenauer was able to brush such demands aside, setting the pattern for his relations with the SPD on rearmament over the next decade, leading a frustrated SPD eventually to dally with extra-parliamentary methods of opposition when it became clear that Adenauer's regime was unresponsive to opposition within the parliamentary system.[4]

With Adenauer pressing on with his rearmament programme, public opposition remained fragmentary and apathetic. The irregular attempts at launching protests against the policy were further impeded by the ruthless actions of the police, and the ease with which they could be portrayed as the tools of communism. The Conference of the Young Generation that met in Darmstadt in March 1952, for instance, drew support from various youth, religious and political groups, and was able to attract 30,000 young people to a peace march in Essen on 11 May 1952. The short-lived campaign they were attempting to launch was effectively brought to an end when a police attempt to break up the banned march by force resulted in one of the demonstrators, 21-year-old Philipp Müller, being shot dead. The shooting acted both as a disincentive for further participation in protests and as an opportunity for red-baiting: *Die Welt* blamed the shooting on 'communists' whom it claimed had fired the first shots.[5] Condemnation of the shooting, and especially concern for its implications for democracy, was notable by its absence and the North Rhine Westphalia Minister President's relatively restrained claim that police should have used water cannon instead of firearms stands out as a rare exception.[6]

The new West German army, the *Bundeswehr*, could only be created after the country had been granted sovereign status, which Adenauer negotiated at the Nine Power Conference in Paris in October 1954, prompting a further round of SPD opposition. The Paris Accords allowed the Federal Republic to join NATO as long as it did not produce atomic weapons, a move vehemently opposed by Schumacher's successor, Erich Ollenhauer, for whom it placed any hope of German reunification in jeopardy.[7] In December the SPD could only engage in heated exchanges that ultimately proved to be fruitless as the *Bundestag* voted to send the Accords to the

4. Drummond, *The German Social Democrats*, pp. 55–6.
5. 'Getarnte FDJ schießt auf Polizei in Essen: Demonstration gegen Generalvertrag, Ein Toter und zahlreiche Verletzte', *Die Welt*, 12 May 1952, p. 1.
6. 'Wasserwerfer statt Schußwaffen', *Die Welt*, 14 May 1952, p. 1.
7. Drummond, *The German Social Democrats*, pp. 132–9 gives an excellent account of the SPD attitude to the Paris Accords and the subsequent Paulskirche movement.

committee stage in preparation for ratification. Faced by Adenauer's two-thirds majority in the *Bundestag* the SPD decided to appeal directly to the German people, taking comfort in the rising tide of vocal opposition to the rearmament policy from trade unions and socialist youth organizations that was starting to express itself in demonstrations. On 29 January 1955, therefore, the SPD gathered more than 600 prominent Germans at the Paulskirche in Frankfurt to protest against the rearmament policy. Those present were asked to sign a 'German Manifesto' demanding negotiation with the Soviet Union on reunification before the ratification of the Paris Accords. The Accords were nevertheless ratified on 27 February despite SPD opposition, and West Germany was granted sovereignty as well as NATO membership in May. The *Bundeswehr* was eventually created in November 1955. By this stage, the German public was also more amenable to the prospect of rearmament, and a 1955 survey found that around two-thirds viewed rearmament as a political necessity.[8] In this climate Adenauer was able to force a bill on the introduction of conscription, albeit with some amendments, through the *Bundestag* in July 1956, despite passionate SPD resistance.[9]

Adenauer's announcement in April 1957 that the *Bundeswehr* should be given tactical nuclear weapons brought SPD outrage and frustration to the boil.[10] There is some disagreement about Adenauer's motives. American troops had stationed 280-mm atomic cannons on German soil in October 1953 and, according to Jeffrey Boutwell, by 1956 American policy had shifted to place an emphasis on the deployment of nuclear weapons to allow for reductions in American ground troops. Having recently won the *Bundestag*'s approval for conscription and the resultant creation of an army of 500,000 men, Adenauer felt he was being undermined by the move away from ground troops, but realized he could not be too critical of his main ally, and the Federal Republic 'was on the verge of being deprived of any significant voice in the shaping of NATO nuclear policy if it continued to stress conventional deterrence'.[11] This interpretation is contested by Matthias Küntzel, who insists that far from being a reluctant partner Adenauer was keen to avoid differentiation in the armaments held by a NATO country, which would have left West Germany as a natural first-strike target as the country least equipped to defend itself. Possession of nuclear weapons would also give Adenauer a bargaining

8. Burns and van der Will, *Protest and Democracy*, p. 76.

9. Drummond, *The German Social Democrats*, pp. 163–71.

10. See 'Wasserstoff-Waffen auch für die Bundesrepublik?', *Die Welt*, 6 April 1957, p. 1.

11. Boutwell, J., *The German Nuclear Dilemma*, pp. 18–19.

chip in influencing American nuclear strategy.[12] Adenauer's announcement prompted a storm of controversy, most notably in the form of the Declaration of the Göttingen Eighteen, in which 18 German nuclear scientists, including four Nobel Prize winners, sent a telegram to Adenauer protesting against the proposed policy. They argued 'for a small country like the *Bundesrepublik*, it would be best for its protection and for world peace for it to renounce possession of nuclear weapons of any kind, expressly and freely, at the earliest opportunity'.[13] A few days later Albert Schweitzer gave a radio speech from Oslo, broadcast around the world on more than 150 radio stations, in which he warned of the dangers of radioactivity from nuclear weapons.[14] This was followed on 26 August 1957 by the Soviet announcement that they had achieved Inter-continental Ballistic Missile (ICBM) capability, followed by the launch of the Sputnik satellite in October, prompting an acceleration in the American ICBM project and a raising of stakes and fears.[15] The following month Polish Foreign Minister Adam Rapacki made his proposal for the creation of a nuclear-free zone in Central Europe, including West Germany, and then in December, in defiance of the Rapacki plan, Adenauer made clear at the Paris NATO conference his desire for short-range nuclear weapons. This rapid succession of developments prompted intense media and political debate in West Germany on the wisdom of nuclear armament.

Once again, the SPD failed to mount effective opposition to Adenauer's plans in the Bundestag, prompting it to seek an extra-parliamentary alternative. On 20 March Adenauer presented to the *Bundestag* his proposal for arming the *Bundeswehr* with tactical nuclear weapons, and despite 'the bitterest parliamentary session in the short history of the FRG' comfortably won the subsequent vote.[16] SPD leaders had already met in Bonn on 20 January to call on party members to 'Kampf dem Atomtod' (fight nuclear death) with demands for an end to atomic test explosions, a ban on equipping armies with nuclear weapons, the exclusion of German scientists from atomic weapons research, and the prohibition of nuclear weapons from German soil.[17] Having been frustrated in the *Bundestag* yet

12. Küntzel, M., *Bonn and the Bomb*, p. 13.
13. The statement is quoted at length in '18 deutsche Forscher warnen vor Atomwaffen', *Die Welt*, 13 April 1957, p. 1.
14. 'Albert Schweitzer mahnte: Beendet die Atomversuche', *Die Welt*, 24 April 1957, pp. 1–2.
15. See 'Russia Fires Test "Super Rocket"', *The Times*, 27 August 1957, p. 8. The ICBM test launch had taken place several days before the Russian announcement.
16. Boutwell, *The German Nuclear Dilemma*, p. 23.
17. Drummond, *The German Social Democrats*, p. 223.

again, Ollenhauer made the first public statement of the newly created extra-parliamentary campaign, *Kampf dem Atomtod* (KdA) on 10 March 1958, just a few weeks after the creation of the Campaign for Nuclear Disarmament (CND) in Britain. The SPD had certainly interpreted the public mood correctly: in 1958 there were 64 per cent of West Germans opposed to arming the *Bundeswehr* with nuclear weapons, and only 17 per cent supported the idea.[18] Starting with a demonstration in Frankfurt on 23 March 1958 the KdA and the *Deutscher Gewerkschaftsbund* (German Trade Union Federation or DGB) then organized a series of protests around Germany throughout the following months. The KdA gained spectacular support for its demonstrations in the following months: as many as 120,000 people may have attended a KdA demonstration in Hamburg on 17 April, and an estimated 40,000 people participated in an anti-nuclear demonstration in Hanover in June.[19] At the end of April Ollenhauer introduced a bill in the *Bundestag* calling for a national plebiscite on whether the West German public wanted an army equipped with nuclear weapons, a return to a tool used by the Nazis which the government was quick to seize on as an attempt to subvert the constitution and undermine parliamentary authority. The SPD then tried and failed to carry out referenda at *Land* level, only for the Constitutional Court to announce in July that regional and national plebiscites were incompatible with parliamentary government. With this blow the SPD was left with the option of pursuing a vigorous extra-parliamentary campaign through the KdA, or admitting defeat and moving on the fight another day within the parliamentary system. Not wishing to give Adenauer any further opportunities to present the SPD as disloyal to the Federal Republic and representative democracy, the party chose to abandon the KdA, which was allowed to wither on the vine over the next few months. *Bundeswehr* troops were eventually equipped with nuclear weapons in late 1959.

By then the SPD had undergone a fundamental reassessment and realignment of its political aims. Having lost three general elections with a policy that promoted a middle way between capitalism and communism, and therefore between America and Russia, the SPD had to face the fact that the majority of the electorate had made it clear they supported the fundamentals of Adenauer's policy. The SPD position had also made it all too easy for Adenauer to raise the spectre of communism. After its worst general election defeat so far in September 1957, in which Adenauer

18. Küntzel, *Bonn and the Bomb*, p. 11.
19. Rupp, H.K., *Außerparlamentarische Opposition*, pp. 289–96 provides a useful chronology of the anti-nuclear demonstrations in Germany.

gained an absolute majority in the *Bundestag* for the first time (270 CDU seats compared to 169 for the SPD), reformers in the party were able to take the initiative. Diane L. Parness, in her history of the SPD, has noted that the reformers generally had practical experience of participation on government in the *Bundestag*, in *Landtage* (State parliaments), many as *Land* Ministers or Minister Presidents, or as Mayors of large cities, like Willy Brandt in West Berlin. As a result they were aware of the necessity for compromise and collaboration with other parties in the name of effective government and pragmatic politics, unlike previous leaders, like Ollenhauer, who were products of the party administrative structure.[20] At Bad Godesberg in November 1959 these reformers were able to persuade the party that if it was to gain power in future it needed to recognize political realities and adopt sweeping reforms. Support for a Marxist programme of social reform was finally swept aside, the SPD's hostile attitude to the Catholic Church was replaced by a more accommodating line, and the emphasis on working-class struggle was abandoned. This was followed up in June 1960 with the announcement of SPD support for NATO. For Parness, Godesberg 'gave the SPD a new image and a successful marketing strategy that the party could use to get its foot in the doors of political power' by ridding it 'of archaic clichés and trappings of a working class struggle no longer relevant to German politics. More importantly, it cast the SPD relations with other social and particularly religious forces in a new light, thereby closing a long chapter of acrimony between socialism and organized religion in Germany.'[21]

By accepting the post-war settlement, rearmament, and the alliance with NATO, as well as gaining a new appeal for middle-class voters and those who had previously voted according to confessional priorities, the SPD made it more difficult for Adenauer to portray it as an illegitimate participant in a system it wanted to overthrow, and strengthened West German democracy as a result. As reformer Fritz Erler argued 'we are fighting not the state, but a false policy of the government and its majority . . . we are fighting not against the state, but for the state, in fact, not the state of the distant future, not the state only in a reunified Germany, but the state in this Federal Republic, which we want to govern'.[22] Its attempt to become a *Volkspartei* (People's Party) with a mass broad-based appeal nevertheless meant it was no longer able to create and lead mass-protest campaigns that questioned the substance of the post-war settlement. In a direct reference to the effects of this consensus politics, Parness points out

20. Parness, D.L., *The SPD and the Challenge of Mass Politics*, pp. 29–30.
21. Ibid., p. 48.
22. Boutwell, *The German Nuclear Dilemma*, p. 32.

that 'the destabilization of European party systems and the decomposition of their voter alignments are primarily due to the inability or unwillingness of traditional parties to meet the new demands of a new society'.[23] With the policy alignments of mainstream parliamentary political parties converging in key areas, and with those parties proving unwilling or unable to address the concerns of single-issue campaigns, whether national or local, extra-parliamentary activity based upon mass-protest movements was one of the few spaces left in the political landscape for public declarations of dissent. In a positive sense this opened the possibility of the creation of genuine public participation in politics, away from the restrictions of party political dogma.

In the case of nuclear rearmament policy, then, the SPD's realignment left room for the formation of an independent protest campaign. The SPD had succeeded in provoking people to action who were not willing to drop the issue of nuclear rearmament according to the dictates of party political strategy. Many of those who were alienated by the SPD's abandonment of the campaign, and its subsequent reform at Bad Godesberg, converged on the fledgling *Ostermarsch der Atomwaffengegner* (Easter March of the Opponents of Nuclear Weapons), formed in Hamburg in 1960 by a teacher, Hans-Konrad Tempel. The organization took its name from the Easter March organized in 1960 as a *Sternmarsch* (literally 'star march' with protesters arriving at a central location from various places) on the nuclear missile base at Bergen-Hohne, where the first nuclear weapons had been stationed the previous year. *Ostermarsch* took the CND Aldermaston marches as its example, and later used a stylized version of the CND badge on its documents. The march opposed 'atomic weapons of every kind and every nation' and it also demanded the unilateral disarmament of 'both German states', the first time unilateral disarmament had been introduced to the debate in Germany. The slogan 'have trust in the power of the individual' highlighted the fact that the Ostermarsch was 'independent of all parties, party-like groups or trade union organizations'.[24] Karl A. Otto has noted that *Ostermarsch* was initially a 'small group of religiously motivated pacifists', and that the appeal to individual conscience, with a belief in non-violent protest at its heart, fitted this tradition. Otto remarks that 'in this way the communist opposition would be excluded from the decision-making committees of the campaign, without being prevented from participating in the marches'. Far from being a haven for revolutionary Marxist activity, then, the *Ostermarsch*

23. Parness, *The SPD*, p. 16.
24. See 'Warum wir marschieren' and the flyer for the 1960 Easter March reprinted in Otto, K.A., *Die außerparlamentarische Opposition*, pp. 51–4.

leadership tried to give 'the overwhelming anticommunist propaganda of the time no evidence for the omnipresent suspicion of communist infiltration'.[25] Relations between *Ostermarsch* and the SPD were particularly strained. The SPD has traditionally had a fractious relationship with other organizations on the Left, and has either sought to assimilate them or actively opposed them. *Ostermarsch*'s position outside the parliamentary system that the SPD embraced at Bad Godesberg precluded the possibility of a mutually beneficial association for both organizations. In 1963 a long article published in the *Ostermarsch* newsletter *Information zur Abrüstung*, entitled 'SPD still against Easter March movement', accused the SPD of conducting a smear campaign. *Ostermarsch* alleged that the SPD had spread false information, and that they had accused *Ostermarsch* of betraying German interests by supporting disarmament in the West.[26] Having denied a role for political parties and other groups, then, *Ostermarsch* did not as yet engage in issues directly related to German politics and democracy.

Ostermarsch rapidly became the leading anti-nuclear organization and represented the start of a broad and sustained extra-parliamentary campaign. Regional committees were rapidly established throughout the country, and although only 1,000 people took part in the first Easter march in 1960, this rose to 23,000 in 1961, to 50,000 in 1962 and to 100,000 in 1963 in the aftermath of the Cuban Missile Crisis.[27] These eventually became the highpoints of an ongoing year-long campaign of local measures, including smaller-scale marches and vigils, most notably marches on Hiroshima Day (6 August) and Anti-War Day (1 September). From 1962 to 1963 the remit of the organization was expanded to reflect the changing, and more openly political, nature of the membership. In September 1962 the suffix *Kampagne für Abrüstung* (Campaign for Disarmament) was added to its name and alongside its traditionally more general aims like 'nuclear disarmament in West and East' and 'détente and nuclear-free zones', it now also campaigned for 'the rule of law and freedom'.[28] This

25. Otto, *Die außerparlamentarische Opposition*, pp. 47–8.

26. 'SPD weiterhin gegen Ostermarsch-Bewegung', *Information zur abrüstung*, November 1963, Nr. 4, Sammlung Werner Röder, ED 387/Band 14, Kampagne für Demokratie und Abrüstung/Ostermarsch, 1961–1969, Institut für Zeitgeschichte, München (henceforth IfZM).

27. Rupp, *Die Außerparlamentarische Opposition*, p. 147. In Britain CND support diminished rapidly after the Cuban Missile Crisis, presenting a strange paradox in comparison with the German experience.

28. Flyer *Ostermarsch der Atomwaffengegner, Kampagne für Abrüstung*, 1963, Sammlung Werner Röder, ED 387/Band 14, Kampagne für Demokratie und Abrüstung/Ostermarsch, 1961–1969, IfZM.

latter answered critics opposed to the campaign, including the SPD, who branded it communist, as well as attempting to placate those members who sought to politicize the campaign further.

These cosmetic changes failed to appease *Ostermarsch*'s critics, though, and a meeting of the Central Committee of the *Ostermarsch* in September 1963 made more fundamental changes. The organization was renamed *Kampagne für Abrüstung* (KfA) and would in future concentrate on promoting a disarmament policy specifically for Germany rather than simply opposing nuclear weapons in general.[29] The new campaign slogans would therefore be 'for nuclear weapon-free zones – against multilateral nuclear power', as well as the more specific 'cut back the armament budget in both parts of Germany' and 'Bonn needs a Disarmament Authority', representing a new focus on the policies of the West German government.[30] In addition, the Central Committee opened up the campaign to participation by other organizations, since the KfA now presented itself as a 'people's movement in the space before parliament'.[31] Although the KfA steadfastly maintained that it did not identify with 'any political organization or political party', the purpose of the campaign was now to encourage 'the political groups and parties in the *Bundesrepublik* to grasp the opportunity to move toward a policy of securing peace'.[32] The organization necessarily became even more politicized in its position toward the Federal government and the nature of the *Bundesrepublik*, and provided a broad base for a variety of organizations and political viewpoints, particularly the entryist activities of groups such as SDS. As such it evolved into an umbrella organization for extra-parliamentary opposition, rather than simply extra-parliamentary protest. This finally found full expression in its further name change in 1968 to the *Kampagne für Demokratie und Abrüstung* (Campaign for Democracy and Disarmament or KfDA). Even in 1964, though, the organization was becoming a more definitely oppositional force within German politics, informed by a critique of individual policies as well as of German democracy in general, rather than simply representing a general pacifist campaign.

---

29. *Information zur abrüstung*, June 1963, Nr. 1, p. 1, Sammlung Werner Röder, ED 387/Band 14, Kampagne für Demokratie und Abrüstung/Ostermarsch, 1961–1969, IfZM.

30. See 'Was ist zu tun?', reprinted in Otto, *Die außerparlamentarische Opposition*, pp. 96–7.

31. See 'Christel Beilmann, "Ostermarsch-Überlegungen"', reprinted in Otto, *Die außerparlamentarische Opposition*, p. 99. Beilmann was the editor of *Information zur abrüstung*, and wrote this statement in July 1964.

32. See 'Erklärung der KfA zur Frage "Sammelbewegung" oder "politische Partei"', reprinted in Otto, *Die außerparlamentarische Opposition*, pp. 99–100.

As such, the KfA helped to fill the void left by the SPD after Bad Godesberg, not just in terms of providing a focus for extra-parliamentary politics on the issue of nuclear disarmament, but also in providing a national forum for those whose views were not represented by the main political parties, especially those who were uneasy with the post-war settlement. In this respect it is perhaps not surprising that *Ostermarsch* was marked by such a great diversity of opinion and was able to attract support that crossed generational and social boundaries. A survey by the *Ostermarsch* regional organizations found in 1965 that among their supporters 11 per cent were workers, 34 per cent were salaried employees, 13 per cent were civil servants, 8 per cent were housewives, 15 per cent were self-employed, 22 per cent were academics and 11 per cent were students. It was established that 19 per cent were under 25 years of age, 76 per cent were between 25 and 50, and 5 per cent were over 50 years old. A similar survey of support for the Easter marches in 1967 discovered 1,416 clergy-men, 1,507 teachers, 486 university lecturers or researchers, 1,378 trade unionists, 1,008 representatives of youth and student organizations, and 891 artists, including 577 writers and journalists.[33] Clearly the APO was not a homogenous phenomenon. This is not to suggest that the APO and the KfA were synonymous. The KfA was the first sustained campaign of protest, and provided the first focus for protest activities by otherwise diffuse and varied groups, but it was one of many organizations that can be placed within the APO camp. From this starting point the APO was able to mushroom out into new protests on a variety of issues by a wide spectrum of organizations as the 1960s progressed. Yet this is only a part of the story and as was shown in the previous chapter the origins of the APO can only be fully understood in the context of more fundamental historical trends, including post-war economic prosperity and the resultant changes in behaviour patterns, including the rise of a youth culture.

Perhaps the clearest example of the way in which the encouragement of freedom of expression by the new youth culture fed into the creation of an APO is provided by the Schwabing Riots. A few weeks before the riots, police were called in by Munich University to break up a jazz con-cert forcibly because it had gone past its official curfew time of 10.00 p.m. The ensuing confrontation escalated to the point where around 2,000 people assembled in protest on Geschwister Scholl Platz outside the main University building.[34] The guitarist in this incident was arrested again in

33. Otto, *Die außerparlamentarische Opposition*, p. 23.
34. See *Bekanntgage in der Sitzung der Vollversammlung des Stadtrates München am 27. Juni 1962*, in the archive of the Deutsche Liga für Menschenrecht, ED 707/12, Schwabinger Krawalle, IfZM. This statement by the police to the City Council of Munich is a detailed, if biased, account of the riots.

the evening of 20 June 1962 along with two other guitarists who were singing in the street in front of a large crowd on Wedekindplatz in the bohemian Schwabing district. The police used loudspeakers to break up the crowd in order to enforce the local curfew. The following day, at around 10.30 p.m., the same guitarist was playing outside a café on Leopoldstrasse, the main commercial thoroughfare in Schwabing. A group of around 500 people watched the performance and sang along but local residents called the police to complain about the noise.[35] When the police arrived and tried to arrest the guitarist the situation rapidly degenerated into a riot which only ended at 1.00 a.m., by which time 41 people had been arrested. Clashes were repeated over the following four nights by thousands of young people, including the young Andreas Baader. By the end 198 people, including 102 students, had been arrested.[36]

From the perspective of the rioters, the events in Schwabing were an expression of frustration at the limitations placed upon young people. In turn, the police response to the riots raised issues about personal freedoms and the basic assumptions supporting democratic rights. The *Allgemeiner Studentenausschuß* or AStA (General Student Committee, or student union) of Munich University stated in its report that the police had indiscriminately beaten anyone in their path so that 'protest against a mistaken police tactic' had quickly escalated into 'opposition against state violence'.[37] The police response to this was heavy-handed to say the least and reflected a disapproval of the new youth culture that exposed deep generational divisions. A particularly striking example of this was the arrest and conviction of two 18-year-olds for dancing the Twist in Leopoldstrasse during one of the riots.[38] At their trial their defence lawyer argued for leniency and the judge took the lack of previous convictions into account, but he argued 'the two young accused have brought a great deal of guilt upon themselves through their behaviour'. He therefore convicted them of the charges and gave them a sentence of six months in a youth detention centre each, suspended on condition of good behaviour. Not only were the

35. See letter from Hans-Jochen Vogel, Oberbürgermeister der Landeshauptstadt München, to Frau Anneliese Friedmann, dated 16 July 1962, Deutsche Liga für Menschenrecht, ED 707/12, Schwabinger Krawalle, IfZM. Vogel was mayor of Munich, and this letter, to a reporter of *Stern* magazine in complaint at an article on the Schwabing riots, is a rich source of detail. In 1974 Vogel became Federal Justice Minister.

36. 'Es waren keine Studentenunruhen … stellt der AStA zu den Schwabinger Krawallen fest', *Süddeutsche Zeitung*, 3 September 1962, Deutsche Liga für Menschenrecht, ED 707/12, Schwabinger Krawalle, IfZM.

37. Ibid.

38. 'Twist auf der Straße – Zwist mit der Polizei', *Süddeutsche Zeitung*, 21 November 1962, p. 11.

police and justice system unable to countenance such behaviour but the ready willingness to use extreme force and prison sentences, out of all proportion to the original 'crimes', highlighted a gulf between authorities and protesters in their understanding of the meaning of democracy and the ways in which it should be defended. It is clear that for the City authorities, the rioters were a threat to democratic freedom and the rule of law. Hans-Jochen Vogel, the SPD Mayor of Munich, declared that 'in the Munich City Council sit many men and women who were hunted down and robbed of their freedom between 1933 and 1945. The police president was also a political victim. They are all, as I am myself, certainly no friends of rubber truncheons', but he justified the police tactics, saying 'the police cannot allow destruction of the peace and law-breaking on the streets of a democratic state in homage to a mistaken concept of freedom'.[39]

The Spiegel Affair followed just months after the Schwabing riots and added to the questioning of the *Bundesrepublik*'s democratic credentials.[40] *Der Spiegel* had established a record for critical investigative journalism, although it has been described rather sanctimoniously by Peter Pulzer as 'well-known for its muck-raking' in his brief account of the Affair.[41] As part of its investigations it had run a series of articles on Defence Minister and CSU leader Franz-Josef Strauß and *Der Spiegel*.[42] The long-running friction between them boiled over when, on 10 October 1962, *Der Spiegel* renewed its attack on Strauß with an article in which it alleged that the General Inspector of the *Bundeswehr*, General Friedrich Foertsch, had informed them of secret plans for a massive expansion in *Bundeswehr* strength. The article went into detail about a report by American observers that suggested the *Bundeswehr* was seriously understrength, as well as cataloguing the current *Bundeswehr* dispositions and the plans for their augmentation.[43] On 26 October the offices of *Der Spiegel* in Hamburg, and the homes of four senior staff members, were raided and searched by police investigating charges that the magazine had compromised national security in the *Bundeswehr* article. The owner, Rudolf Augstein, was arrested and detained in custody until February 1963, while the author of

---

39. Letter from Vogel to Frau Anneliese Friedmann, dated 16 July 1962.

40. Books on the Spiegel Affair are legion. Bunn, R.F., *German Politics and the Spiegel Affair* is not among the most up-to-date or comprehensive, but is still a good introduction to the subject. Also interesting are Williams, *Adenauer*, pp. 503–14, and Irving, R., *Adenauer*, pp. 183–7.

41. Pulzer, P., *German Politics 1945–1995*, p. 73.

42. See 'Affären: Kapfinger', *Der Spiegel*, 31 May 1961, pp. 40–5 for the article that sparked the earlier 'Fibag affair', also involving Strauß in corruption charges.

43. 'Bundeswehr', *Der Spiegel*, 10 October 1962, pp. 32–53.

the article, editor Conrad Ahlers, was arrested in Spain where he was on holiday. He was flown back to Frankfurt, where West German police arrested him at the airport. These actions had been carried out by police acting under Federal orders from the Ministry of Defence, and in contradiction of laws limiting the right of Federal authorities to bypass the *Land* Interior Ministries who controlled policing.

In the public and official response to the raids differences in attitudes to democracy were again evident. The parallels with the knock on the door in the middle of the night favoured by the Nazis when removing opponents was not lost on the editors of *Der Spiegel*. A few weeks after the raid the magazine featured a cartoon of Adenauer leading a child resembling Hitler, complete with the familiar moustache, with 'German Democracy' written on the front of his *Lederhosen*. Adenauer has a copy of *Der Spiegel* in his pocket and is saying 'so young, and already a moustache'.[44] Letters to the magazine included a note of solidarity from *Gruppe 47* writers, and one member of the public wrote that 'as a former supporter of the Nazis I protest most strongly against the arrest of the Spiegel editor'. Others attacked *Der Spiegel*, writing 'when I heard about Augstein's arrest I wanted to give a donation to the Salvation Army for a celebratory concert'.[45] The press both in Germany and abroad condemned the arrests as undemocratic, while the German Journalists' Union attacked the censorship in advance that it alleged was the purpose behind the police raid.[46] Yet Adenauer, far from distancing himself from the raids, told the *Bundestag* 'Augstein committed treason, and I find that nasty; he carried out a general hate campaign also against the coalition partners.' The Interior Minister, Hermann Höcherl, even went so far as to argue that although the government had acted 'somewhat outside the law' nonetheless 'reproaches on moral grounds cannot be made by anyone' because the government had acted to defend democracy.[47]

In the following weeks the crisis deepened. On 9 November Strauß was forced to admit to the *Bundestag* that he had ordered Ahlers's arrest in Spain and that his previous denials of involvement had been lies.[48] On 19

44. *Der Spiegel*, 21 November 1962, p. 29.
45. 'Briefe', *Der Spiegel*, 7 November 1962, pp. 5–18.
46. See "Das Ansehen der Staatsführung steht auf dem Spiel", *Der Spiegel*, 7 November 1962, pp. 22–47, and 'Vorzensur und Meinungsfreiheit', *Der Spiegel*, 7 November 1962, p. 62. The former is a collection of newspaper articles on the raid from German and foreign newspapers, while the latter is a collection of statements from German and international press organizations.
47. 'Bonn', *Der Spiegel*, 14 November 1962, p. 43.
48. "Ich habe mit der Sache nichts zu tun", *Der Spiegel*, 28 November 1962, pp. 53–5 is a chronological reconstruction of Strauß's statements on his involvement in the Affair.

November Dr Wolfgang Stammberger (FDP), the Minister for Justice, resigned in reaction to the undermining of his authority inherent in the lack of consultation with him in launching the police raids. He was joined by the four other FDP members of Adenauer's cabinet, thereby forcing Adenauer to dissolve the coalition government on 27 November. Adenauer was able to form a new coalition with the FDP on 7 December only after agreeing to resign as Chancellor in October 1963. The parliamentary investigation into the Affair found in February 1963 that Strauß had indeed lied to the *Bundestag*, and that the checks and balances in Federal and *Land* laws to prevent such actions by central government had been breached in pursuit of Strauß's personal vendetta with *Der Spiegel*. Augstein called the Adenauer government a 'regime of incompetence', but he also acknowledged that 'in the "Frankfurter Allgemeine" I read: "If the Spiegel is the only Opposition in Germany, that is not good for the Federal Republic". No, gentlemen, it is not good for the Federal Republic, and if you are not to be intentionally blind, you will have to take notice.'[49]

The Spiegel Affair revealed the best and worst of the democratic system in the Federal Republic. On the negative side of the balance sheet, it brought the government's inability to deal with dissent into stark relief, along with its difficulty in striking a balance between protecting democracy and undermining it. Many of the checks and balances, particularly the sacrosanct insistence on local rather than Federal police jurisdiction, had patently failed to work, and apart from his resignation Strauß got away scot-free. He was even able to resurrect his career in government just four years later when he returned as Finance Minister in Kurt-Georg Kiesinger's cabinet. For Germans of all political persuasions the Affair revived memories of arbitrary governmental actions under the Nazis that flouted the law with impunity. For supporters of APO campaigns the Affair added to a growing suspicion of the *Bundesrepublik* and its leaders; above all, for those on the road to revolutionary activity the Spiegel Affair reinforced a view of the *Bundesrepublik* as an intolerant and undemocratic state. On the other hand, though, the checks and balances within the system eventually reined in the government's excesses. Through vocal opposition it was made clear that 'Chancellor democracy' did not entail unaccountable and unrepresentative government. On the contrary, the various political parties, the *Bundestag*, the *Länder*, the press, the legal system, and above all the German people were aware of the need to make the government accountable for its actions, and were willing to act in order to protect democracy.

49. Augstein, R., 'Regime der inkompetenz', *Der Spiegel*, 28 November 1962, p. 37.

Nevertheless, the dismissal of dissent as evidence of communist infiltration, the willing resort to violence by the police, and the illegal activities of those in government confirmed or created suspicions about the nature of democracy in the *Bundesrepublik* that would be added to repeatedly in the coming years. For those in authority, however, the growing violence of demonstrations, the lack of respect for norms of behaviour and deference, the hurtful accusations of Nazism, and the questioning of the post-war settlement that took place ever more vociferously as the decade continued showed that the fabric of West German society and democracy was at risk. This in turn was used to justify a continuous escalation of the harsh measures deployed to deal with the problem, so that the solutions to the 'problem' threatened democracy in themselves.

Part II
1965–1967

University Reform

From the mid-1960s students began to take part in a wider variety of protests than previously, and in particular they became increasingly concerned with the issue of university reform. Their disquiet rapidly moved beyond its initial concentration upon courses and student participation in government to include a far-left critique of the *Bundesrepublik* in general. Having become the dominant force in universities, far-left organizations used them as a source of ongoing confrontation as well as a base for their activities in wider APO engagements. Above all the confrontation over university reform highlighted contrasting interpretations of the role of universities, of the lessons of the Nazi past, and of the meaning of democracy.

The Nazi past was perhaps the key issue informing attitudes to university reform in the 1960s by prompting a fundamental reassessment of the very nature of West German universities. The almost complete failure of universities to oppose Nazi incursions on their autonomy has been well documented.[1] In her history of German higher education Rosalind Pritchard has noted that the model of German universities established by Alexander von Humboldt at Berlin University has been blamed for creating the conditions in which the Nazis were able to co-opt universities so easily.[2] Pritchard describes a classical model of German universities based upon an ideal of introverted personal enlightenment rather than the creation of a critical academic community. She suggests that the influence of Romanticism and neo-humanism, personified by Humboldt's friend and colleague Friedrich Schiller, was especially strong in emphasizing a cloistered disengagement from wider society in the pursuit of a personal

1. Despite its age Weinreich, M., *Hitler's Professors,* first published in 1946, is still the classic account of academic collusion with the Nazis. For a contemporary account see Klemperer, V, *I Shall Bear Witness,* especially p. 134, and *To the Bitter End,* p. 34.

2. Pritchard, R.M.O., *The End of Elitism?,* pp. 34–5. Berlin University is now the Humboldt University, with its main buildings on Unter den Linden, in what was the Soviet zone. Hahn, H.J., *Education and Society in Germany* covers similar ground. See also Jahrausch, K.H., *Deutsche Studenten 1800–1970.*

understanding of the world and the attainment of *kultur* and *innerlichkeit* (inwardness).[3] German universities were ivory towers indeed, divorced from the everyday realities and social needs of ordinary Germans, and populated by academics determined not to dirty their hands with political issues. When challenged by the Nazis the lack of an academic tradition of critical political participation and debate meant universities were unable or unwilling to defend either themselves or German democracy.

In both the Nazi period and the 1960s, then, universities faced a clash between two views of the purpose of universities and academic work. On the one hand academics looked to a classical tradition of academic discourse free of party political dogma and which concentrated on the production of research that was as objective as possible. Research for its own sake, a contemplative approach, and purely academic debate were the foundations of academic life. University courses concerned themselves with the creation of a general critical faculty that was applicable throughout life outside the university. Vocational courses were therefore unnecessary, and had no relevance for the social background of the majority of students. On the other hand, with varying degrees of emphasis, stood a model that recognized the inherent subjectivity of academic work, and which called for academic engagement with political and social issues. At least for the Left of the 1960s the Nazi period represented the failure of the former model, necessitating reform toward the latter model in the post-war period. For many academics, in contrast, Nazi policies toward universities represented the complete victory of the latter model, which was to be avoided at all costs in the post-war period. It could be said that the periods before and after the Nazi seizure of power characterized the extremes in an ongoing negotiation between two conflicting sets of demands and viewpoints, but this was emphatically not the stand-point of far-left protesters of the 1960s. For post-war university reformers, nationalism was viewed as providing the seedbed in which Nazism was able to establish itself, and as such both it and its practitioners were to be removed from academia if democracy was to be preserved. For the far left, moreover, political activity by university staff and students was in itself insufficient if carried out within parameters for political debate that were set by an acceptance of the post-war settlement. Instead, they presented a critique of universities in which Nazi propaganda of the 1930s and 1940s was replaced by the capitalist indoctrination of the post-war settlement,

3. Pritchard, *The End of Elitism?*, pp. 17–40 is a detailed account of the foundation of Berlin University and of the various aspects of the classical model of German universities that encouraged separation from the real world.

which was viewed as Nazism in a democratic disguise. Universities were therefore to become an arena for political combat, and for many academics who were determined to avoid a repeat of past mistakes, student demands, especially those from the Left, were all too reminiscent of the politicization required by the Nazis and, more recently, by the Soviets.

The intractable debate on the role of universities provided a source of conflict from the very start of the post-war period. The *Report of University Reform*, produced by the Allies in 1948, insisted on the need for a fundamental change in attitudes within universities, and an emphasis upon their role in educating young people for a role in society rather than upon research. This was rejected out of hand by *Rektors* (Vice Chancellors or Principals) in January 1949, and in the absence of a desire to impose reform from outside, universities remained largely unchanged.[4] Fears of subordinating critical academic debate to political dogma and of subjecting the independence of universities to the demands of industry meant the creation of a modified form of the classical model, in which academics engaged in critical debate on current affairs, while seeking to preserve the independence of research. Having learnt from the Nazi past, numerous academics overtly took part in political activity, especially on issues such as nuclear weapons that had a moral dimension that appealed across party lines: academics were a significant group in the anti-nuclear campaign, and German academics made the Declaration of the Göttingen Eighteen. In contrast to the press in the Nazi period, the post-war press was also replete with letters and articles by academics sharing their views on current affairs. Many courses, particularly in the humanities, remained detached from engagement with the contemporary world, and the problem of applying a university education to the practical demands of employment was an issue that exercised student protesters throughout the 1960s, including students of vocational subjects such as engineering. Harald Husemann has talked of a failure to seize the opportunity for reform in 1945. This left problems for the future that led directly to the confrontations of the 1960s.[5] In light of the generational model advanced in the previous chapter, it is notable that not until the mid-1960s did student dissatisfaction prompt open confrontation with university authorities.

Once again these tensions were particularly exacerbated by the continued presence of former Nazis at universities after 1945. As elsewhere, a serious shortage of qualified staff forced the Allies to allow the return of

---

4. Husemann, H., 'Anglo-German Relations in Higher Education', in Hearnden, *The British in Germany*, pp. 167–9 gives a useful account.

5. Ibid., pp. 169–70.

former Nazis after a process of denazification. Geoffrey Bird, a member of the Education Branch of the Control Commission for Germany from 1945 to 1951, estimated that 'if the appointment of everyone who had been technically a member of the Nazi organization had been disallowed there would have been very few qualified university teachers left'.[6] Although 4,000 Nazi academics were removed from their posts by the Allies in 1945, they were eventually allowed to return, many going on to hold senior posts: Hans Wenke, who became the founding *Rektor* of the Ruhr University, wrote in 1934 that 'the protection of the race' was 'a necessity for the future of the German people'. He was forced to resign as *Rektor*, though not as an academic, when his Nazi past became known. Similarly Theodor Maunz was forced to resign as Bavarian Culture Minister, with direct influence on universities, when it was discovered that in 1936 he had declared promotion of 'the National Socialist world view' as the purpose of all German university lecturers. Again, he was allowed to remain in his post as a Law Professor.[7]

The issue of student representation was a further area of continuity with the past since university government remained firmly in the hands of senior academic staff. Representation beyond this was limited, and even at the Free University (FU) Berlin student representation was not without its flaws and frustrations. The FU Berlin was established in the elegant suburb of Dahlem, in the American sector, in 1948 at the height of the Berlin Airlift.[8] It was set up by West German students and academics in direct opposition to the politicized institutions being created by the Soviets. As such state interference was discouraged by the creation of a *Kuratorium*, the equivalent of a Council, that included representatives from the Berlin City government and the university as well as at least one student. It was given the most liberal constitution of any West German university and, unlike any other university, the 'Berlin Model' allowed for student representation at Faculty level, as well as on the academic Senate. These student representatives were taken from the elected members of the student parliament, the *Konvent*. In theory, then, this was a democratic

6 Bird, G., 'The Universities', in Hearnden, *The British in Germany*, p. 148.

7. 'Gesellschaft: Professoren', *Der Spiegel*, 19 February 1968, p. 42. This extensive article provides an overview of the development of German universities, including the Nazi period, and an analysis of the student demands for reform.

8. See Tent, J., *The Free University of Berlin* for a detailed account of the history of the University. See also Rabehl, B., *Am Ende der Utopie*. Rabehl was a senior member of SDS in the 1960s and a personal friend of Rudi Dutschke. His book is a critique of the University as a tool of capitalism, and as such it gives an invaluable account of SDS activities at the University.

system that allowed for participation in debate on all issues by all sections of the academic community of the university. The personal relationships, consensus about the aims of the FU, and the atmosphere of compromise necessary to make this situation work were only possible in a small institution where both staff and students were engaged in the exciting task of constructing a new university model. While these relationships were based upon the mutual respect created in a common struggle, as James F. Tent argues 'unfortunately no one found a mechanism with which to institutionalise this mutual respect in the university constitution'.[9] With the evolution of a larger and more impersonal university in the 1950s, in which more traditional relationships of deference and authority between staff and students became the norm, the government of the university became centralized in the hands of senior staff and the *Rektor*. Added to this was the presence of a rapidly expanding group of junior members of staff who, because they had not featured in the FU at its foundation, were given no representation within university government. Campaigns to change this situation in the 1950s met with no success, so that by the mid-1960s frustrated students and junior members of staff, at the FU and at other universities, were willing to combine in attempts to claim the rights they felt were consistent with democracy.

It must also be recognized that the FU became heavily politicized in the 1950s, but not in the sense of creating a balanced political environment in which staff and students could engage in open and critical political debate, as had been the intention of its founders. In West Germany in general, and the FU Berlin in particular, rabid anti-communism was the dominant norm in student politics in the 1950s and 1960s, with the FU proving to be particularly receptive to students from the Soviet zone who had suffered persecution at the hands of the communist authorities. In this environment, despite the simultaneous emphasis upon the need for academic freedom, the study of Marx was almost impossible at the FU. Conservative organizations, and particularly the CDU student arm, the *Ring Christlich-Demokratische Studenten* (the Circle of Christian Democratic Students or RCDS), remained the majority political grouping in student politics throughout the 1950s and early 1960s, both at the FU and elsewhere. The Right was further strengthened in 1958 when the Supreme Federal Court ruled that the FU ban on the formation of far-right duelling societies (*Burschenschaften*) was illegal, despite the belief that they had provided key sources of support for the Nazis in the 1920s and

9. Tent, J.F., 'The Free University of Berlin: A German Experiment in Higher Education, 1948–1961', in Diefendorf et al., *American Policy*, p. 253.

1930s.[10] This does not mean that the student body was completely quiescent on other issues: expressions of concern about the Soviet invasion of Hungary, the Algerian civil war, and above all student involvement in the campaign against German rearmament, exposed the tensions and contradictions in the FU system, resulting in concerted attempts to oppose a politicization of the university. Although stopping short of the bitter confrontations that marked relations between students and the FU authorities from the mid-1960s, it is clear that the anxieties and mutual hostility displayed in later protests were already being given manifestation, albeit less violently, in the 1950s. There was of course a paradox here since the desire by many academics to prevent politicization was selective in actively promoting outspoken anti-communism while branding any attempt to oppose this view, or to encourage critical political debate, as inherently undemocratic. It is a position that is instructive for attitudes both on the role of the university and on democracy in West Germany in general. By the mid-1960s, with the arrival of a new post-war generation that was not so wedded to conservative viewpoints, who wanted universities to live up to the democratic rhetoric used to oppose the Soviets, and who were frustrated by university resistance to such demands, far-left critiques about the nature of post-war democracy and the role of former Nazis found a receptive audience in the reformist majority.

The first large-scale protests over higher education came in 1965 in reaction to overcrowding. The number of students registered at universities had risen from 123,154 in 1952 to 205,346 in 1959 and then to 274,392 in 1964. This rate of expansion, a doubling of numbers in 12 years, made it impossible for university resources to keep pace. This forced universities to refuse entry to qualified students because of insufficient places, with the prospect of a worsening situation with the arrival of the baby-boom generation.[11] The government responded to the crisis by announcing the creation of new universities, but this proved insufficient to placate between 100,000 and 300,000 people, including both students and academics throughout West Germany, who took part in a day of protests organized by students from Freiburg University on 1 July 1965. Known as the *Aktion 1. Juli*, it was supported by the national student organization, the *Verband Deutscher Studentenschaften* (Union of German Student Societies or VDS), and represented the largest single demonstration on the issue of university reform in the 1960s, and even involved the circulation of 250,000

10. Ibid., pp. 247–50.
11. See Statistisches Bundesamt Wiesbaden (ed.), *Statistisches Jahrbuch, 1953*, pp. 94–5, *Statistisches Jahrbuch, 1960*, p. 108, and *Statistisches Jahrbuch, 1969*, p. 79.

flyers.[12] This was just an opening shot, and the rather genteel and decorous form of the mass meetings stands in stark contrast with the openly confrontational style of protests that were to follow in the coming years.

Aktion 1. Juli nevertheless produced a wide-ranging critique of higher education. Students demanded equality of opportunity in gaining university entrance, and noted '5 per cent of working class children study at German universities, in England 25 per cent, in the USA 30 per cent'. Appeals for the establishment of a national education policy, with national financial planning, rather than *Land* control of these areas, were combined with calls for a 'revaluation of education policy in light of the requirements of defence, economic, foreign and social policies'.[13] In line with this inclusive and integrated view of higher education, students also requested the introduction of comprehensive state financial support for students, rather than the reliance upon parental assistance that was the lot of most German students.[14] Many of these demands were recurrent themes in the years ahead, but students had yet to make the leap to a revolutionary analysis.

The FU Berlin was perhaps the key location in the development of such an analysis. Although most German universities experienced student unrest of various kinds in the 1960s, students at the FU Berlin remained the most vociferous and radical in their demands for reform. The FU was also the scene of the first concerted campaign of protest for reform at an individual university rather than the previous national campaign to reform higher education policy in general. Indeed, the first skirmishes, surrounding the Kuby Affair, brought the democratic credentials of the university into question and allowed the Left to portray the university as intolerant of alternative views of the post-war settlement because, ultimately, it was a capitalist contrivance. The origins of the confrontation went back to the 1950s: in 1958 the writer Erich Kuby had given a speech at the FU in which he commented on how 'unfree' the Free University was, after which the Senate and *Rektor* banned him from speaking at the University.[15] The

12. '1. Juli – Proteste und Hoffnungen', *Politica*, June 1965, HIfS. This was a student journal from Münster. See also *Freiburger Studenten Zeitung*, July 1965, pp. 11–12.

13. Peter Schönefuß, 'Nicht am 2. Juli vergessen', *Freiburger Studenten Zeitung*, July 1965, pp. 13–14.

14. See flyer *Aktion 1. Juli*, Sammlung Schlemper, ED 328/353, IfZM.

15. Parts of the speech are quoted in 2. *(abschließende) Beschlußempfehlung des 1. Untersuchungsausschusses – V. Wahlperiode*, p. 9, Rep 14/845, Landesarchiv Berlin (henceforth LB). This is a report by a committee of investigation set up by the Berlin *Parlament* in 1967 to examine the disturbances at the FU Berlin. It provides exhaustive detail on the development of the student protests.

actions of the university authorities had prompted an outcry from the student body but nothing more. When, in the Spring of 1965, the FU AStA invited Kuby to give a speech to students, the situation had changed. The speech, on the subject of 'restoration or new beginning?', or whether the *Bundesrepublik* was a genuine break with the past or a continuation of the Nazi regime, was banned on 8 April 1965 by the *Rektor,* Professor Herbert Lüers. Kuby gave the speech at the Technical University (TU) Berlin on 7 May instead.

Student groups such as the SDS, the *Liberaler Studenbund Deutschlands* (Liberal Student Federation of Germany or LSD), the *Humanistische Studentenunion* (Humanist Student Union or HSU) and the *Sozialdemokratischer Hochschulbund* (Social Democratic University Federation or SHB) responded by calling a mass protest meeting on 7 May. This was the first such protest meeting to take place at a German university, but in future the mass meeting would be used regularly by the Left as a tool of direct participation and representative decision-making, bypassing elected bodies such the *Konvent*. Around a thousand students condemned 'the scandalous banning of the speech' and asked 'what does Rektor Lüers understand as "free"?'.[16] The protesting students passed a resolution which was then signed by 3,000 students and sent to the *Rektor*, famously demanding that he allow them to 'listen to anyone, at any time, on any subject, and to discuss it with them', in direct imitation of the demands of students at Berkeley, California.[17] Faced with the *Rektor*'s continued intransigence, staff and students at the Otto-Suhr Institute held a lecture strike on 18 May.

The Senate responded to the student objections by confirming the powers of the *Rektor* and dismissing their demands as incompatible with those powers.[18] On 28 May the AStA representative Wolfgang Lefèvre (SDS) even took the unprecedented step of using the assembly of the University in celebration of registration for the new Semester to attack both the *Rektor* and the Senate. The *Rektor* attempted to diffuse the situation on 4 June by declaring that there had never been a ban on Kuby speaking, but that there had simply been no rooms available. Kuby made a diplomatic reply to this olive branch on 17 July by stating that his

16. Flyer *Freie (???) Universität*, Sammlung Schwiedrzik zur Studentenbewegung, ZSg 153/2, BK.
17. Flyer *Offener Brief*, file 00108 Berlin 1965, Dokumentationstelle für unkonventionelle Literatur, Bibliothek für Zeitgeschichte, Stuttgart (henceforth BfZS).
18. *2. (abschließende) Beschlußempfehlung des 1. Untersuchungsausschusses – V. Wahlperiode*, p. 10 reprints the decision in full.

comments in 1958 had been misinterpreted and that he had merely suggested the university had been named in a way that it did not reflect its origins, unlike the Humboldt University. Having saved face, the *Rektor* finally allowed Kuby to give a speech at the FU Berlin on 11 November.

This was not the end of the matter, and as was to happen so often in the protests of the coming years, the initial source of conflict rapidly escalated to include new and unexpected issues. The situation spiralled out of control, positions became entrenched, and dialogue between the two sides became increasingly hostile. On 14 May Dr Ekkehard Krippendorff, a research assistant at the Otto-Suhr Institute, wrote an article in the *Spandauer Volksblatt* in which he attacked the FU *Rektor* over the Kuby Affair. Calling his article 'A demonstration for our freedom' Krippendorff accused the *Rektor* of 'political and intellectual censorship' and equated the Kuby Affair with 'an attack and threat on the internal freedom of Berlin'.[19] The *Rektor* dismissed Krippendorff's accusations of censorship as 'grotesque and libellous', and Krippendorff was forced to give a personal apology to the *Rektor* for his comments.[20] Rather than letting the issue lie, however, on 10 June the *Rektor* informed Krippendorff that his contract, which ran out on 30 September, would not be renewed. Professor Kurt Sontheimer, the Director of the Otto-Suhr Institute, and Professor Gilbert Ziebura, Krippendorff's immediate superior, protested to the *Rektor* that he had not consulted them before making his decision. They contended that in bypassing the democratic structures of the university he had equated loyalty to the *Rektor* with loyalty to the university, and that he 'wanted to make an example'. The Nazi past loomed large in the debate: another memorandum on the issue, this time by Sontheimer and Ernst Fraenkel, referred to a 'reversion to the period of absolutism'.[21] After a series of mass protests by students, the Berlin Senator for Science and Art eventually intervened as the *Land* official responsible for universities, and Krippendorff was re-employed as a member of staff at the FU on a new stipend.[22] Until 1965 the student body had been largely quiescent and the

19. 'Eine Demonstration für unsere Freiheit', *Spandauer Volksblatt*, 14 May 1965, Sammlung Schwiedrzik zur Studentenbewegung, ZSg 153/2, BK.

20. Quoted in *Memorandum über die Entlassung meines Assistenten Dr Ekkehard Krippendorff* by Prof. Dr Gilbert Ziebura of the Otto-Suhr Institute, 22 June 1965, file 00108 Berlin 1965, BfZS.

21. Ernst Fraenkel and Kurt Sontheimer, *Die Freiheit in der Universität Berlin*, file 00108, Berlin 1965, BfZS.

22. See *Chronologischer Abriß der Ereignisse an der Freien Universität Berlin ab April 1965*, Sammlung Schwiedrzik zur Studentenbewegung, ZSg 153/1, BK. This is a chronology of events at the FU produced by the AStA in 1967.

Rektor had generally been able to act as he saw fit. That assumption, and the *Rektor*'s view on what constituted actions that were consistent with democracy, had been challenged by students and staff for the first time in the Kuby and Krippendorff Affairs, but these were merely the opening skirmishes of the conflict.

The exchange of salvoes was renewed again with the start of a new academic year in the autumn. From this point onward the Left, and particularly the SDS, made a concerted effort to gain the upper hand in student politics through confrontations with the newly elected *Rektor,* Professor Hans-Joachim Lieber. At the end of November Lieber rose to the bait and banned SDS from using FU rooms for an exhibition on the Vietnam War. A few days later he insisted that SDS show two American films about Vietnam alongside three north Vietnamese films in an SDS event because he wanted all sides of the case to the presented. The *Rektor* argued that the event was intended to attack the American position in Vietnam, and 'I saw in that a failure to meet the original request and the original intention.'[23] For Lieber a tension existed between 'the demand of student groups and the student representatives for . . . use of the University for their political opinion forming as well as their political actions, fully independent and free of every Administration' and the duty of the *Rektor* as the representative of the University to uphold the laws of the institution. This created 'a conflict for the institution. We believed we could see a conflict coming right from the start of my Rectorate that would be independent of the behaviour of individuals'.[24] To some extent this was an accurate assessment, but Lieber failed to grasp that his consistent failure to produce a measured response to confrontational tactics played into the hands of the Left and exposed him and the University to accusations of undemocratic behaviour.

It is ironic that the university with the most liberal and inclusive form of government should have been such a breeding ground for student radicalism, but its origins as an American-sponsored institution made it an obvious target for far-left charges of indoctrination in the creation of a hegemonic capitalist reality. The presence of an outspoken group of 'anti-authoritarian' SDS members around Rudi Dutschke at the FU Berlin was particularly important, and it is crucial to understand the motivations of

23. Statement by *Rektor* Lieber in *1. Untersuchungsausschuss (V. Wahlperiode) 48 (10. Öffentliche) Sitzung, Dienstag, den 5. Dezember 1967*, p. 5, Rep 014/841, LB. This is a transcript of the oral evidence given by Lieber to a Berlin *Parlament* committee of investigation.

24. Ibid., p. 3.

this group if the events at the FU are to be understood.[25] Not only did this group come to dominate the protests at the FU, but the other groups on the Left gravitated toward it. The SDS had been created in September 1946 as the student arm of the SPD. After the adoption of the Bad Godesburg programme the retention of a Marxist critique by SDS, and its open criticism of the SPD, made it an embarrassment for its parent party. It was jettisoned in 1961, to be replace by the SHB, and from this point it developed an ever more radical and openly revolutionary world-view.[26] In the mid-1960s it split into two main camps, with the majority, controlling the Federal Committee, favouring an entryist policy of infiltration within organizations such as VDS and the KfA, with the ultimate aim of creating a society based upon traditional Marxist lines. In contrast the anti-authoritarian minority, based mainly in Berlin originally, favoured a method of direct confrontation. Bernd Rabehl, a member of the Federal Committee of the SDS in the late 1960s and an anti-authoritarian activist at the FU, has acknowledged that 'the anti-authoritarian revolt lived off the protests, the teach-ins, the Congresses, the conflict'. It was an ad hoc improvised development in which 'theories were always thought of in terms of provocation'.[27] Understanding the revolutionary motivations that informed these tactics, and which differed markedly from those of the traditionalist wing, is crucial.

Curiously, there has been some debate as to whether the SDS was a revolutionary organization. Claus Leggewie has even gone so far as to suggest that when the SDS theorist Rudi Dutschke, who came to prominence in the FU Berlin confrontations, attacked the 'fascism inside the structure' of West German society, he did so 'more out of concern for the republic than out of destructive anti-democratic tendencies'.[28] Although Dutschke undoubtedly viewed his theoretical stance as democratic, it is nonetheless absurd to suggest that he was working to reform the *Bundesrepublik* rather

25. Pritchard, *The End of Elitism?*, pp. 86–97 makes the mistake of ignoring protests before 2 June 1967 and fails to recognize the split within SDS created by the anti-authoritarians. She uses the 1961 SDS document *Hochschule in der Demokratie,* produced by the traditional SDS wing, erroneously as the basis for SDS attitudes to higher education for the rest of the decade, when the anti-authoritarians had a very different agenda.

26. On the early history of SDS see Fichter, T., *SDS und SPD* and Albrecht, W., *Der Sozialistische Deutsche Studentenbund (SDS).* Also useful is Fichter and Lönnendonker, *Kleine Geschichte des SDS.*

27. Rabehl, *Am Ende der Utopie*, p. 248.

28. Leggewie, C., 'A Laboratory of Postindustrial Society: Reassessing the 1960s in Germany', in Fink et al., *1968,* p. 286. See also Schmidtke, M.A., 'Reform, Revolte oder Revolution? Der Sozialistische Deutsche Studentenbund (SDS) und die Students for a Democratic Society (SDS) 1960–1970', in Gilcher-Holtey, *1968,* pp. 188–206.

than to overthrow it. Even a superficial survey of any 1960s SDS document produced independently of other organizations makes it perfectly
clear that revolution was the primary aim; the constant promotion of the
term 'revolution' is something of a give-away.

If there was a debate within SDS on revolution, it concentrated on the
methods of bringing a revolution about and the form of society it would
create rather than the question of whether a revolution was desirable. The
tactics of the anti-authoritarian wing of the SDS were, in part, informed by
a desire to use issues like university reform as a springboard from which
to launch an attack upon capitalist society. This is seen in the numerous
variations on the mantra that protests on university reform were ultimately
concerned with 'the social function of education'.[29] This 'social function'
would not be attained through reform within a capitalist system but via the
replacement of capitalism and parliamentary democracy with direct
participation through *Rätedemokratie*, or government through people's
councils. A survey by *Der Spiegel* in June 1968 found that only 13 per cent
of SDS members believed that the government and parliament represented
the people, and also that 40 per cent disagreed with the view that *Rätedemokratie* was the only real form of democracy, giving a clear indication
of the splits within the organization.[30]

Although careful not to make a specific call for the overthrow of the
Bundesrepublik, Dutschke stated in 1967 that he viewed *Rätedemokratie*
as a method of ensuring the 'uninterrupted continuation of the Revolution
in all areas of social life', and this included universities.[31] In a later interview he followed the Marcusian line in declaring that 'the new form of
fascism is no longer found in a party or one person, it exists in all institutions of late capitalism. Day to day the people in these institutions, from
factories to universities, from schools to churches are given authoritarian
training'. He continued, 'our political tactic of provocation (happenings,
sit-ins, go-ins, etc.), in order to destroy the system at its weakest points,
has proved reliable in the first phase of our struggle'.[32] For the anti-
authoritarians universities served the needs of industry through the provision of unthinking technocrats or non-political cogs in the capitalist
machine who were unable to look beyond the premises upon which the

29. Kadritzke, U., 'Zum Verhältnis von Politik und Protest', *FU Spiegel*, Dezember
1966, p. 5.

30. 'Studenten', *Der Spiegel*, 10 June 1968, pp. 54–5.

31. 'Wir fordern die Enteignung Axel Springers', *Der Spiegel*, 10 July 1967, p. 30.

32. 'Rudi Dutschke in Prag: Liberalisierung oder Demokratisierung?', *Konkret*, May
1968, p. 22.

Bundesrepublik was founded. The imposition of *Rätedemokratie* at universities, whether by stealth or by overthrowing university governments, would allow for courses that challenged the capitalist world-view. Whatever their success in this, their tactics were undoubtedly effective in prompting reactions from authorities that could be described by the SDS as removing the democratic façade to expose the fascist reality beneath. Those in authority were consistently confused by protesters' refusal to act according to the 'rules of engagement', and only gradually came to understand that the issues were being used as a platform for provocation. The two sides often talked across each other, with little understanding of the language and viewpoints of their opponents.

SDS gained its first success in December 1965 by winning six seats in the *Konvent*. Along with the 12 seats won by the SHB, LSD, HSU, and the left-wing *Argument Club*, this meant a gain of just one seat for the Left, but it confirmed the general trend away from the conservative groups, who won 17 seats; this was the final year in which the Right was a significant force in the *Konvent*. Since there were 81 seats available the Left groups remained a minority, but they were able to wield disproportionate influence because, unlike other groups who were working within the university constitution, the SDS was simply using the system as a means to an end. This fundamental difference in assumptions put non-revolutionary groups at a disadvantage from the start, leaving them bewildered and outmanoeuvred by the SDS's aggressive manipulation of systems and situations.

For instance, a small bomb was detonated during an SDS discussion on the Vietnam War at the TU Berlin on 28 January. It caused no injuries and only broke some windows but it prompted the FU *Rektor* to ban a similar SDS meeting planned for 31 January, despite opposition from the AStA and *Konvent*. On the same day the university received an anonymous bomb warning, and the rooms to be used for the banned meeting were closed during a police search. This prompted a general ban on using rooms for political meetings on the grounds that they could only be used for festivals, research or education. The AStA, which resigned in protest, declared 'the possibility for free, full debate is no longer present, if events, that are for political education, are exiled from the rooms of the university'.[33] An attempt by the AStA to get the decision overturned by appealing to the Berlin Senator for Science and Art backfired when the latter supported the stance of the University. This was a setback, but the SDS had succeeded

33. Quoted in *2. (abschließende) Beschlußempfehlung des 1. Untersuchungsausschusses – V. Wahlperiode*, pp. 12–13. See also 'Dokumentation zum Richtlinienstreit, *FU Spiegel*, May 1966, pp. 8–9, BfZS. This long article reprints the key documents in full.

all too easily in provoking the authorities, and the relationship between the student representative organs and the *Rektor* was steadily worsening.

A new crisis, over plans to limit the duration of study, prompted a greater outpouring of student anger than ever before. By the mid-1960s the FU had more than 15,000 students, despite an intended capacity of around 10,000 students. In an attempt to solve the overcrowding problem the University proposed a limitation on the number of semesters for which a student could register (*Zwangsexmatrikulation*). On 14 February 1966 the Registration Committee of the Law Faculty became the first to implement such restrictions by limiting students to 9 semesters, after which students would be forced either to graduate or leave the university. The student representatives in the Law Faculty resigned their positions but this did not stop the Medicine Faculty from announcing similar proposals at the start of May. In response the student *Konvent* called for a referendum on the issue, to be held at the end of June. The moderate FU Berlin student newspaper, *FU Spiegel*, felt the policy was a step backward toward greater exclusivity and that 'whoever supports the limitation of studying time without reform of courses as a valid measure, may not be surprised if tomorrow the state uses statistics to cut funding for expansion'.[34] The *Rektor* refused permission for students to use FU rooms for the referendum on the grounds that the FU constitution allowed for student votes only on issues that were under their own administration, not those which were the shared responsibility of the university community in general. He also looked to the Nazi period, in which referenda were used to bypass existing democratic structures.[35] After both the *Rektor* and the *Konvent* appealed in June to the Senator for Science and Art, the latter gave his support to the *Rektor* and confirmed that students could not use FU rooms to hold the referendum.

The crisis came to a head when, on 20 June, the Court of the University effectively banned the referendum by refusing AStA representative Knut Nevermann's request for rooms. The next day around 2,000 students held a mass meeting of all Faculties organized by the SDS which decided to hold a sit-in occupation of the Henry-Ford building, during a Senate meeting. At around 3.00 p.m. on 22 June 1966 approximately 3,000 students occupied the hall of the building, and began the first sit-in to be held at a German university. By 9.30 p.m. the occupation had become a full-blown teach-in, involving the participation of senior members of staff.

34. 'Ohne Nutzen und elitär', *FU Spiegel*, May 1966, p. 5, BfZS.
35. Statement by *Rektor* Lieber to *1. Untersuchungsausschuss (V. Wahlperiode) 50 (11. Öffentliche) Sitzung, Donnerstag, den 7. Dezember 1967*, p. 11, Rep 014/841, LB.

Among the messages of support read out to the students was a letter from the VDS, which re-emphasized the need for a root-and-branch rethink of universities, saying 'the reform of study must begin with the definition of the educational purpose of university study'.[36] When the Senate meeting ended at 10.00 p.m. it became known that the decision to ban the use of FU rooms for political purposes had been reversed and the debate continued in triumph.

The sit-in was the first mass public meeting in which Rudi Dutschke expounded the theories of the anti-authoritarian wing of the SDS and his speech helped to gain greater awareness and support among students for the anti-authoritarian message. Having quoted from Marx he asserted that

> the call of the student opposition for the democratization of universities should not be separated from the historical process of the democratization of society . . . We lead the dispute with our backs to the Wall, without illusory hopes, but we lead it constantly and convincingly, through the uninterrupted organization of protests and information campaigns to enlarge the anti-authoritarian camp.[37]

This SDS domination of the sit-in was reflected in the resolution passed by the assembly before dispersing, which followed the essence of Dutschke's speech: student demands went beyond the ending of forced deregistration to include 'the necessity to work together with other democratic organizations in society in order to carry through their demands'.[38] The sit-in was the perfect example of SDS manipulation and provocation tactics, giving them political weight that far outweighed their numerical strength, and it would be a mistake to view the sit-in as a spontaneous expression of popular discontent, although numerous people who attended no doubt felt it was. SDS member Siegward Lönnendonker has admitted that during the sit-in the various messages of solidarity read out to the assembled students had been arranged well in advance 'but they were read out to the assembly as if they'd been sent spontaneously. In fact, the occupation's direct democracy included a number of well-planned dramatic techniques'.[39] Having gained this success in the sit-in, the SDS were then outmanoeuvred by the authorities who realized the situation had got out of hand and refused to

36. *Solidaritätserklärung des Verbandes Deutscher Studentenschaften*, Berlin 1966, file 00110, BfZS.

37. Quoted in Dutschke, G., *Rudi Dutschke*, p. 103.

38. 'Resolution verabschiedet von der versammelten Studentenschaft der Freien Universität Berlin auf dem Sit-in am 22/23. Juni 1966', *FU Spiegel*, July 1966, p. 7. See also *FU Spiegel*, July 1966, p. 6, for one of the many excellent chronologies of the sit-in.

39. Fraser, *1968*, p. 127.

rise to the SDS bait again. Attempting to diffuse the situation through the kind of inclusive, co-optive tactics that the Left viewed as 'repressive tolerance' and which Arthur Marwick has termed 'measured judgement', the university authorities accepted the *Konvent*'s call for a commission to debate proposals for the reform of the University.[40] This was quickly established with representatives from across the university community.

The *Rektor*'s victory was short-lived, and the SDS simply raised the level of provocation. On 26 November 1966 the *Rektor* took part in a mass discussion on university reform. After two hours of uneventful debate a group of students, mainly SDS members, climbed onto the stage and seized the microphone from the *Rektor* and read out the text of a flyer that was simultaneously being distributed throughout the hall. Written by the 'Provisional Committee for the creation of a self-run student organization', this flyer accused the AStA of being in league with the Senate and insisted students should 'refuse to allow ourselves to be turned into *Fachidioten* [specialist idiots] by professorial *Fachidioten*'. Instead students were urged to implement reform themselves, as the only group qualified to do so.[41] The *Rektor* left the hall, after which the AStA representative broke up the meeting amid scenes of chaos. This new extreme shocked much of the student body, to the extent that the *FU Spiegel*, normally a stalwart supporter of the student case, condemned the 'uncouth methods that are unworthy of discussion' that had put the student body on the defensive just when constructive discussions over reform were finally taking place.[42]

Far from damaging the Left, the demonstration gained the support of students in the *Konvent* elections in December, in which the Left achieved a majority for the first time. During the campaign the SDS dismissed the new reform commission as an attempt by the university 'to make the student members of the commission partners in their compromise deals, so they can defend their measures to students better later on'.[43] Although

40. See Dutschke, R., 'Die Widersprüch des Spätkapitalismus, die antiautoritären Studenten und ihr Verhältnis zur Dritten Welt', in U. Bergmann et al., *Rebellion der Studenten*, p. 73 for Dutschke's application of Marcuse's theory of repressive tolerance to the campaign against the Vietnam War. The *Konvent*'s proposal was put forward in 'Memorandum zur Reform des Studiums der Freien Universität Berlin', *FU Spiegel*, July 1966, p. 8, BfZS.

41. Quoted in *2. (abschließende) Beschlußempfehlung des 1. Untersuchungsausschusses – V. Wahlperiode*, pp. 15–16.

42. 'Tumult bei der Diskussion mit dem Rektor über Studienreform', *FU Spiegel*, December 1966, p. 4.

43. *Was will der SDS?*, Berlin 1966, file 00110, BfZS. This flyer, dated December 1966, deals directly with the *Konvent* election campaign.

the vast majority of students did not vote for the Left, the 11 seats for conservative groups compared with 6 for SDS and 15 for other Left-oriented groups effectively gave the Left control of the *Konvent*. This was followed by the appointment of *Konvent* and AStA representatives who were either members of Left organizations or sympathetic to them, deepening the stalemate with the *Rektor*, who had demanded that the AStA provide the names of the 'Provisional Committee'. This continued until 26 January 1967 when, on the orders of a local judge, the police raided SDS Berlin headquarters on the Kurfürstendamm and took away files containing membership cards. Police Chief Erich Duensing later recalled that the raid 'poured oil onto the fire, and the uniformed police and the police in general were brought into disrepute . . . the powder-keg was blown up'.[44] The next day around 2,000 students took part in a demonstration on the issue, and followed this with another the next day, at which the Mayor of Berlin, Heinrich Albertz (SPD), distanced himself from the police raid when faced by placards bearing the message 'Big Heini is watching you.'[45] The demonstration had not given the three days' advance notice to police that was required in Berlin, and so was not strictly legal, but faced with the prospect of rioting the police were unwilling to break it up. In a telling statement Duensing later called it 'a black day for the police' and worried that 'police officers would soon not know how they could intervene' in such situations, revealing a reluctance to deviate from the letter of the law that would inform police actions in subsequent events.[46] Later in the day another demonstration was held, which was attended by around 3,000 people including trade-union members and Günter Grass. The outcry was so great that on 31 January the membership cards were returned to the SDS unopened. Later in the year the legal investigation into the events of 26 November 1966 was quietly dropped. The SDS had won another very well publicized victory.

It was quickly followed up. When SDS members of the hippie commune *Kommune I* were arrested for allegedly trying to assassinate US Vice President Hubert Humphrey (discussed in Chapter 5), their names were forwarded to the FU *Rektor* with a view to further disciplinary proceedings. This was followed on 19 April by a Senate decision to ban the *FU*

44. Quoted in *1. Untersuchungsausschuß (V. Wahlperiode), 4 (öffentliche) Sitzung, Freitag, den 23. Juni 1967*, p. 4, folder 'Untersuchungsausschuß 2. Juni 1967', Aktenbestand des Sozialistischen Anwaltskollektivs, HIfS. This reprints Duensing's oral testimony to the committee of investigation into the events in Berlin on 2 June 1967.

45. Quoted in 'Berlin: Studenten', *Der Spiegel*, 6 February 1967, p. 39.

46. Quoted in *1. Untersuchungsausschuß (V. Wahlperiode), 4 (öffentliche) Sitzung, Freitag, den 23. Juni 1967*, p. 5.

Spiegel from publishing reviews of seminars and lectures. When the *Rektor* issued an ultimatum demanding that the AStA promise to cease these reviews, around 2,000 students held another mass meeting of all Faculties in the hall of the Henry-Ford Building, despite warnings from the *Rektor* that this would be considered as an illegal sit-in. At about 10.30 p.m. the *Rektor* summoned the AStA representative, Hartmut Häußermann (SHB), to tell him that the mass meeting should be brought to an end or the police would be deployed. When Häußermann repeated these demands to the mass meeting, the students declared a sit-in and elected Häußermann and Nevermann leaders of the protest. When the RCDS representative accused the Left groups of a lack of tolerance and democracy, Dutschke took the stage, saying 'tolerance with appalling representation is clear partisanship against the victims of the government, and we can not make ourselves guilty of that'. He continued by outlining issues about democracy and legality that would preoccupy the Left in the coming years:

> the call for democracy underpins the democratic maturity of the people in this state. If this maturity does not exist, if it is systematically made impossible, then every action for the creation of a critical consciousness is democratic! Legality is a fetish, for the maintenance of these illegal methods of government in society and in the university, around which at the moment we discuss demo-cratic attitudes, and the academic Senate continues its undemocratic attitudes.[47]

Attempts by Senate members and the *Rektor* to bring the sit-in to an end were met by jeers and around midnight the *Rektor* requested help from the police, who dragged around 100 of the remaining 800 protesters from the hall. The Berlin Police Chief, fearful of the repercussions of the police action, then sent a message to end the police deployment, and the students who had been dragged outside returned to the sit-in. The protest only ended at 1.30 a.m., after the passing of a resolution to hold another mass meeting in the same place during the next meeting of the Senate on 3 May.

Not realizing that he was playing the SDS's game the *Rektor* naively relied on previously trustworthy methods and in an attempted show of strength brought charges against Nevermann, Häußermann, his fellow AStA representative Bernhard Wilhelmer, Lefèvre and Dutschke, all of whom had addressed the assembly. In protest the *Konvent* passed a resol-ution in which it condemned the disciplinary measures, and called another referendum that asked whether students wanted to reject its resolution. The referendum naturally became a vote on the future of the university, with

---

47. Quoted in Dutschke, G., *Rudi Dutschke*, pp. 119–20.

conservative student groups supporting the *Rektor*'s pleas for students to vote 'yes', while the Left united around the 'no' campaign. The *Rektor* confused the situation further by releasing an open letter in which he argued that 'if the student body rejects the *Konvent* resolution . . . then, and only then, will the way be free to refrain from enforcing the disciplinary measures that all members of our University dislike equally'. This forced the AStA and *Konvent* into a campaign in which they opposed the *Rektor* by tacitly agreeing to the disciplinary proceedings.[48] The rhetoric of the campaign was more bitter than had been imaginable even the previous year: a pro-AStA flyer, responding to the *Rektor*'s description of the sit-in as a 'fascist mob', declared that the *Rektor* 'eliminates the formal right of citizens' democracy (freedom of assembly, freedom of speech, etc.) through brutal terror'.[49] Similar themes were taken up in a flyer signed by all the AStA representatives since 1956, who claimed 'the Berlin Model is under threat', and took the view that 'without independent student representation there is no Free University'.[50]

The final result of the referendum, held from 3 to 10 May, made it clear that the issue had fundamentally split the University. The 'no' vote of 4,709 or 46.1 per cent only narrowly defeated the 'yes' votes of 4,383 or 43.3 per cent. Although this was a victory for the *Konvent* and the AStA, the fact that only 67.1 per cent of students voted, and more than 10 per cent of votes were invalid, meant that the *Burschenschaft Germania*, along with other conservative groups, was able to claim that 'the AStA no longer represents the majority of the students'.[51] For the Left such objections could not cloud the fact that they had scored an unprecedented victory over the *Rektor* of a West German university.[52] They had not only challenged existing democratic structures, but in so doing had publicly undermined previously accepted norms of deference to authority. *Rektors* had previously been able to act in an arbitrary fashion, assuming this was acceptable in preserving democracy and academic freedom, especially from communist incursion. The FU *Rektor* had now been told that he was

48. Quoted in *Bericht des Rektors der Freien Universität Berlin für den Untersuchungs-sausschuß des Abgeordnetenhauses von Berlin*, p. 34, Rep 014/843, LB. This is a long report by the *Rektor* on the disturbances at the FU, submitted to the official investigation by the city government of Berlin.

49. *Sit-in und Faschismus*, Berlin 1967, file 03791, BfZS.

50. *Das Berliner Modell ist in Gefahr*, Berlin 1967, file 03791, BfZS.

51. See flyer *Kommilitonen! Der Asta vertritt nicht mehr die Mehrheit der Studenten!!!*, Berlin 1967, file 03792, BfZS.

52. *Bericht des Rektors der Freien Universität Berlin für den Untersuchungsausschuß des Abgeordnetenhauses von Berlin*, p. 34, Rep 014/843, LB.

wrong, that students wanted inclusion in government, and that they were willing to take it for themselves if necessary. He had been publicly humiliated and shown that his authority had definite limits. *Der Spiegel* accurately summed up the importance of the student victory in the FU referendum as 'a milestone in the history of the FU – and above all in the history of West German higher education. For the first time in academic memory a student majority at a German university has – at least relatively – opposed the almost unanimous wishes of its professors'.[53] This was the last act in this phase of the campaign for university reform: the shooting of Benno Ohnesorg just a few weeks later altered the political landscape completely, and before returning to the campaign for university reform the development of the rest of the APO needs to be described.

---

53. 'Berlin: Studenten', *Der Spiegel*, 5 June 1967, p. 58.

–4–

The Vietnam Campaign

Whether appealing to pacifism, humanitarianism or international revolutionary solidarity, for protesters the Vietnam War was without question the most emotive issue of the 1960s. As with so many other aspects of the decade, perceptions of the Vietnam campaign are loaded with misconceptions: slogans such as 'love and peace', 'make love, not war' and 'peace, man' spring directly from the protests against the Vietnam War, and yet have little to do with the kind of campaign conducted in West Germany. All of these slogans came from the American anti-Vietnam movement, which was much more heavily influenced by the counterculture. In Germany, where pacifism was prominent in the early campaign, the far left gradually gained a dominant position, eventually coming to set the tone of the campaign. The galvanizing influence of the War for the far left is easily understood: opposing views could always be dismissed by pointing to Vietnam and asking whether a War in support of a succession of unelected and corrupt regimes could be described as defending freedom. From the start of the protests through to the terrorist campaigns of the 1970s, the Left used the War as the ultimate proof of the moral bankruptcy of the capitalist powers, while the support given to the Americans by the government of the *Bundesrepublik* was presented as yet more evidence that West Germany was still a fascist state.

The strength of feeling generated by Vietnam is difficult to underestimate. Support for American intervention in Vietnam was never clear-cut in West Germany, so that as early as March 1966 just 44 per cent of people said America was defending freedom against communism, as opposed to 25 per cent who felt the Americans had no right to be there, and 33 per cent who were undecided.[1] This limited approval of American policy diminished further as the War dragged on, and a survey carried out by *Der Spiegel* in February 1968 found that 67 per cent of people in the 15-to-25 age range approved of the anti-War protests that were sweeping the country by that stage, while 63 per cent of 19-to-22-year-olds were willing to protest

---

1. Noelle-Neumann, E. (ed.), *The Germans*, p. 475.

against the War.[2] Another survey, carried out in the same month, showed that 60 per cent of West Germans disapproved of American soldiers fighting in Vietnam, with 35 per cent worried that the conflict could trigger a third world war. Some 42 per cent also believed the Americans were committing atrocities, although this figure rose to 63 per cent for students and to 61 per cent for opponents of the War in general. A truce was the solution supported by a majority, 54 per cent, with only 24 per cent arguing for the immediate withdrawal of American troops.[3] Of course, this survey was carried out when public opinion in all Western countries was becoming disillusioned with war, and it is essential to recognize that protests against the War were initially slow to develop and originally gained only limited support.

Although direct American military involvement began in March 1965, it was not until the autumn of 1965 that regular protests against the War began to take place. The early campaign was not dominated by any one organization or viewpoint, and several groups were usually involved in the organization of each protest, often representing various shades of socialism, from social democracy and trade unionism to revolutionary Marxism. Party political and revolutionary rhetoric was kept to a minimum and the aims of the campaign were sufficiently vague to be acceptable to a wide spectrum of views. The campaign was fundamentally informed by pacifist and humanitarian considerations, but went beyond an opposition to war in general. While it was not supportive of the revolutionary aims of the North Vietnamese, it did support the application of the terms of the 1954 Geneva Agreements, which ended the war of liberation against the French. This divided the country in two along a demilitarized zone on the seventeenth parallel, with the communists to the North and an American-backed regime in the South. The Geneva Agreements stipulated that this was only to be a temporary solution, and that national elections should be held in 1956 to allow for the unification of Vietnam under a single democratically elected government. When it became clear that the communists would win such elections, America refused to allow the elections to go ahead. The enforcement of these conditions were central planks in the pacifist campaign against the War in numerous countries, including West Germany.

The KfA and SHB positions provide good examples of the multi-faceted nature of the campaign, in which the desire for Vietnamese self-determination, along with humanitarianism, were common themes. A list of demands reproduced in a 1966 KfA flyer used the common phrase 'Vietnam to the

2. 'Zwei drittel zum Protest bereit', *Der Spiegel*, 19 February 1968, p. 40.
3. 'Diesen Krieg kann niemand gewinnen', *Der Spiegel*, 4 March 1968, pp. 30–1.

Vietnamese' and called for 'no support for the US policy in Vietnam', a direct attack on the German government's support for American policy, that marked an important step in the KfA's evolution into an oppositional organization.[4] For KfA, then, Vietnam was both a moral issue, and a part of its new critique of the *Bundesrepublik*. In 1967 it called for 'an end to any support for this American war in Vietnam by the Federal Government' as well as urging supporters to 'make a stand for the end of the bomb attacks on North Vietnam, and for a peace in Vietnam based upon the Geneva Treaty'.[5] The following year, having changed its name to *Kampagne für Demokratie und Abrüstung* (KfDA), it added to this list by appealing for 'the removal of all foreign troops from Vietnam.'[6] In common with almost all groups that took part in anti-Vietnam War protests the SHB accused the Americans of *Völkermord* (genocide) and repeated the call for the enforcement of the Geneva Agreements. The Americans' support for the latest in a succession of corrupt regimes, under Marshal Ky, 'oppresses every opposition with the methods of terror'. Going beyond the KfA position, but stopping short of outright support, the SHB described the communist Viet Cong as a 'national liberation army', suggesting 'whoever reproaches the Vietnamese with forcefully seeking self-determination is simply cynical or takes an indirect part in their oppression'. This prompted the demand 'leave Vietnam alone, give Vietnam the right of self-determination!'.[7]

With the emergence of far-left groups, especially the anti-authoritarian wing of SDS, as the main force in the Vietnam campaign, the dominance of the pacifist-humanitarian stance within the campaign was short-lived. Pacifist elements remained, and as at the FU Berlin the influence of the far left was certainly out of all proportion to its size. Yet the desire to drive

4. Taken from flyer *4. März. Auftaktkundgebung zum Ostermarsch 1966*, Sammlung Dr Werner Röder, ED 387/Band 14, Kampagne für Demokratie und Abrüstung/Ostermarsch, 1961–1969, IfZM. This is a flyer from the Munich section of the KfA.

5. Untitled flyer, Kampagne für Abrüstung, November/Dezember 1967, Sammlung Dr Werner Röder, ED 387/Band 14, Kampagne für Demokratie und Abrüstung/Ostermarsch 1961–1967, IfZM.

6. *Aufruf zum Ostermarsch '68*, file 00124, BfZS.

7. Sozialdemokratischer Hochschulbund, *Demonstration gegen Völkermord*, October 1967, file 03791, BfZS. Marshal Nguyen Cao Ky took control of the South Vietnamese government in June 1965, replacing General Nguyen Khanh. In January 1964 Khanh had himself seized power from Duong van Minh, who in turn had seized power from Ngo Dinh Diem in November 1963 in an American-backed coup, during which Diem was murdered. Nguyen Van Thieu effectively edged Ky out of power in September 1967. All of these regimes were corrupt and undemocratic, but enjoyed American support because of their anti-communism.

the campaign toward a revolutionary agenda combined with the anti-authoritarian Left's provocative tactics often presented other groups with a fait accompli and gave the far left the ability to seize the initiative. For the far left, pacifism amounted to lily-livered vacillation that did nothing to challenge capitalist hegemony. This is not to suggest that the far left were unconcerned with humanitarian issues, or that far-left groups did not want an end to the war in Vietnam, but rather it is to acknowledge that revolutionary considerations were given far greater importance. For the SDS in particular the Vietnam War was seen as yet another example of Western cultural imperialism of the kind that it felt had been carried out by the Americans in Germany. According to this interpretation the North Vietnamese were engaged not simply in a war of liberation, but were at the sharp end of an international revolutionary struggle against capitalism. It was the duty of the far-left groups in West Germany to support the North Vietnamese in their struggle by launching an effective campaign of opposition in Germany. This included demands for the immediate withdrawal of American troops, criticism of the support for the American policy in Vietnam given by the West German government, and attempts to bolster the North Vietnamese war effort with blood donations and collections of money.

The SDS's critique of capitalism and the *Bundesrepublik* meant it was able to take its activities beyond universities to include a more direct confrontation with state authorities and the German public. The national accounts for the SDS in 1966 show that even at this early stage the Vietnam campaign was allocated by far the largest amount of money in the SDS budget in comparison with amounts for any other issue or project. Out of a total 6,522 DM available, 1,833 DM, or just under a third of the total, was spent on Vietnam alone.[8] The protest activity that this financed was varied, encompassing demonstrations, film screenings, national conferences, flyer distribution, and collections for medical help to North Vietnam. As in other areas these protest methods were a source of disagreement within the SDS and from an early stage the anti-authoritarian group at the FU Berlin used the Vietnam campaign to challenge the traditionalist wing within the SDS and to outrage the City authorities. On the night of 3 to 4 February 1966 members of the Berlin anti-authoritarian

---

8. *Aufstellung der Verbindlichkeiten der gruppen gegenüber dem BV*, Sammlung Schwiedrzik zur Studentenbewegung, ZSg 153/7, BK. These are accounts presented to the annual national SDS conference held in Frankfurt from 1 to 4 September 1966. They show that by far the largest financial contributor was the Munich section, followed in order by those of Hamburg, Frankfurt and Berlin.

group, including Dutschke and Rabehl, took part in the so-called *Plakat-aktion* (poster protest), in which 5,000 anti-Vietnam War posters were put up throughout Berlin. This was perhaps the single most important event in making the general public in Berlin aware of the presence of the anti-authoritarian campaign. In sensationalist melodramatic style, the poster began by attacking the Chancellor, Ludwig Erhard and the *Bundestag* parties for supporting 'murder through Napalm bombs! Murder through poison gas! Murder through atomic weapons!' It went on to say:

> the people of Asia, Africa and Latin America are fighting against hunger, death and inhumanity. The former slaves want to be human beings. Cuba, Congo, Vietnam – the answer to the capitalists is war. The rulers are maintained with armed strength. Trade is secured through the wartime economy. East and West are coming to an accommodation with each other ever more at the cost of the underdeveloped countries. Now only taking up arms remains for the oppressed. For them the future is called: Revolution . . . How much longer will we allow murder to be committed in our names? Americans get out of Vietnam! International liberation front![9]

The various facets of the anti-authoritarian position are introduced here: identification with liberation campaigns, rejection of both the capitalist West and the totalitarian regimes of the Soviet East, declarations of solidarity with North Vietnam, and finally the inclusion of the Vietnam War into an international campaign of socialist revolutionary struggle that incorporated protests in Europe.

The *Plakataktion* was followed the very next day, 5 February, by the first mass Vietnam demonstration to be held in Berlin. This was organized by a number of groups, including LSD, SHB, HSU, *Argument Club* and SDS, after the FU *Rektor* banned SHB from holding a Vietnam event on FU land. The aims were non-specific, insisting on 'no further escalation of the war! Negotiations on the basis of the Geneva Agreements! Peace for Vietnam!'[10] Around 2,500 people took part in a peaceful march through the centre of Berlin, after which about 200 of the more militant protesters held a sit-down strike outside the American Embassy. Around ten to fifteen people pulled the American flag down to half-mast and then pelted the Embassy with eggs. Two SDS members were among the five people arrested for this, and although the other participating organizations later

9. *Zur Information für SDS-Genossen: 1. Text des Flugblatts 2. Plakattext. Inform-ation über Vietnam und Länder der Dritten Welt. Berlin, Mai 1966, Nr. 1,* file 00110, BfZS.
10. See the flyer *Demonstration,* file 00110, BfZS.

distanced themselves from the egg throwing, describing those who threw the eggs as ' a few hotheads', SDS refused to do so.[11]

A socialist attack on America and American property was a red rag (literally) to a bull, especially in Berlin. The press response, especially from the titles in the right-wing Springer publishing empire, was to condemn the protest as the work of communists. The tabloid *Bild* declared 'two million Berliners will not allow themselves to be led by the nose by 1500 muddled heads', and the broad-sheet *Berliner Morgenpost* stated 'the politically idiotic and rowdies should be ruthlessly removed from the universities' and wanted to 'send the hooligans to East Berlin'.[12] The protests were described as a 'shameful event' by *Die Welt*.[13] Ernst Lemmers, the Chancellor's Special Representative in Berlin, lamented that Americans were giving their lives 'for freedom' in Vietnam, while in Berlin they were subject to 'such loutish treatment'.[14] This vitriolic response was totally out of proportion to the seriousness of the event, especially as this was the first large Vietnam protest in Berlin.

The attitude of the city authorities was equally uncompromising, particularly from Pastor Heinrich Albertz (SPD), the Senator for the Interior and later Mayor of Berlin. Jacques Schuster, Albertz's biographer, has been able to say – with justification – that as a result of this minor egg-throwing incident 'two worlds collided, two irreconcilable mentalities, that only shared one similarity: black and white thinking'.[15] Schuster presents Albertz, who had responsibility for the Berlin police, as courting police loyalty and quotes him as referring to the police as 'my men'.[16] Under Albertz the Berlin police, which had become ever more militaristic in nature in the 1950s, were armed with Walther automatic pistols and

11. *Rote haus im schwarzen Pelz?*, Munich file 03473, BfZS. This declaration by organizations including HSU, LSD, SHB and SDS, dated 11 February 1966, was sent to Berlin Interior Senator Albertz, the *Land* representatives of the CDU, SPD and FDP, press agencies and all German AStAs and student newspapers.

12. Both quoted in Lenz, R., 'Foltern für die Freie Welt: Der Vietnam-Krieg im Spiegel der deutschen Presse, *Konkret*, March, p. 18. This is a useful survey of press attitudes both to the War and to the protests. 1960s protest movements, in Germany and elsewhere, were particularly poor at dealing with the media, and regularly complained of misrepresentation. See Gitlin, T., *The Whole World is Watching* for the classic account of media coverage in America, and Hilwig, S.J., 'The Revolt Against the Establishment: Students Versus the Press in West Germany and Italy', in Fink et al., *1968*, pp. 321–49.

13. Conrad, B., 'Ein empörendes Schauspiel', *Die Welt*, 7 February 1966, p. 2.

14. 'Lemmer verurteilt scharf "Pöbeleien" gegen die USA', *Die Welt*, 7 February 1966, p. 1.

15. Schuster, J., *Heinrich Albertz*, p. 191.

16. Ibid., p. 148.

wore uniforms that made them resemble soldiers. Albertz oversaw a massive increase in police numbers and spending so that twice as much money was spent on police as on the entire *U-* and *S-Bahn* transport system. There were more than 10,000 uniformed police officers, 3,000 riot police, 1,400 plain-clothes officers and 5,000 reservists 'to protect against a mass invasion of communists'. *Der Spiegel* noted that there were more police officers per head of population in Berlin than in any other *Land* in Germany and that 'the fire-power of the Berlin police is greater than [that of] a German infantry division in the Second World War'.[17]

Schuster portrays Albertz as someone who viewed study as a privilege, for whom student protest should be directed solely against East Germany. Albertz viewed protesters as an East German 'fifth column' and supported the heavy-handed tactics of Berlin police in dealing with demonstrators.[18] When, on 8 February, 300 outraged citizens took part in a CDU protest outside the American Embassy, supporting US policy on Vietnam, and attacked the egg-throwing incident with what Gerhard Bauß has described as 'fascistic violence, during which opponents of the Vietnam War were beaten in the *S-Bahn* to East Berlin', Berlin police did nothing to intervene.[19] Any act of protest that was not aimed against East Germany, whether peaceful or not, was identified as a threat to democratic freedom and so was not to be tolerated. Not only were lines of opposition clearly delineated early in the conflict by this uncompromising stance by the press, the state and the police, but when the confrontation expanded and escalated there was no room for moderate opinion on either side. Further escalation, and ever more violence, was the result.

The next major events in the campaign against the War were the peaceful Easter demonstrations from 9 to 11 April 1966 by the KfA, and these provide clear evidence of the already established lines of division. Although the KfA held small-scale local protests throughout the year, the Easter marches still represented the zenith of its annual activity. An account by marcher Rolv Heuer of the march from Duisburg to Essen gives a graphic illustration of the diversity of the participants, while also getting in a dig at those who saw the march as communist propaganda. He wrote,

17. 'Berlin: Polizei', *Der Spiegel*, 17 July 1967, p. 36. This article quotes the same figures as those used by Schuster.

18. Schuster, *Heinrich Albertz*, pp. 189–90.

19. Bauß, *Die Studentenbewegung*, p. 174. Ernst Lemmers was a speaker at this demonstration, during which he thanked the Allies for continuing to protect Berlin. See 'Sympathie-Kundgebung vor dem Amerika-Haus', *Die Welt*, 9 February 1966, p. 1.

there are track-suit types, people with knickerbockers and beautiful red knitted stockings, parka socialists, every-day-a-good-deed Christians . . . but also – more in the middle and that is the majority – people whom we really can't categorize, completely normal, ordinary citizens who don't draw one's attention . . . and so are seldom noticed. Are you disappointed? Did you expect FDJ supporters? Ulbricht himself?[20]

During the march there was a constant stream of abuse from bystanders, and march slogans, including the classic 'hey, hey, LBJ, how many kids have you killed today?', were mixed with shouts of 'hooligans', or 'like Russians, you understand – put them all in a sack and then use truncheons'. Although the marches passed off peacefully, the battle lines were being drawn.

On 22 May 1966 the SDS collaborated with other organizations, including the SJD, the KfA, SHB and LSD, in holding a Vietnam Congress in Frankfurt am Main under the title *Vietnam – Analyse eines Exempels* or 'Vietnam – Analysis of an Example.' Even though around 2,000 students from various organizations attended the conference, the SDS controlled the programme and debates.[21] Speakers included Conrad Ahlers, Oskar Negt, and the Frankfurt School philosophers Jürgen Habermas and Herbert Marcuse who were so influential in informing the anti-authoritarian SDS world-view. As well as attacking the American military campaign, and the impact of this upon the civilian population, the *Kongreß* claimed that the roots of 'the armed war of opposition against the semi-fascist Regime in Saigon . . . lie in the unbearable exploitation and the reign of terror that the Diem Regime, as well as all of the later Saigon Regimes, has meant for the people'.[22] It was the first national congress on the subject and marked the fact that the SDS was now the dominant force within the Vietnam campaign. Yet the anti-authoritarian wing of the SDS played only a limited role. The *Plakataktion* had been an embarrassment to the traditionalist Federal organization, and the threats by the Berlin group to disrupt the

20. Heuer, R., 'Mein Ostermarsch "Marschieren wir gegen den Osten? NEIN! Marschieren wir gegen den Westen? NEIN"', *Konkret*, May 1966, pp. 22–4. Knickerbockers and stockings are the traditional clothing for country walkers or ramblers. FDJ stands for *Freie Deutsche Jugend* or Free German Youth, the youth organization of the East German ruling SED, that was banned in West Germany in 1954. Ulbricht was the East German head of state.

21 See the pro-Viet Cong SDS pamphlet *Vietnam "Analyse eines Exempels" Information über den Studentenkongreß am 22. Mai 1966 in der Universität Frankfurt*, Sammlung Schwiedrzik zur Studentenbewegung, Zsg 153/10, BK.

22. Quoted in Riehle, E., 'Vietnam – Analyse eines Exempels', *Studentenzeitschrift TH Stuttgart*, June 1966, p. 19, BfZS.

Congress unless they were given control of its organization exposed deep rifts within the SDS, making for strained relations both within the organization and with the other groups participating in the Congress, many of whom threatened to pull out at the last minute. In the event, the Federal SDS organization successfully navigated a course between being too radical for the LSD and the SHB and not radical enough for the anti-authoritarians, thereby avoiding the promised disruption.[23] This was only a temporary stay of execution, though, and the anti-authoritarians were soon setting the pace within the SDS campaign against the War.

Indeed, by the autumn SDS influences were manifesting themselves clearly in protests organized by groups such as the SHB and the KfA. Statements now went so far as to make direct comparisons between American policy and Nazism, with the German government's support for American policy seen as support for a fascist war. For instance, demonstration in Munich on 28 November 1966, organized by the SDS, the SHB and the *Hochschulausschuß der Kampagne für Abrüstung* (University Committee of the KfA), took place in parallel with demonstrations in America. It was publicized by a flyer that complained at how 'unreservedly does the Federal Government build roads in Vietnam for US troops, sends poison gas specialists to Vietnam, and helps to construct concentration camps on the coast of South Vietnam'. The organizers went on to say that 'in our name the Federal Government subsidizes a regime that needs not only one, but "six or seven Hitlers"'.[24] Such statements became ever more common as the anti-authoritarian revolutionary aspects of the campaign gained supremacy.

Anti-authoritarian dominance was, of course, particularly visible at the FU Berlin. In December, just days after the disruption of the speech by the *Rektor*, the SDS antagonized the authorities further by disrupting an RCDS meeting on Vietnam. RCDS groups across Germany followed the pro-American line, arguing that Vietnamese in both North and South wanted only peace, but that pro-Chinese socialists were only interested in dominating the country at any cost. For the RCDS, German socialists 'believe in the final victory of socialism' in Vietnam and 'it cannot be denied: at numerous West German universities the misfortunes of Vietnam are abused by radical socialists, in pursuit of hypocritical agitation'. It

---

23. Bauß, *Die Studentenbewegung*, pp. 178–80 gives a particularly useful account of this episode.
24. *Es ist kein Zufall*, November 1966, Sammlung Werner Röder, ED 387/3, IfZM. The quotation refers to a speech by Ky in which he said he needed people like Hitler in Vietnam.

asked 'does this cheap show help the Vietnamese people in any way?'[25] In an act of provocation the RCDS invited the South Vietnamese Ambassador, Nguyen Qui Anh, to a discussion at the Henry-Ford Building of the FU Berlin on 6 December, at the same time as an SDS Vietnam film event in the same building. This gave the SDS the opportunity to confront the enemies of North Vietnam directly, and on the night, in a classic display of provocation tactics, SDS members demanded that the Ambassador come to their event to discuss the War. He refused and instead invited them to come to the RCDS debate. The SDS members took him up on his offer to the extent that the theatre was so overfull that people had to sit on the steps, and of the 400 people present, only 150 were RCDS supporters. As soon as the Ambassador tried to speak he was interrupted by catcalls from members of the crowd, some of whom tried to seize the microphone from him. After a struggle the Ambassador left the hall, decrying the fairness of the proceedings, and the SDS members remained to hold a mass meeting on Vietnam in which it was agreed that they should send a telegram of support to protesting students at Berkeley, California. The SDS-led AStA supported the protest but the *Rektor* was appalled 'that a representative of a foreign government, which maintains diplomatic relations with the *Bundesrepublik*, was forced to leave an event to which he was expressly invited' and believed it was 'regarded as badly damaging to the reputation of the University by a large section of the University'. He also questioned whether the SDS, as a disruptive organization, any longer met the requirements of the University constitution.[26]

With feelings now running high, the police violence during the Vietnam demonstration in Berlin on 10 December ratcheted up the tension even further. This demonstration, which was an important precursor to events on 2 June 1967, is worth looking at in some detail along with its corollary on 17 December. The demonstration took place on the afternoon of Human Rights Day, along with simultaneous protests in London and New York. It was originally to have been a march by several thousand people spread along Tauentzienstrasse and the Kurfürstendamm, the main shopping streets in West Berlin. Before the march could reach these streets police units attacked it because the front of the march had taken a wrong turn. The protesters pushed on to hold a mass meeting at Wittenbergplatz, on Tauentzienstrasse, before making their way down Tauentzienstrasse to the Kurfürstendamm. The march was subject to police attacks throughout,

---

25. *Was will das vietnamesische Volk?* Sammlung Werner Röder, ED 387/3, IfZM. This is a flyer produced by RCDS at Frankfurt am Main University in 1966.

26. *Bericht des Rektors*, pp. 18–19, Rep 014/843, LB.

with fierce clashes taking place in streets throughout the whole area until the evening when the march came to an end and most of the protesters dispersed.

One eyewitness repeated his version of events in *FU Spiegel*, although he withheld his name, choosing to make it known only to the editor. Having left a café on the Kurfürstendamm he was confronted by a row of police vans and officers, opposite a group of protesters singing Christmas carols. 'Without issuing even one of the much-written-about warnings to disperse, the police forced themselves into the group, who spontaneously shouted "Gestapo" against the use of rubber truncheons. It was clear that the intention of the police was to force the demonstrators into violence against their will, in order to have "the right to hit back"'. He saw one protester break away from the main group, who was then set upon by police who beat him 'repeatedly when the young man already lay helpless on the floor'. When the witness asked one of the officers for his service number he was taken away under arrest. The fact that the police labelled him a communist gives a clear indication of their motivations.[27]

The veracity of the testimony is given weight by a mass of supporting eyewitness evidence, including a collection of statements produced by the FU Berlin AStA. Witness X, for example, attended the mass meeting on Wittenbergplatz and then made his way down Tauentzienstrasse toward the Kurfürstendamm. At the Gedächtniskirche (Memorial Church), on the junction of these two streets, his route was blocked by crowds:

> I found myself on the edge of the group of marchers, which was moving slowly in the direction of the Kurfürstendamm. Police officers behind us attempted to keep us moving with shouts, pushes and kicks. Suddenly my arm was grabbed by one of the policemen and I was dragged onto the road. More policemen . . . sprang at me from behind and brought me down. While I lay on the ground I was kicked numerous times by the police, and I was kicked and punched when the officers pulled me up and dragged me to a police van. I was then literally thrown into the van and hit about by the policemen sitting inside, one of whom punched me in the face.[28]

After the demonstration had come to an end a small group of SDS members and supporters, among them future *Kommune I* members such as

---

27. 'Bericht eines Betroffenen', *FU Spiegel*, January 1967, p. 9, BfZS, provides details and an eyewitness account of the demonstration.

28. Eyewitness X, *Dokumentation über das Vorgehen der Berliner Polizei anläßlich der Dokumentation vom 10.12.1966 und 17.12.1966*, p. 10, Aktenbestand des Sozialistischen Anwaltskollektivs, file Diverses Demonstration I, HIfS.

Dieter Kunzelmann, held a 'Christmas happening' on the corner of the Kurfürstendamm and Joachimstalerstrasse. One of those present remembered 'a large group stood around a Christmas tree with an American flag and two caricatures (Johnson and Ulbricht), attempting to give expression to their protest over the false peace (Christmas in Germany) and terribly brutal war (in Vietnam) by spontaneously singing Christmas carols'. After they had set the tree and the caricatures alight, which the witness is careful not to include in his account,

> in the middle of singing I was suddenly shoved from behind and taken away with the shout 'come with me you rowdy'. On the way to the 'Green Maid' [police wagon] . . . my minder and I came to a group of policemen who looked as though they were about to march into action. Three of these hit me in the stomach. After this totally unmotivated attack I asked my 'protector' if it would be possible to identify these policemen. In answer my arm was painfully pulled behind my back. I allowed myself to be pushed along without resistance because I was worried about being totally beaten up.[29]

Rather than encouraging peaceful protest, the police tactics seem to have intended to stop protest altogether. Such actions confirmed enmity and prejudices for both sides, bringing the state's commitment to free speech, and to law and order into question. Professor Dr Jacob Taubes of the Philosophy department at the FU attended the demonstration as an observer. In a letter to Heinrich Albertz after the demonstration, he described it as 'civilized' until the violent police intervention, which he claimed was unprovoked. He continued 'in a country, in which not long ago wearers of state uniforms carried out the worst crimes, such uniform wearers should strictly hold themselves in check while implementing the required measures. Shouting, arrests, and acts of violence against young students who are simply holding discussions, reawakens all too evil memories'.[30] The Nazi past was evoked by another eyewitness who argued that the police violence was intended 'to indulge the tools of established powers once again'. The witness warned of the 'risk for German democracy that lies in such police actions that point to the dangerously short memories of German police officers who have learnt nothing from their history'.[31] Perhaps most significantly the FU AStA sent a letter to Minister Albertz on 12 December in which it congratulated him on his nomination for the office of Mayor of Berlin (to which he was elected on 14 December)

---

29. Eyewitness XIV, *Dokumentation über das Vorgehen*, pp. 13–14.
30. Letter dated 20.12.66 quoted in ibid., pp. 1–3.
31. Eyewitness VI, ibid., p. 8.

and then attacked the violent police tactics. They protested 'that many officers and numerous police actions have damaged the principle of deploying proportionate methods'. They demanded that police should wear their service numbers on their uniform and that Albertz 'should have a care that the actions of the police do not undermine the foundations of democracy in future'.[32] Albertz sent the letter straight back without reply.

A follow-up demonstration was organized for 17 December, this time in protest at the police tactics employed on 10 December. This took the form of a march along the Kurfürstendamm with protesters simultaneously engaged in debates and flyer distribution on the pavements. The protest was completely peaceful, but the police had refused permission for it to be held and were under orders to break it up. Once again they resorted to violence and indiscriminate arrests, which, to their embarrassment, included the arrest of the respected reporters Kai Hermann of the newspaper *Die Zeit* and Walter Bartel of the *Kölner Stadtanzeiger*. Again, eyewitness testimony points to police tactics informed by fear of dissent and the enforcement of the letter of the law. On the way to meeting friends in a café, witness IX met them instead on the corner of Fasanenstrasse and the Kurfürstendamm. Two police cars pulled up near them but

> we knew there was a demonstration that wasn't allowed and we didn't want to be suspected of belonging to it. We scattered, even though we could scarcely have been a hindrance to the traffic. Suddenly a plain-clothes officer came to me and four other policemen overpowered me. These dragged me to the police van and brought me to the police prison. I was detained there without being told on what grounds. I was released around 22.00 hours, having been arrested around 15.10 hours.[33]

Far from viewing police actions as problematic, after these events Albertz was intent on cracking down on protesters even further. His demands that the FU take action against SDS members involved in the demonstration, and the police raid on SDS headquarters in search of membership cards, must be seen in this context. In early January the Berlin Senate debated whether to ban demonstrations in the city. Although a ban was rejected for the moment, during the debate Professor Dr Dilschneider argued 'a small radical group is terrorizing a German University with 16,000 students. That is political infiltration. I would like to track down the source, that runs

32. Letter from the FU AStA to Heinrich Albertz, dated 12 December 1966, Aktenbestand des Sozialistischen Anwaltskollektivs, file Diverses Demonstration I, HIfS.

33. Eyewitness IX, *Dokumentation über das Vorgehen der Berliner Polizei anläßlich der Dokumentation vom 10.12.1966 und 17.12.1966, Bericht über die Demonstration am 17. Dezember 1966*, p. 22.

from West to East'.[34] In response to the recommendations of Police Chief Erich Duensing, affectionately known to his officers as 'truncheon Erich', Albertz allowed the creation of *Greiftruppen* (snatch squads) of plain-clothes officers armed with automatic pistols who were to target and arrest ringleaders in future demonstrations. The *FU Spiegel* summed up the attitude of many protesters when it said that for some officers the use of violence was 'embarrassing, but some show the light in their eyes when the citizenship lessons of Patriarch Heinrich, who resides under the freedom bell, includes hammering political nonconformists with trunch-eons'. On the subject of dissent it insisted 'before Christmas Eve Pastor and Social Democrat [Albertz] told a Senate speaker "Berlin doesn't need any agitators". Berlin needs these agitators very much, whose behaviour creates wide publicity for the absurd conduct of police who don't need grounds, but only seek leave to pester, hit, and arrest demonstrators and bystanders.'[35] Far from learning that unwarranted violence and heavy-handedness by the police only inflamed the situation further, and added justification to claims that basic civil liberties were at risk, the Berlin auth-orities added more oil to the fire.

It would be a mistake to concentrate solely upon events in Berlin since in an increasingly volatile atmosphere protests against the Vietnam War intensified around the country. On 18 February 1967 a typical series of demonstrations were held simultaneously in Hamburg, Frankfurt and Erlangen. In Frankfurt protesters threw smoke bombs at the police and held a sit-down demonstration in the middle of the road, using passive res-istance against police who tried to arrest them. In Erlangen a mass meeting under the title 'Peace for Vietnam' attacked the Saigon regime as being unrepresentative of the wishes of the majority of Vietnamese.[36] A flyer advertising this demonstration, which was organized by SDS and SHB groups at Erlangen-Nürnberg University, again raised the spectre of the Nazi past. It asked 'is "Western freedom" being protected in Vietnam?', and replied 'American SS units, known as Green Berets and leathernecks, move murdering and burning through the villages and towns of South Vietnam. Ten thousand rice growers are crammed into concentration camps with women and children.' It went on to say 'Hitler said: how will

---

34. 'Studenten pöbeln gegen Bürgermeister', *Bild Zeitung*, 13 January 1967, Sam-mlung Schwiedrzik zur Studentenbewegung, ZSg 153/1, BK.

35. 'Mal Bummeln gehn', *FU Spiegel*, January 1967, p. 7, BfZS. This account of the demonstration includes a photograph of a protester being dragged along by his feet by police officers.

36. 'Wieder Demonstration gegen den Vietnamkrieg der USA', *Erlanger Tageblatt*, 20. February 1967, p. 1, Sammlung Mehringer, ED 308/box 11, IfZM.

our people train themselves to fight against the insanity of democracy? Air Marshal Ky said: we need five Hitlers in South Vietnam. Chancellor Kiesinger said: South Vietnam belongs to the free world.'[37] Such comments were given added resonance by the fact the Kiesinger, who had been head of the Grand Coalition government since December, was a former senior official in Goebbels's Propaganda Ministry.

The Nazi theme was raised again during the Easter marches for 1967 that took place across Germany from 25 to 27 March. The KfA also continued its long-running trend toward open criticism of politics in the *Bundesrepublik* to which it added new fears for the future of German democracy. A KfA flyer aimed at Munich schoolchildren exhorted them to march 'for peace and democracy, so that tomorrow we must not march for fascism and war'. On Vietnam itself strident rhetoric condemned the fact that 'every day Americans bomb hundreds of Vietnamese to death – because they want to protect freedom, so they say. We hear that the Federal government supports this War morally and financially.' The KfA now took this reasoning a step further to declare 'we see that old Nazis are always still involved and that young Nazis are joining them. We see that democratic rights and freedom of opinion could be fully removed.'[38] Although they did not follow the SDS in calling for a North Vietnamese victory, or for international revolutionary solidarity, the KfA was adopting as much of the SDS line as it could while remaining a pacifist organization.

In another demonstration in Munich, on 8 May, the SDS once again employed tactics of provocation against what were seen as authoritarian police restrictions. A protest meeting of around 800 to 1,000 people at the Löwenbräukeller in the city centre formed itself into a protest march through Briennerstrasse to Prinz-Carl-Palais as had been arranged in advance with the police. A heavy police presence lined the route, and when the marchers moved on to the American General Consulate, which was not covered by the pre-arranged plan, the police intervened. The protesters threw eggs and bottles at the police and following clashes they were chased through side streets. Around 15 demonstrators held a sit-down demonstration on one side of Von-der-Tan-Strasse, blocking the traffic in the process. When the police tried to direct traffic up the other side of the road, the demonstrators moved to that side and were arrested by the police. A number were later given prison sentences and fines for their involvement.[39]

37. Untitled Flyer, February 1967, Sammlung Mehringer, ED 308/box 11, IfZM.

38. *Das erwarten Manche von uns*, Sammlung Werner Röder, ED 387/3, IfZM.

39. *Rechtshilfe der APO München 1968–1969, II. Vorfall am 8.5.1967 (amerikanisches Konsulat)*, p. 4, ED 713, IfZM. This excellent collection gives details of the APO cases defended by this human rights organization across Germany.

The national SDS campaign continued with a drive for donations or *Spendenaktion* that was called in May 1967 under the title 'Pro-Vietcong – pro-North Vietnam.' This was one of many such requests by the SDS. In one of the clearest statements to date of their attitude toward the campaign, they announced 'the War for the achievement and preservation of democratic rights and social progress is fought on many fronts: in this case the *Bundesrepublik* is also a front, even if conditions are not comparable with those in Vietnam. For that reason: help Vietnam!'[40] This exhortation may ostensibly have requested humanitarian aid for Vietnam, and fell short of a call to arms, but it could be read as such, and would soon be followed by more explicit appeals for armed intervention. In the meantime collections of money were made to provide the North Vietnamese with weaponry. In the same month the *Vietnam Komitee* of the Free University, including members of the SDS, the SHB and the LSD, announced that they would be carrying out collections of money at the University, in the American living quarters and in the City 'for the South Vietnamese Liberation Front'. They stated 'this collection should equip the Vietnamese people with all the kindness and material that is necessary to preserve themselves as people', in other words, with weapons.[41] At the end of the month these collections began without the permission of the FU *Rektor* and in defiance of his authority.

This collection took place just days after the SDS held a protest at the FU during the visit of the Federal President, accompanied by Mayor Albertz, and members of the Federal Cabinet, for a celebration of the 125th anniversary of the creation of the *Pour le Mérite* Order. As the guests left the hall in which the celebration had taken place, SDS members broke through the police cordon and shouted pro-Vietnamese slogans at the assembled politicians. The *Rektor*'s assessment was that 'although the police were quickly masters of the situation the impression made by this action [upon the politicians] by radical students was catastrophic'.[42] The presence of heavily armed of Berlin police officers, and the security implications of the protest action in the presence of so many VIPs, meant the consequences of the protest could have been much worse. On the same day, 21 May, the FU Berlin Senate resolved that the SDS no longer conformed to the rules on political organizations at the FU and banned it from participating in the student political system.

40. 'Pro Vietcong – Pro nordvietnam', *Facit*, May 1967, p. 4, AFAS.

41. *Resolution des Vietnam-Komitees an der Freien Universität Berlin*, 26 May 1967, Sammlung Schwiedrzik zur Studentenbewegung, ZSg 153/17, BK.

42. *Bericht des Rektors*, p. 34, Rep 014/843, LB.

The *Konvent* responded to the Senate decision in two unprecedented ways. First, on 26 May it passed a resolution on Vietnam in which it redefined its role within the University, making it openly political for the first time. Charging America with genocide in Vietnam, the *Konvent* asserted its democratic position as a mandate 'that can only be fulfilled together with the social function of the university'. For the *Konvent*, 'university research cannot shrink from its task in a society that declares its purpose to be the freedom of the individual'. It continued 'for that reason university research can only ignore a genocide like that in Vietnam if it has accepted a social role in which it is a subject, and others are the object'.[43] This was the clearest indication yet that the *Konvent* had become an SDS tool and that its engagement in political issues beyond the University, as well as its redefinition of the role of the University, was an unambiguous break with tradition. The *Konvent* then responded directly to the Senate decision on the SDS. On 31 May it described the effective banning of the FU Berlin SDS as 'a continuation of the authoritarian measures of the University bureaucracy against the real democratic activity of oppositional student groups'.[44] It called for the AStA and the student population to oppose the decision with demonstrations, sit-ins and strikes, and announced a mass protest meeting to be held in the Henry-Ford Building on 3 June. Although this campaign was overtaken by Benno Ohnesorg's death on 2 June, these events exemplify the way in which the Left was able to fall back on Vietnam as a catch-all. Those in authority who supported Vietnam could be discredited and their authority challenged or rejected.

The Vietnam campaign began with, and remained informed by, humanitarianism. By 1967, however, the tone and momentum of the campaign was coming under the sway of anti-authoritarian SDS members, by whom it was linked with other issues, including the campaign for university reform, as part of the Left's revolutionary critique of the *Bundesrepublik*. Having identified the North Vietnamese struggle as a key part of an international revolutionary movement, the Left was moving inexorably toward the use of weapons in support. The actions of those in authority lent momentum and credence to the adoption of ever more radical and violent stances.

---

43. 'Beschluß des Konvents vom 26.5.1967 zu Vietnam', in *2. (abschließende) Beschlußempfehlung des 1. Untersuchungsausschusses – V. Wahlperiode – vom 3. Juli 1968*, pp. 59–60, Rep 014/845, LB. This is a large document, quoted in full in this source.
44. Quoted in *Bericht des Rektors*, p. 35, Rep 014/843, LB.

Conspiracies and Counter-conspiracies?

In carrying out research on West Germany in the 1960s, it quickly becomes clear that many people believed in the existence of a variety of conspiracies. Protests opposed to new Emergency Laws, the showing of racist films, or the electoral successes of the NPD, all shared the common fear of a conspiracy to revive Nazism. The provocative satirical activities of *Kommune I* sought to expose the authoritarian nature of government. By highlighting literalness and pedantry in the application of the letter of law, it left authorities open to mockery and charges of using the legal system in a conspiracy to silence dissent. *Kommune I* also played successfully upon popular fears about communist conspiracies that supposedly intended to overthrow the *Bundesrepublik*. Belief in these various conspiracy theories created an atmosphere of mutual mistrust and fear that eventually boiled over in June 1967. There is no factual evidence that these conspiracies existed, but belief in their existence was both widespread and deeply entrenched.

Proposals for new *Notstandsgesetze* (Emergency Laws), one of the most controversial issues of 1960s Germany, prompted a long-running protest campaign in which both the KfA and the DGB were able to harness widespread fears for democracy among Germans from all walks of life. The idea of amending the constitution to include emergency powers for government in times of national crisis was first put forward by Gerhard Schröder at a police conference on 30 October 1958. The following October he announced more detailed plans for Emergency Laws that would allow the government to suspend civil liberties either locally or nationally in the event of a natural disaster, invasion, or general strike. The administration of such crises remained in the hands of the Allies, so any constitutional amendment would mean an extension of Federal authority and the removal of the external counter-weight and guarantee of German democratic rights represented by the Allies. On the other hand, it would also be a step toward international acceptance as a full-fledged democracy capable of looking after its own interests and no longer at risk of a reversion to Nazism. Above all, the proposals raised the spectre of the Nazi period once again: Hitler had after all gained power in 1933 by invoking the dictatorial powers provided for by Emergency Laws in times of crisis.

The process of amending the constitution over the next decade was tortuous. In February 1960 the *Bundesrat* raised objections to the use of the new laws in industrial disputes and after heated debates in September of the same year the *Bundestag* rejected the bill and sent it back to the committee stage. The CDU, for whom the amendment was a pet project, consistently promoted the reform despite these setbacks and in June 1965, during Ludwig Erhard's Chancellorship, a new bill was put before the *Bundestag*. According to this amended proposal, while the decision to enact the Emergency Laws for internal crises would lie with *Land* presidents or *Land* parliaments, the declaration of a national state of emergency because of an external threat could be made by the *Bundestag*, by an 'emergency committee', or by the Chancellor in conjunction with the President. This enactment would allow for censorship of the press, the suspension of *Länder* authority, a ban on freedom of assembly or freedom of forming unions or associations, a removal of the right to chose one's employment, withdrawal of legal guarantees of personal freedoms, as well as the ability to introduce forced labour and to deploy the police to resolve internal disputes.[1] The bill failed when, in a vote in the *Bundestag* on 24 June 1965, it received 167 votes against, mainly from SPD members, and 238 votes for, far short of the two-thirds majority required for a change to the Constitution. The CDU was nevertheless determined to get the bill through the *Bundestag* successfully, and spent the next year or so debating the next course of action. Far from bringing the confrontation over the Emergency Laws to an end, the defeat of the bill simply took it into a new and more intensive phase. In August Adenauer argued for the creation of a Grand Coalition with the SPD and FDP, in which the CDU would put aside its many deep-seated differences with the SPD in order to neutralize opposition to the *Notstandsgesetze*. Although Erhard rejected the plan, Federal President Heinrich Lübke (CDU) expressed his support for a Grand Coalition in December 1965.

From the late 1950s until the mid-1960s the campaign against the Emergency Laws was dominated by trade unions under the umbrella of the DGB. The main objections to the proposed laws are succinctly summarized by the resolution passed by the DGB at its annual conference in

---

1. Quoted in *Arbeitskreis Notstandsgesetze, I Informationsblatt zum Notstandsverfassungsgesetz*, Munich file 03474, BfZS. This flyer was released in 1965 by the newly created Emergency Law Working Group based in Munich. It was formed by members of the GASt, HSU, KfA, LSD, SDS and SHB.

1965. For the DGB 'the existing emergency regulations . . . not only are sufficient but already threaten the framework of democracy partly themselves (Chancellor democracy, national treason by journalists, etc.)'.[2] Parallels with the Nazi take-over in 1933 were regularly drawn upon in the campaign. A 1966 GASt (*Gewerkschaftlicher Arbeitskreis der Studenten* or Student Trade Union Working Group) flyer presented a stark choice between democracy on the one hand and on the other a 'moulded society' in which the Emergency Laws would destroy the democratic freedoms of the majority of the populace. According to GASt this 'moulded society' would act in the interests of big business, 'who brought Hitler to power'.[3]

Student groups began to take a significant role within the campaign from about 1965, followed in 1966 by the KfA, representing a major realignment both of the opposition to the Emergency Laws and of the APO in general. The change was most immediately expressed in the Congress held in Bonn on 30 May 1966 under the title *Die Demokratie vor dem Notstand* (Democracy facing the Emergency). This was organized by student groups such as the SDS, HSU, SHB and LSD, but all of the main speeches were by academics rather than by students, on subjects including 'crisis and parliamentary control', 'press freedom in a state of emergency' and 'the right to strike and civil service'.[4] The Congress took place against a background of DGB demonstrations across the country in the weeks leading up to the readings of the bill in the *Bundestag*. Crucially, Gerhard Bauß explains that student groups never dominated the campaign against the Emergency Laws in the same way as they did within the Vietnam campaign. Although he inexplicably plays down the influence of the KfA he is accurate in maintaining that it was mainly the 'traditional' wing of the SDS that became involved in the campaign against the Emergency Laws. Unlike the anti-authoritarian wing they actively encouraged the dominance of the labour movement, particularly the DGB and its constituent trade unions.[5] Nevertheless, Bauß does acknowledge that the SDS distributed around 100,000 flyers on the subject at German universities in the period leading up to the *Bundestag* readings.[6] The involvement of

2. Quoted in *Nein zu den Notstandsgesetzen!*, Munich file 03474, BfZS. This April 1966 GASt flyer urged the DGB to reiterate its opposition to the Emergency Laws, which it did at its annual conference in May. The reference to 'treason by journalists' is to the *Spiegel* Affair of 1962.

3. *Arbeitskreis Notstandsgesetze, VI Akademiker zwischen Notstand und Mitbestimmung*, Munich file 03474, BfZS.

4. Untitled GASt flyer by Hans Wölcken, dated 24.5.65, Munich file 03475, BfZS. This flyer gives the programme for the Congress.

5. Bauß, *Die Studentenbewegung*, p. 132.

6. Ibid., p. 128.

students and later the broad cross-section of opinion that the KfA was able to mobilize was crucial in providing wide-ranging mass support for the campaign when it reached a climax later in the decade.

The origins of KfA involvement are difficult to pin down, with local groups including the issue in their literature and protest activities before the official statement on the Emergency Laws by the Central Committee in May 1966. This statement acknowledged that KfA local organizations were already participating in the co-ordination of efforts against the Emergency Laws in both Frankfurt and Berlin and insisted that the KfA should put opposition to the laws 'at the forefront' of its national campaign.[7] This was a new departure for the KfA. Its concerns with nuclear weapons and the Vietnam War were at least related directly to peace, whereas the campaign against Emergency Laws was preoccupied with specific questions about Germany's democratic future, combined with related concerns that the laws would mean a return to fascism, totalitarianism, and wars of conquest. This was an acknowledgement that the KfA's concern with single issues such as nuclear weapons led logically to a more fundamental questioning of the motivations and vested interests that informed decision-making within the German political process. This was particularly so in light of the growing influence of organizations like the SDS. An SDS document released in September 1966 that recommended expansion of the KfA campaign aims is of particular interest in this respect. After saying that the KfA's decision to support the protests against the Emergency Laws had made it '*the* central meeting place of the living opposition in the *Bundesrepublik*', the SDS stated:

> A section of the ruling classes is driving toward an ever more authoritarian position: they want to secure their interests against every political or social opposition through openly violent oppression . . . In this position you should no longer regard the struggle against the Emergency Laws as part of your peace campaign. It represents much more a life and death question of the movement itself. As by far the most popular political meeting place for opposition in the Federal Republic the Campaign may not only be led from the viewpoint of disarmament. It must make it clear how the Emergency Laws stand in opposition to peace as well as to the political and social freedoms of the majority of the population and its different groups.[8]

7. 'Beschluß des Zentralen Ausschusses der KfA zur Einleitung einer Kampagne gegen die Notstandsgesetzgebung (Mai 1966)', quoted in Otto, *Die außerparlamentarische Opposition*, pp. 123–4.

8. 'Vorschlag des SDS zur Erweiterung der Kampagne (1966)', quoted in ibid., pp. 127–8. SDS emphasis.

While this gives an excellent summary of the SDS position, it is essential not to overestimate the SDS influence within the KfA. The SDS had been instrumental in politicizing the KfA, but its Marxist model of capitalist conspiracy was not repeated in KfA statements. Rather, the KfA emphasized concerns for the future of democracy in light of the potential threat posed by the *Notstandsgesetze*. The SDS claim that the KfA's involvement in the Emergency Law campaign made it the central APO organization is somewhat grandiose and smacks of flattery. Yet it is true to say that the protests against the Emergency Laws mobilized support from more people, and from a greater cross-section of German society, including a greater variety of age groups, than any other issue.

The DGB, the SDS and the KfA set about combining their forces in local *Aktionsausschuß* or Action Committees, many of which had enjoyed de facto existence, if not official KfA recognition, for some time. This pooling of resources also made possible the organization of the national Congress *Notstand der Demokratie*, or 'the crisis of democracy', held in Frankfurt on 30 October 1966. The Congress was attended by 8,000–9,000 people and included 420 academics, 650 priests and theologians, and 1,200 'intellectuals', reflecting the concern at the proposed laws through all strata of German society. There were also 24,000 participants in the final rally.[9] This became an annual event between 1966 and 1968, and Karl A. Otto has described the co-operation of the SDS, the KfA and the trade unions in 'Action Committees', and especially in the *Notstand der Demokratie* Congresses, as the 'historical culmination point' of the APO. He justifies this claim by arguing that resources could be concentrated on the three contributing groups 'because the whole organizational spectrum of the APO was more or less integrated during the high point of 1967–68 in the mobilization campaign of the KfA, the SDS and the committee of *Notstand der Demokratie*'.[10] While this may overemphasize the role of the Congresses in particular, and the *Notstandsgesetze* campaign in general, at the expense of the massive amount of protest activity taking place on other issues, it is true to say that this sustained convergence of resources and organizations was unique. This is explicable by the fact that strength of feeling on the *Notstandsgesetze* was augmented by fears of the imminent demise of democracy through the creation a Grand Coalition in December 1966.

Chancellor Erhard's regime collapsed as a result of an economic crisis in November 1966, leaving the way open for the resurrection of plans for

9. Bauß, *Die Studentenbewegung*, p. 137.
10. Otto, *Die außerparlamentarische Opposition*, p. 41.

a Grand Coalition. The chance to play a part in government that had eluded the SPD for the entire post-war period proved to be too much, and on 1 December a Grand Coalition between the CDU/CSU, the SPD, and the FDP was announced. The SPD leader Willy Brandt was installed as Foreign Minister, and Kurt-Georg Kiesinger, the CDU Minister President of Baden-Württemberg, took over as Chancellor. With the creation of this government several perceived threats to democracy presented themselves at once. Most obviously, the parliamentary opposition was not simply nullified, it was incorporated into the apparatus of government. Protest became the only way in which people could make their voices heard and an increasing number of people did exactly that when faced with the prospect of the Grand Coalition passing the Emergency Laws with no parliamentary opposition to keep a check on their implementation. The SHB, the LSD and *Die Falken* held a pre-emptive mass-protest meeting at Wittenbergplatz in Berlin as early as 28 November against the formation of a Grand Coalition, while the GASt and the LSD in Munich held a demonstration on 30 November. In an appeal to SPD voters who 'wanted to elect an alternative to the CDU/CSU' and who had been 'deceived', the demonstrators proclaimed

> the CDU/CSU and their economic paymasters are using the SPD for their anti-democratic plan. (Lücke: 'we need the Grand Coalition in order to bring the Emergency Laws before the *Bundestag* this year.') With the help of the Emergency Laws the opposition will be eliminated. The elimination of the opposition is a step toward the moulded society. The moulded society is the totalitarian state in pseudo-democratic packaging.[11]

Even two years later a survey of students by *Der Spiegel* found that 66 per cent of all students, including 90 per cent of SDS members, 79 per cent of SHB members, and even 48 per cent of RCDS members, believed the Grand Coalition was anti-democratic.[12] Jürgen Seifert, a member of the traditional wing of the SDS, has said that for him the Grand Coalition 'marked the real beginning of a student movement' because 'a parliamentary democracy without a real opposition led many youth to think that we were pretty close to an authoritarian state. The Emergency Laws gave people a concrete notion of what such an authoritarian state would mean'.[13] For many, predictions of a return to fascism were at risk of becoming reality, with no parliamentary opposition, rabid press opposition to dissent,

11. *An alle SPD – Wählen*, Munich file 03474, BfZS.
12. 'Studenten', *Der Spiegel*, 10 June 1968, p. 55.
13. Quoted in Fraser, *1968*, p. 124.

and an authoritarian use of police violence against protest acting as mere precursors to a seizure of power by the Right.

Such concerns were not allayed by the personnel of the new government. Not only did it include the previously disgraced Franz-Josef Strauß as Finance Minister, but the Chancellor, Kiesinger, was formerly a Nazi party member who had been head of the international radio propaganda section acting under Goebbels from the Foreign Ministry. The Springer newspaper *Die Welt* wrote disapprovingly in January 1967 about a 'spontaneous and wild demonstration' on the Berlin Kurfürstendamm by several thousand students of the Berlin TU who attacked plans for Kiesinger to lay a wreath at the memorial to the victims of Nazism as tactless.[14] In a speech in January 1967 Günter Grass described Kiesinger, as well as Hans Globke, as anti-Nazis: Kiesinger had apparently acted to block anti-Jewish broadcasts by the Nazis while Globke claimed to have worked to limit the Nuremburg racial laws. Although a loyal supporter of both Brandt and the SPD, Grass found it impossible to refrain from expressing his opposition to the Grand Coalition. He asked what could be said to young people about the fact that an 'old Nazi' had become Chancellor, and answered

in 1945 we lost a war, on 1 December 1966 the Federal Republic lost the peace. It capitulated before the past and future at the same time, but the cost of this further capitulation will not have to be paid by Herr Kiesinger or Herr Wehner, this expense will come home to us . . . who were too young to be able to assess the bad times before and after 1933.[15]

Grass' concerns reflected widespread unease with the Grand Coalition that went beyond the APO and informed a number of anti-Nazi protests that took place in the period before the death of Benno Ohnesorg that took place while anti-*Notstandsgesetze* protests continued to rumble on.

Various anti-Nazi demonstrations were concerned with both internal and external fascism. Unlike the Peace or the *Notstandsgesetze* campaigns, these protests were carried out overwhelmingly by the young, reflecting the post-war generation's ability to point to the moral failings of those who had supported and experienced Nazism. Moise Tschombe's state visit to Germany in December 1964 was particularly controversial. Tschombe was the separatist President of the Congolese province of Katanga, who had been implicated in the murder of Patrice Lumumba, the President of the Congo, in 1961. Students argued that the capitalist West was supporting

---

14 'Tausend Studenten forderten die Beachtung der Grundrechte', *Die Welt*, 25 January 1967, Sammlung Schwiedrzik zur Studentenbewegung, Zsg 153/1, BK.

15. "Ausserdem hat der Mann verdienste", *Der Spiegel*, 30 January 1967, p. 21.

his corrupt regime because Katanga was a rich source of raw materials. Students in Munich condemned 'the financial support of murder and terror by German tax money' and suggested further that the material support given to Tschombe by the West meant 'the oppressors of the Congolese people are also our oppressors'.[16] Groups in Berlin, including the emerging anti-authoritarian wing of the SDS, even claimed Tschombe's troops were 'South African and South Rhodesian racists, former French OAS officers and former SS people'.[17] Upon Tschombe's arrival in Berlin on 18 December police plans to take a secret route from Tempelhof airport to Rathaus Schöneberg failed to prevent around 400 organizing a demonstration at the airport. The confrontation continued at Rathaus Schöneberg, where around 150 protesters were involved in violent clashes with the police. Rudi Dutschke recorded in his diary that onlookers told the demonstrators to 'beat it back to the East'. Dutschke later described the demonstration as 'the start of our cultural revolution [the anti-authoritarian campaign], in which all the previous values and norms of the Establishment were brought into question, that concentrated itself primarily in action, and in which action was presented the explanation of the meaning and purpose of the action'.[18]

Two years later, after heavy involvement in protest over Vietnam, university reform and the Emergency Laws, the Berlin SDS was once again involved in violent clashes with police in anti-Nazi demonstrations. On the evening of 2 August 1966 SDS students and members of African student groups held a demonstration at the Astor cinema on the Kurfürstendamm against the film *Africa Addio* by the Italian director Gualtiero Jacopetti. The film had already been banned as racist in Italy and England, and the left-liberal newspaper *Der Abend* described Jacopetti as a well-known 'racist, colonialist fascist'.[19] The demonstrations against the film are instructive examples both of SDS provocation tactics and of the police and press reaction, as well as marking the start of a new level of violence in the tactics of the Berlin police as a precursor to the clashes during the Vietnam demonstration in Berlin on 10 December 1966. The protest on 2 August took place during the film's première showing when students in the audience interrupted the film with whistles, boos and choruses of

16. Flyer *Die Einladung des Mörders Tschombe ist eine Billigung seiner verbrechen*, Berlin 1964, file 00107, BfZS.

17. Flyer *Flughafen Tempelhof*, Berlin 1964, file 00107, BfZS.

18. Quoted in Dutschke, G., *Rudi Dutschke*, pp. 60–1.

19. Raimund le Viseur, 'Es gab großen Krach', *Der Abend*, 3 August 1966, file Africa Addio, Aktenbestand des Sozialistischen Anwaltskollektivs, HIfS. This article also gives a detailed description of the demonstration on 2 August.

abuse. When around fifty protesters stormed the stage the police intervened and violent clashes ensued for over an hour, resulting in damage to the cinema and the seats. Afterwards the protesters formed a committee of five which brought charges against the film, arguing that it breached Berlin city laws on racism and Federal laws on slander of a head of state (Jomo Kenyatta) and so should be banned. On 3 August Police Chief Duensing announced that he had arbitrarily decided to ban the next demonstration against the film on 4 August. In a letter sent to the SDS the next day he betrayed the siege mentality of the Berlin police by justifying the ban on grounds that 'communist demonstrators will use the demonstration for their purposes', meaning the 'demonstration will destroy public security and order'. Ominously, he warned that 'the police have been instructed to prevent by any means the carrying out of this event [i.e., the demonstration]'.[20] A small demonstration outside the cinema on 3 August ended peacefully, but the *Berliner Morgenpost*, hinting at the prejudices that would inform the press uproar over the next few days, described in scandalized tones how 'numerous members of SDS and many coloured African students' had attended.[21]

The SDS wholeheartedly seized the opportunity the ban gave them to bait the authorities, and defiantly went ahead with the demonstration on 4 August. According to the police report around 600 to 800 people assembled outside the cinema in the early evening. Over a loudspeaker the police ordered the crowd to disperse, and when this failed around 300 police used force to break up the demonstration. The police arrested 43 people, including the West Berlin secretary of the East German FDJ, adding to fears of communist infiltration.[22] Statements by individual officers provide some insight into their attitudes toward protesters and the enforcement of the law: *Polizeioberwachtmeister* Heinz-Günter Koch, who said the police were there 'to arrest hooligans', was involved in the police action on the Kurfürstendamm at around midnight. When the police faced groups of protesters shouting 'race hate' they formed snatch squads to arrest 'the loudest shouters'. Koch arrested a Ruth Fleischmann because she was an 'especially loud shouter' and a 'leader'.[23] Koch's colleague

20. Letter from Erich Duensing to SDS Landesverband Berlin, dated 4 August 1966, file Africa Addio, Aktenbestand des Sozialistischen Anwaltskollektivs, HIfS.

21. 'Protest gegen 'Africa addio': Polizei verbot Studenten-Demonstration', *Berliner Morgenpost*, 4 August 1966, file Africa Addio, Aktenbestand des Sozialistischen Anwaltskollektivs, HIfS.

22. Quoted in '"Africa Addio" am Kurfürstendamm abgesetzt', *Die Welt*, 6 August 1966, file Africa Addio, Aktenbestand des Sozialistischen Anwaltskollektivs, HIfS.

23. Testimony of *Polizeioberwachtmeister* Heinz-Günter Koch, dated 22.8.1966, file Africa Addio, Aktenbestand des Sozialistischen Anwaltskollektivs, HIfS.

Gerhard Bahrke also said that the police aimed to arrest 'shouters' and to this end he arrested a Wolfgang Titze who was taking part in choruses of shouting.[24]

The testimony given to the police by demonstrators who were arrested adds to this picture of police heavy-handedness. Udo Vehof, an architecture student at the TU Berlin, took part in the protest outside the cinema at the start of the evening carrying a placard marked 'race hate' along with (illegal) SS runes. When asked about this by the police he replied that he wanted 'to document that under this symbol race hatred has already happened to a considerable extent and in criminal ways'. He was arrested later that night because he failed to listen to police loudspeaker orders to clear the area. The investigating officer repeatedly asked Vehof about this, and seemed unable to comprehend why he would ignore such an order.[25] Ullrich Pfütze, who saw the film on 2 August, decided it was racist and attended the demonstration on 4 August out of curiosity. He spent most of the evening in the Café Zuntz on the Kurfürstendamm, but when he left at around 11.00 p.m. he was caught up in the demonstration. He stopped at his bus stop to get a bus home, and was arrested when the police moved through the area. Again the police officer interviewing him had difficulty in understanding why he did not leave the area when ordered. He told the officer, 'on the corner of the Kurfürstendamm and Joachimstalerstrasse the police began an arrest sweep. I observed an officer who in my view performed his duty over-eagerly. He went here and there arresting people. I had the impression that it was fun to him to take hold of people as hard as possible'. When asked whether he viewed this officer as a Nazi he replied 'yes – I had the impression that the method of arrest did not match the behaviour of the demonstrators. The intervention was too forceful and I believe it can be compared to "Nazi methods"'.[26] On 5 August the distributors withdrew the film from the Astor, but the City authorities still permitted them to show it at small suburban cinemas.

The decision to withdraw the film was welcomed both by the press and by Heinrich Albertz, who was still Interior Senator. In a portentous public statement he backed the actions of the police and argued 'destroying furniture is no argument against a film, however much one disagrees with it. It is not acceptable that film censorship is practised, especially through

24. Testimony of *Polizeioberwachtmeister* Gerhard Bahrke, dated 22.8.1966, file Africa Addio, Aktenbestand des Sozialistischen Anwaltskollektivs, HIfS.

25. Testimony of Udo Vehof, file Africa Addio, Aktenbestand des Sozialistischen Anwaltskollektivs, HIfS.

26. Testimony of Ullrich Pfütze, dated 12 September 1966, file Africa Addio, Aktenbestand des Sozialistischen Anwaltskollektivs, HIfS.

violence'. He warned 'there will not be any more riot scenes in West Berlin. We will take drastic measures'.[27] Perhaps predictably the press reaction was rabid and sensationalist, condemning the protesters as communists and paying great attention to the presence of an FDJ member. The Berlin daily *BZ*, a Springer title, described the skirmishes with police as 'a scandal' and declared 'Terror is no argument!' It continued 'The SED people are ever present when it comes to staging riots. And we will never fall back before them!'[28] In a city where feelings were already running high, demonstrators viewed with distaste the sight of the state and press rushing to defend a racist film through violence.

State and press attitudes were not the only factors contributing to fears of a Nazi revival: the growing support for the neo-Nazi NPD was a particular cause for concern among both protesters and those loyal to the *Bundesrepublik*. The party was created in November 1964 when various small right-wing organizations unified under the leadership of former Wehrmacht officer Adolf von Thadden. As well as being anti-communist and pro-family they demanded an end to proclamations of German collective guilt for the Nazi past, and argued that Germany was being oppressed by foreign powers. This meant German war criminals were in prison 'while thousands of foreign war criminals walk around free'.[29] During the economic crisis that led to the demise of the Erhard government in 1966 the NPD made successive gains in *Land* elections, to the dismay of the press and the main political parties. On 6 November they gained 7.9 per cent of the vote in *Land* elections in Hesse, which gave them representation in a *Land* government for the first time. This was followed by a 7.4 per cent share of the vote in Bavarian *Land* elections on 20 November. They were also active at universities through their student arm, the *Nationaldemokratische Hochschulbund* (National Democratic University Federation or NHB), which established a branch at the FU Berlin during the referendum campaign in May 1967 as part of the 'yes' campaign against the Left. Their campaign aims included 'quiet and order at the Free University, a ban on the SDS and all of their supporting groups' and 'sharp disciplinary measures against all who stirred up trouble in recent times'.[30]

Students across Germany responded with demonstrations against the NPD, among which protests by staff and students of Erlangen-Nuremberg

27. 'Keine zensur durch Radaubrüder', *Bild*, 6 August 1966, p. 2.

28. 'Gleich drei Skandale und ein Machwerk', *BZ*, 6 August 1966, p. 2.

29. 'Grundungsaufruf der Nationaldemokratische Partei Deutschlands (NPD), 1964', quoted in *Demokratische Aktion*, p. 5, ED 716/1, IfZM.

30. *Nationaldemokratische Hochschulbund an der Freien Universität (NHB), Endlich!*, Berlin file 00116, BfZS.

University in December 1966 are representative. As early as 1928 the AStA at Erlangen-Nuremberg had been the first in the country in which Nazis had gained a majority, and shortly afterward the professorial bodies also came under Nazi control in the 'brown university'. In response to NPD election victories in Erlangen the AStA reminded staff and students of the Nazi history of the University and called them to a memorial march and mass meeting in Erlangen on 9 December 'so that all right-wing tendencies are rejected in the region around our University'.[31] Around 2,000 students and staff took part in the march, carrying placards with messages insisting 'our uni [*sic*] is and will not be brown'.[32] The NPD's electoral success continued unchecked, though: the following April they received 6.9 per cent of votes in Rheinland-Pfalz (Rheinland-Palatinate) *Land* elections, and 5.8 per cent in Schleswig-Holstein. On 4 June, just two days after the Ohnesorg shooting, the NPD gained 7 per cent of votes in *Land* elections in Niedersachsen (Lower Saxony). The NPD were a marginal force and their relatively small electoral successes certainly did not suggest a groundswell of popular support for a new Nazi regime but, in light of the Nazi past, the Grand Coalition, the *Notstandsgesetze* and the highly charged atmosphere of the late 1960s, they had disproportionate significance. The state's refusal to ban them despite a readiness to ban the KPD hardly allayed fears on the Left that democracy was once again under threat from the Right.

The activities of *Kommune I* (commune 1) certainly fuelled suspicions that the state authorities were colluding to stifle opposition, while also proving particularly effective at inflaming the loathing of protesters by the press and police. The *Kommune* was established on 1 January 1967 in Berlin and from 1 May it was located at Kaiser Friedrich Strasse 54 in Charlottenberg, just a few streets to the south of the Deutsche Oper. Some of the sixteen founders, such as Fritz Teufel and Rainer Langhans, were members of the SDS, and were at least nominally registered students at the FU Berlin. Others, including Dieter Kunzelmann, were not members of any political organization, but had been active in protests in Berlin for some time: Kunzelmann was a key figure in the development of the anti-authoritarian wing of the SDS in partnership with Dutschke. The *Kommune* was defined by Rainer Langhans as a 'political group with a shared living area' and by Kunzelmann as 'a political group that seeks to combine

31. *Kommilitoninnen, Kommilitonen!*, Sammlung Mehringer, ED 308/11, IfZM. This is a flyer by the AStA announcing the demonstration.
32. 'Die Uni ist nicht braun', *Erlangen Stadt und Land*, 10/11 December 1966, Sammlung Mehringer, ED 308/11, IfZM.

political and human existence'.[33] In a letter to his parents Teufel (literally 'devil') described the new commune as 'a revolution of everyday life, an abolition of private property, a breaking of the achievement principle, a proclamation of the pleasure principle'.[34] The *Kommune* fused an alternative hippie lifestyle, including long hair, unkempt and colourful clothing, drug-taking, free love, collective nudity, and so on, with political activity in the form of satirical provocation, in a way that bears comparison with the activities of the Yippies in America.

Kommune I was anti-authoritarian, revolutionary in outlook, and provocative toward authority, and in contrast with their stern-faced counterparts on the Left, members were hedonistic, theatrical, and mocking: Teufel even described himself as a 'polit-clown'. The phrase 'make love not war' may seem applicable to the group, but its openly confrontational style and its active engagement with political issues made it very different from the personal hippie 'revolution in the head' which usually shunned politics and made its challenge to society through personal lifestyle choices. Vietnam provided the main focus for its political activity, and the support given to the North Vietnamese cause stands in complete contrast to the pacifist outlook of hippie groups in other countries. Although a host of other communes were established across the country in imitation of *Kommune I*, none of them succeeded in publicizing themselves and the new alternative lifestyle in the way that *Kommune I* did so spectacularly: the members of *Kommune I* have after all been described as 'the pop-stars of the student revolt'.[35]

The first and perhaps most famous (or infamous) success for *Kommune I* took place in advance of US Vice-President Hubert Humphrey's visit to Berlin on 6 April. The FU Berlin AStA planned a demonstration against the Vietnam War during Humphrey's visit to the galleries in Schloß Charlottenberg, just a few streets from the *Kommune I* building.[36] A few days beforehand, *Kommune I* set about making plans to attack Humphrey's entourage at Schloß Charlottenberg.[37] The police got wind of the plan, and

---

33. Testimony by Rainer Langhans dated 1 August 1967, and testimony by Dieter Kunzelmann dated 25 October 1967, file 56, Aktenbestand des Sozialistischen Anwaltskollektivs, HIfS. These are statements given to police as part of the investigation into events on 2 June 1967.

34. Quoted in von Uslar, M., 'Einer, der gern saß', *Der Spiegel*, 9 June 1997, p. 72. This is a retrospective of Teufel's career during and after *Kommune I*.

35. Hüetlin, T., 'Die Tage der Kommune', *Der Spiegel*, 30 June 1997, p. 100.

36. See the flyer *Empfäng für Humphrey*, Berlin file 00107, BfZS.

37. Statements to the police by Volker Gebbert, Rainer Langhans and Ulrich Enzensberger, all dated 7 April 1967, file 64, Kommune I I, Aktenbestand des Sozialistischen Anwaltskollektivs, HIfS.

raided the *Kommune I* building in the belief that an assassination attempt was being planned. In total 11 members of the commune were arrested and taken into custody while the police searched the building. Details of the planned attack were released to the press who, the next day, outdid even their own previous efforts and splashed sensational headlines across their front pages about an attempt to kill Humphrey. With complete certainty the cover of *Bild* declared 'Berlin: Bomb attack on US Vice-President' and the *Berliner Morgenpost* announced 'Assassination attempt on Humphrey foiled by Criminal Police: FU Students completed bombs with explosives from Peking'. The next day they were forced to backtrack and admit that the supposed assassination attempt was actually a police fantasy: the 'bombs' were made from blancmange, quark, and cakes. *Der Spiegel*, rejoicing in the humiliation of its competitors, gleefully suggested that *Kommune I* had put Humphrey's life at risk from cholesterol-rich butter-cream.[38] The 11 'assassins' were not released until the early hours of 7 April because the judge would not believe the police report in light of the frenzied press response. Far from apologizing for their mistake Duensing reasserted that the police had acted to preserve the 'life or the health' of the US Vice-President.[39] Members of *Kommune I* became household names in the wake of the *Pudding Bomben Attentat* (blancmange assassination attempt) in April 1967 and over the next few years both the press and the police exacted revenge for their humiliation.

The perception that both sides were engaged in conspiracies was undoubtedly exacerbated by generational differences, and in many respects *Kommune I* was merely an extreme expression of changes that were happening throughout Western societies. Without those changes the formation of a community as bohemian as *Kommune I*, in which every aspect of daily life was potentially shocking for older generations, would not have been possible. Before looking further at *Kommune I*, then, it is worth taking time to look at these changes, particularly concentrating upon the importance of the post-war economic boom in making general changes in behaviour patterns possible. Attitudes to sex had certainly changed: a survey by *Der Spiegel* in June 1967 found that only one in six students believed women

38. Köhler, O., 'Mord', *Der Spiegel*, 17 April 1967, p. 61. This article includes facsimiles of several front-page headlines in reaction to the *Attentat*, including those quoted here.

39. See *Kommune I, Gesammelte Werk gegen uns*, pp. 9a–9b, Broschüren DO2212, BfZS. This reprints a letter from Berlin Interior Minister Wolfgang Büsch's, dated 19.7.67, on charges brought by Kunzelmann and Ridder against Duensing as a result of the inaccuracy of his statements. The letter includes details of Duensing's statement. The document as a whole is an extensive collection of material relating to, and assembled by, *Kommune I*.

should be virgins when they married.[40] When two researchers at the Hamburg Institute for Sexual Research attempted to carry out a survey of student attitudes in 1968, six universities refused permission, but in contrast to this attitude among older generations, 60 per cent of the 3,666 students asked to fill in the extensive 280-question survey took the time to do so, in itself evidence of a more open attitude to sexual matters.[41] The survey found that, in contrast to the Imperial, Weimar and Nazi periods, duty toward society, religion, public morals, the family, and the state were rejected in favour of personal needs and decision-making.

A total of 65 per cent of male and 57 per cent of female students had already lost their virginity. Although only every twelfth female student was taking the contraceptive pill, 54 per cent of sexually active 20- to 21-year-olds had had a sexual partner, 27 per cent had had two or three, five per cent had had four or five, and 14 per cent had had more than six. Among those 20- to 21-year-olds who were not sexually active, the decisions of only two-fifths of women and a third of men were informed by moral, usually religious considerations. Even then, only 42 per cent of churchgoers supported strict abstinence before marriage. The researchers found that in all the categories the majority of respondents supported a liberalization of the law against homosexuality, which was still illegal. Combined with the fact that 90 per cent of Catholic students approved of the use of contraceptives, the researchers concluded that there was a tolerance for 'the self-regulation of sexual life without legal interference by the state'.[42] These developments were described as evidence of an ongoing sexual reform rather than a sexual revolution, because for more than 95 per cent of respondents the ideal was still a stable monogamous relationship and almost 50 per cent of single students remained virgins. In fact, rather than pointing to a sexual revolution in the 1960s, changes in attitudes and behaviour patterns in the 1960s seem to have been consistent with long-term trends. This view is confirmed by Jonathon Gathorne-Hardy in his biography of Alfred C. Kinsey when he says that both Kinsey's research and a similar survey carried out in Britain indicated 'that people became *aware* of sexual changes in the '60s which seem to have taken place in the '50s'.[43] Similarly, David Allyn, in his history of the sexual revolution, insists that 'people told the truth . . . about their sexual

---

40. 'Was denken die Studenten?', *Der Spiegel*, 19 June 1967, p. 31.

41. 'Studenten: Sex-report', *Der Spiegel*, 26 August 1968, pp. 46–50.

42. Giese, H., 'Revolution oder Liebe?', *Der Spiegel*, 26 August, 1968, pp. 51–4.

43. Gathorne-Hardy, J., *Alfred C. Kinsey*, p. 400. These conclusions are based on survey evidence about trends in the median age of first intercourse, which fell consistently throughout the post-war period.

histories' and 'when enough people told the truth, the life of the nation [the United States] was transformed'.[44] It is certainly the case that sex was more openly discussed and represented in the media than ever before. In acknowledgement of the fact that attitudes to sex had changed fundamentally, in particular that it was now a question of personal choice rather than state interference, both the Kiesinger and Brandt administrations introduced a series of reforms to the laws on sex. On 1 September 1969 the law banning homosexuality was repealed and adultery ceased to be a prosecutable crime. In November 1973, despite opposition from the CDU, a root-and-branch liberalization of sex laws made pornography for adults legal and clarified the law on homosexuality to make it punishable only for acts with the under-aged.

These new freedoms were made possible by an environment of economic prosperity and stability. The availability of contraception undoubtedly played a part, but the fact that so few women were taking the contraceptive pill suggests it would be easy to overestimate the importance of this issue: in February 1968 the *FU Spiegel* reported that only 4 to 6 per cent of female students were taking the contraceptive pill. Besides concerns that the pill entailed personality-altering hormones, availability was also an issue. When *FU Spiegel* conducted a survey of 176 Berlin gynaecologists and asked which of them would be willing to prescribe the pill to unmarried women, they found that of the 96 who replied only 49 would give the pill to unmarried women.[45] Other forms of contraception are curiously missing from the surveys, although Hermann Korte has stated that by 1970 other methods of birth control were being used by more people, from all sections of society, than ever.[46] Nevertheless, even the availability of contraception, and dealing with the economic consequences of unplanned pregnancy, are dependent upon wealth or the existence of a generous public health and social welfare service, and usually both. This explanation is central to an understanding of the development of liberal sexual attitudes throughout the Western world in the post-war period. As has been discussed, prosperity creates new opportunities, personal freedoms and expectations.

Youthful rebellion is an age-old phenomenon, but by the 1960s young people had the means to indulge in it as never before. The April 1967 survey in *Der Spiegel* found that 37 per cent of students had an income of between 200 and 299 DM per month, 28 per cent had between 300 and

---

44. Allyn, D, *Make Love, Not War*, p. x.
45. 'Anti-Baby Pille für Studentinnen', *FU Spiegel*, February 1968, p. 24.
46. Korte, H., *Eine Gesellschaft im Aufbruch*, p. 86.

399 DM per month, and 16 per cent had more than 400 DM per month. Only 19 per cent had less than 200 DM and were forced to live at home with their parents.[47] This is put into perspective by a survey of the Ruhr University in Bochum in October 1967 which found that 34 per cent of students had their own car.[48] Anti-authoritarianism was a central aspect of student rebellion, but it was also a key feature of the new youth culture, including the consumption of products, and engaging in activities, that were aimed specifically at, and were often produced by, the young. In its long lead article on youth culture in October 1967 *Der Spiegel* expressed the shock that seemed to be shared by older generations throughout the Western world at mini-skirts, pop music, and the whole panoply of youth culture, all of which seemed to celebrate youth at the expense of age. In West Germany alone the age group between 14 and 24 was spending 23.8 billion DM on consumer goods and entertainment a year by 1967. The record industry, which was worth 400 million DM, was overwhelmingly aimed at the young, with 'serious music' only representing 20 per cent of production. Young people spent their money on clothes above all else, with 4.8 billion DM devoted to this single area. The result was a massive change in the high street, with the Neckermann chain of department stores giving more than 40 per cent of its store space to youth clothing by 1967, whereas even in the previous year it had allocated only 10 per cent.[49] All of these statistics and statements, including those on sex, would have been unthinkable even a decade beforehand. Conspicuous consumption, the easy gratification of desires, non-conformity with the behaviour codes of previous generations, including sexual permissiveness, new expectations and opportunities for different lifestyles were all opened up to the post-war generation. *Kommune I* was a part of this development, however much it parodied capitalism.

Kommune I's form of rebellion was not universally appreciated on the Left, however, and it soon found itself jettisoned from its collective membership of the SDS. In the run-up to the May 1967 referendum at the FU Berlin, *Kommune I* members distributed flyers in the name of the SDS to the *Rektor*, the AStA, and the various student organizations. In this they accused the student population of being boring careerists and urged them not to take part in the referendum.[50] The flyer had not been approved by the SDS, for which *Kommune I* was a 'horror commune', and they seized

---

47. 'Was denken die Studenten?', *Der Spiegel*, 19 June 1967, p. 31.
48. *BSZ: Bochumer Studenten Zeitung*, 9 October 1967, p. 3, AFAS.
49. 'Kultur: Gesellschaft', *Der Spiegel*, 2 October 1967, pp. 154–70.
50. Dutschke, G., *Rudi Dutschke*, pp. 123–4 on the expulsion of *Kommune I* from SDS.

the opportunity to punish such 'indiscipline' by throwing *Kommune I* out. Giving equal importance to personal lifestyle choices and political activity, even seeing the former as a political activity, was impossible for many SDS members to take on board, including anti-authoritarians who could only remain at best sympathetic to *Kommune I*. *Kommune I* had already reprinted Wilhelm Reich's book *The Function of the Orgasm* and Ulrich Enzensberger has stated that 'we took the line that a fulfilled individual life of freedom and the freeing of desires is directly linked to meaningful political work'.[51] This was anathema to the traditional wing of the SDS, and went too far for most anti-authoritarians with their dynamic emphasis on action. In response *Kommune I* mocked the 'poor SDS'.[52]

Having been sent packing by the SDS, *Kommune I* then gave the police an opportunity to exact some revenge. On 22 May the Brussels department store *A L'Innovation* burned down leaving more than 300 people dead. Two days later *Kommune I* members, notably Teufel and Langhans, distributed a series of flyers (numbered six to nine) on Vietnam at the FU Berlin. In flyer number six they described how a Belgian group of Vietnam activists had set fire to the building and said 'it could encourage other groups in other cities, not only in Belgium, to use the power of this big happening [*sic*] in similar actions'.[53] In flyer seven they went so far as to declare 'a burning store with burning people conveys for the first time in a major European city the crackle of the Vietnam feeling . . . that we have missed in Berlin for so long'.[54] Flyer eight asked 'when will the Berlin stores burn?' and chuckled 'burn, ware-house, burn!'.[55] The police seized their chance and on 8 June Teufel and Langhans were charged with 'inciting life-threatening arson'.[56] In the period after the Ohnesorg shooting the trial over these flyers would be one of a series involving *Kommune I* members, all of which became causes célèbres that brought the justice system into question.

51. Quoted in Chaussy, U., *Die drei Leben des Rudi Dutschke*, p. 137.
52. See *Kommune I, Gesammelte Werk gegen uns*, pp. 16–17, Broschüren DO2212, BfZS.
53. 'Neue Demonstrationsformen in Brüssel erstmals erprobt', quoted in *Strafsache*, pp. 17–21, file 65, Kommune I IIa Brandstiftung Diverses, Aktenbestand des Sozialistischen Anwaltskollektivs, HIfS. This extensive document collects together the details of the case against Teufel and Langhans.
54. *Neu! Unkonventional!*, Berlin file 00116, BfZS.
55. *Wann brennen die Berliner Kaufhäuser?*, Berlin file 00118, BfZS. 'Ware-house' is the German term for department store.
56. See *Strafsache*, p. 2, file 65, Kommune I IIa Brandstiftung Diverses, Aktenbestand des Sozialistischen Anwaltskollektivs, HIfS.

By June 1967, then, the conflict between protesters and those in authority had escalated to the point where the patience of both sides was being tested to the full. For protesters the Emergency Laws, the Grand Coalition, the government's support for the American intervention in Vietnam, a growing support for the NPD, a refusal to ban either the NPD or racist films in the name of free speech in contrast to the ban on the KPD, police raids on the FU Berlin and the SDS offices, police bans on demonstrations, and police violence, all in the name of defending democracy, combined to produce distrust in the democratic credentials of the *Bundesrepublik* and doubts for the safety of German democracy in the future. For those in authority the growing presence of the far left, fear of communist infiltration, the provocation tactics of the SDS, violent protest tactics, vocal opposition to the *Bundesrepublik* and the post-war settlement, accusations of Nazism, public humiliation at the hands of *Kommune I*, and a youth culture that challenged traditional values, whether in terms of clothing, long hair, attitudes to sex, attitudes to authority, and so on, meant that protesters posed a threat both to democracy and to accepted value systems. This volatile mixture of views that were diametrically opposed finally exploded on 2 June 1967 with the killing of Benno Ohnesorg.

– 6 –

The Shooting of Benno Ohnesorg:
The Turning Point

It is a strange fact that although various brief accounts of the shooting of Benno Ohnesorg on 2 June 1967 have been written in both English and German, no attempt has ever been made to reconstruct events in detail. The meaning of the date is so familiar that former protesters refer simply to '2. Juni' and folders in archives are labelled in the same way, no further explanation being necessary. Perhaps this familiarity goes some way to explaining why the events have never been examined in depth by historians: there may be an assumption that the facts are long established and that only the most basic thumbnail sketch is necessary in any account of the period. To repeat this mistake here would be a travesty, as the events surrounding the shooting are far from straightforward and Ohnesorg's death represents one of the most controversial episodes in post-war West German social history, with far-reaching implications for German democracy. Ohnesorg's shooting by a plain-clothes police officer prompted tens of thousands of students to become politically active for the first time; it raised the stakes for demonstrators to a new and potentially fatal level; it confirmed many in their suspicions that West German democracy was either under threat from, or had already been destroyed by Nazism, and led directly to a rapid escalation in violence that culminated in terrorism. Singling out any other event in the period before or after 2 June 1967, including any of the events of 1968, as representing the key turning point in the development of the protest movements of the 1960s would be completely inaccurate. More than any other event 2 June exposed and deepened fault lines of opinion throughout West German society. It is not too extravagant to say that Ohnesorg's death changed the political landscape irrevocably.

The events of Friday 2 June 1967 centred on the controversial state visit of the Shah of Iran, Mohammed Reza Pahlavi. Students at the FU Berlin accused him of being a corrupt dictator with a record of human-rights abuses.[1] This was repeated by Ulrike Meinhof in an open letter to the

---

1. *Informationen über Persiah und den Shah*, B/166/1315, VDS, BK.

Shah's wife, published in *Konkret* in advance of the Shah's visit.[2] Even Mayor Albertz, when faced with the prospect of dealing personally with the Shah during his visit to Berlin, told the Berlin Senate 'don't leave me alone with this tyrant'.[3] On 1 June the Berlin FU AStA organized a debate on conditions in Persia, during which Dr Bahman Nirumand, an Iranian opponent of the Shah, spoke out against the Shah's government. Now that the AStA was dominated by the Left the event was naturally a platform for political declarations and gestures by far-left organizations. The committee of investigation that was later set up to look into the events of 2 June stated that at least one speaker demanded a massive show of force against the police, and another declared sympathy for an assassination attempt against the Shah.[4] Whatever the truth of these accusations, it is clear that placards for the demonstration on 2 June were distributed and plans were made by the SDS for the use of missiles such as eggs, tomatoes and bottles against the police. Feelings were running high and alongside these plans for provocation were expectations of police violence that prompted discussions on how demonstrators could protect themselves.

Not only did previous police behaviour and statements suggest that these expectations were realistic, but unknown to the demonstrators the police were involved in advance planning for the demonstrations that made violent clashes a probability. The Federal Interior Ministry gave the Shah's visit the highest security rating and level of risk, Security Level 1, meaning police had to plan for a possible assassination attempt. Far from giving the police a green light for breaking up demonstrations, the Ministry explicitly recognized the risk posed by heavy-handedness: 'the security of the imperial guests is alone the task and purpose of all police measures. Chanting, placards, etc., are basically to be ignored as long as they do not disturb the peace too badly. Police measures should under no circumstances create a greater threat to public security and order than the reasons for the intervention.'[5] The police were to intercede only in cases involving violence, or where the demonstrators were deemed to be a risk to security. In theory this meant a 'hands-off' approach, but in fact it was used to justify police violence in the name of security.

At around midday on 2 June the first demonstration against the Shah took place outside Rathaus Schöneberg involving a wide cross-section of

---

2. Meinhof, U.M., 'Offener Brief an Farah Diba', *Konkret*, June 1967, pp. 21–2.

3. Quoted in Schuster, *Heinrich Albertz*, p. 199.

4. *1. Beschlußempfehlung des 1. Untersuchungsausschusses des Abgeordnetenhauses von Berlin, V. Wahlperiode, vom 18. September*, p. 98, Rep 014/1017, LB. See also *Bericht des Rektors*, pp. 36–7, Rep 014/843, LB.

5. *1. Beschlußempfehlung des 1. Untersuchungsausschusses*, p. 93.

age groups, including pensioners and children. The majority, however, were young people, especially students. Around 2,000 to 3,000 protesters and bystanders formed up behind crash barriers set up by the police on the far side of the square, opposite the Rathaus. They carried placards with messages such as 'down with the military dictator' and 'welcome to Berlin Mr. Dictator' while shouting slogans including 'murderer get out of the Rathaus' and 'police state'.[6] In front of the Rathaus was a cordon of police, and between the police and the demonstrators was a group of about 100 Iranians, ostensibly supporters of the Shah but actually members of the Iranian secret service organization, Savak.[7] These agents soon got involved in verbal exchanges with the demonstrators opposing the Shah. Eyewitness Wendula Dahle, remembered, 'around 15–20 Shah supporters went to the right hand corner of the cordoned area . . . broke down the barriers, and the police let them past. A group of them were armed with poles (from placards) and blackjacks . . . they hit not only demonstrators but also the bystanders, such as housewives and pensioners.'[8] This took place in full view of the police, who did nothing to stop them, even though the Iranians were hitting people with thick wooden poles that measured 4 to 6 feet in length. The police report into the incident says that both sides attacked each other with sticks (for which there is no evidence at all), and that the demonstrators responded by throwing missiles which injured three police officers and one of the Iranians. As a result four demonstrators were arrested for breach of the peace.[9]

Here was the first evidence that the police interpretation of their security role would be selectively applied. The police had made no plans to cordon off these Iranians and they had no orders on how to deal with them, even though it was likely that their presence would inflame the situation. The committee of investigation into the 2 June events took the view that a lack of orders had led to moral paralysis, so that although the police had the general task of keeping the peace, in this case they were concentrating on carrying out specific orders regarding the demonstrators.[10] Even this

6. Ibid., p. 94.

7. See for instance 'Geheimdienste: Savak', *Der Spiegel*, 16 October 1967, pp. 64–7, for an article on Savak, including its involvement in events on 2 June and one of the infamous photographs of Savak agents attacking the crowd.

8. See *Übersicht über die Ordnung des Materials und der Auswertung, IX Schöneberger Rathaus*, file 56, Aktenbestand des Sozialistischen Anwaltskollektivs, HIfS. This is an extensive police report collecting eyewitness testimony of the events on 2 June.

9. *Berlin-Besuch des iranischen Kaiserpaares*, file 127, Aktenbestand des Sozialistischen Anwaltskollektivs, HIfS. This is a Berlin police report on the visit of the Shah.

10. *1. Beschlußempfehlung des 1. Untersuchungsausschusses*, p. 99.

generous interpretation suggests a selective and uncritical stance by the police that saw demonstrators as the main problem, and which heightened the likelihood of violence. Once the Shah had left the Rathaus the demonstration quickly melted away, to take part in further protests during the Shah's tour of the city when further clashes took place, both with the police and the Iranian secret service agents. By the evening, then, feelings were running high on both sides.

The protesters finally regrouped outside the Deutsche Oper at around 6.30 that evening. The Shah and his wife were to watch a performance of *The Magic Flute* in the company of the Mayor of Berlin and the Federal President, Heinrich Lübke. Between 3,000 and 6,000 demonstrators and bystanders assembled outside the opera house to await their arrival. The building is on the north side of a large road, Bismarck Strasse, which runs straight from west to east, where it eventually reaches the Brandenburg Gate. The demonstrators were assembled behind crash barriers constructed by the police along Bismarck Strasse, opposite the opera building, with a building site behind them bordered by a wall approximately seven to eight feet in height. Access to the road was prevented by barriers that wrapped around the pavement corner of Bismarck Strasse and Krumme Strasse (literally 'crooked street'), which ran north to south along the eastern side of both the opera house and the building site. The police were lined up along the centre of the road, facing the demonstrators, who were carrying placards with messages such as 'murderer get out of Berlin' and 'no dictators as guests of a free state'.

At around 7.20 the Savak members arrived, and were kept on the other side of the street by the police. The demonstrators opposite shouted abuse at them, and hurled eggs, tomatoes, smoke bombs and then stones from the building site. Individual protesters were dragged over the crash barriers by the police on suspicion of throwing missiles. They were hit by police officers, often by several at a time, while lying on the ground. Christoph Hönig, a 32-year-old teacher, remembered 'around four to five uniformed officers came over the barrier into the crowd and brought individual people from the crowd onto the road . . . a young man was hit many times while he was taken over the Bismarck Strasse, although I couldn't see him resisting'.[11] Demonstrators responded by shouting 'SA, 'SS' and 'Gestapo' at the police, which just enraged them further.

By 7.45 two police officers had been injured by missiles, and shortly afterward Duensing decided that the demonstrators should be cleared from

---

11. Statement to the police by Christoph Hönig, 12 July 1967, file 56, Aktenbestand des Sozialistischen Anwaltskollektivs, HIfS.

Bismarck Strasse because they were too much of a security risk. Police were to move the demonstrators west from the edge of Krumme Strasse, using truncheons if necessary. They made loudspeaker announcements but many protesters later stated that they either didn't hear these, or they were unintelligible. Whatever the case, the demonstrators had nowhere to move to: those at the corner of Krumme Strasse could only follow the orders of the police by pushing back the crowd of people further along the street, who had not heard the order to move. When the demonstrators failed to respond police moved in swinging truncheons just after 8.00 p.m., having been given the order 'Knüppel frei', giving them permission for free use of their truncheons. Protesters could only get out of the way by jumping over the wall behind them or by jumping over the crash barriers into the arms of officers who were waiting to hit them.[12] Police gave demonstrators the stark choice of being trampled, getting beaten by police, or fighting back. Not surprisingly, many chose to fight back and the demonstration descended into the most violent battle between protesters and police so far in the post-war period. The police even deployed a water cannon to scatter the crowd, although it was clearly impossible for the protesters to disperse. Although it cannot be denied that the demonstrators had provoked the police by throwing missiles, this had been entirely predictable, and the police had anticipated the probability that they would have to deal with this. It could be that the police realized on the day that they had misjudged the location of the demonstration. Whatever the case, instead of using tactics that would keep disturbance to a minimum, they created a situation that encouraged a massive explosion of violence.

Scores of eyewitnesses provided testimony of the ferocity of the police tactics. Heinz-Dieter Kretzmer, a 23-year-old Engineering student, gives a graphic account: at the height of the police 'clearing action', Kretzmer and a friend tried to take some pictures of police officers who were attacking demonstrators. An officer objected to this, saying 'come back again tomorrow, then you'll get a good hiding, communist pig, go back over to the [Eastern] Zone'. When they refused to hand over the camera they were attacked with truncheons. Kretzmer managed to escape these officers and later commented,

> Everything looked to me like chaos. I saw police officers climb over the barriers and noticed a violent hand-to-hand fight. I heard shouts of 'murderer' and also

12. See 'Knüppel frei', *Der Spiegel*, 12 June 1967, pp. 41–6 for a description of the events of 2 June. The sequence of events described in this article differs from that given in this chapter in several details, though not in substance, showing the confusion about events that existed in the aftermath of the shooting.

chants that I couldn't understand. I didn't hear any loudspeaker announcements . . . The officers who had invaded the crowd held their batons in raised hands . . . I also saw how the officers made use of their batons and noticed how numerous demonstrators were dragged over the southern side of Bismarck Strasse toward the Deutsche Oper, to the lines in the middle of the road, and during the dragging they were beaten with truncheons by the police officers. In one case a police officer kicked a demonstrator who had broken free and fallen over.[13]

For many of the police the demonstration seems to have been an opportunity for avenging previous insults and actively opposing communist infiltration. One bystander on 2 June, Paul Fröhling, who said he did not support the demonstration, wrote in complaint to Duensing after he had been attacked by police officers who told him 'you filthy communists will be thrown back over the Wall'.[14]

Some groups of demonstrators were able to escape the police cordon or jump over the wall of the building site to run down the side streets, especially Krumme Strasse. Snatch squads of plain-clothes policemen were in operation in this area and running battles were taking place with police all along the street. At the end of Krumme Strasse, at the junction with Schiller Strasse, was a ground-floor car park, under 66 to 67 Krumme Strasse, into which a number of demonstrators fled. The building, which has hardly changed since the events of 2 June, is a block of apartments supported by pillars on the ground floor, so that the car park is open on all sides, with only a small wall topped by railings facing the street. The police mounted a 'clearing action' to force the demonstrators from this car park. This created another pitched battle and toward the end of this, at about 8.30, when the police had already gained control of the area, the FU Berlin student Benno Ohnesorg was shot in the head by plain-clothes officer Karl-Heinz Kurras, a member of the *Abteilung I* (Battalion I, political crimes) snatch squad. Ohnesorg was taken to hospital, where he died later that evening after an operation to remove a 7.65 mm bullet from his brain. In the meantime the violence at the Deutsche Oper continued, with the police eventually clearing the streets, only for the clashes eventually to spill over onto the Kurfürstendamm a few streets to the south. It was only at around 12.30 a.m. that the fighting came to end, by which time 44 demonstrators had been arrested, and the same number of people had been

13. Statement to the police by Heinz-Dieter Kretzmer, 31 July 1967, file 56, Aktenbestand des Sozialistischen Anwaltskollektivs, HIfS.

14. Undated letter from Paul Fröhling to Police President Duensing, file 127, Aktenbestand des Sozialistischen Anwaltskollektivs, HIfS.

injured, including 20 police officers. In a massive operation the police had deployed 3,905 uniformed officers, 77 members of *Abteilung I*, and 144 members of its sister unit *Abteilung K*. They had even received four anonymous bomb threats.[15] One senior officer made a point of ending his report by saying 'I would like to remark that I have never experienced such an uproar before in my 19 years of service.'[16]

In the days that followed the shooting, a storm of protest swept across German cities, with hardly any universities untouched by the outrage that poured forth, and almost all major cities experiencing demonstrations of some kind. Tens of thousands of students took to the streets, many of them for the first time. Most of the demonstrations took the form of memorial marches for Ohnesorg in which the behaviour of the police was attacked, and anguish for democracy was expressed. At a demonstration in Ulm, for instance, protesters carried placards reading 'the Benno Ohnesorg case: a symptom', or 'democracy shot down, dictatorship protected'.[17] In Hamburg, which the Shah toured on 3 and 4 June, the demonstrations were particularly violent, with clashes between police and protesters on both days of the Shah's visit. Concerns at the precedent set by Ohnesorg's shooting may have been justified: Hans Peter Herbst, a philosophy student, saw how a plain-clothes officer waved his pistol at demonstrators, and then put it back under his coat when demonstrators tried to report this to uniformed officers. Holger Oehrens, chief editor of the Hamburg student newspaper *Auditorium*, was arrested by police when he tried to photograph police violence outside the Rathaus. At the police station where he was charged an officer told him, in clear reference to Ohnesorg's death, 'shut your mouth, stupid boy. The next time we'll do the same as in Berlin.'[18] The Shah flew home from Hamburg on Sunday 4 June, by which time Ohnesorg's death was being seen by students as symptomatic of fundamental flaws in the Federal Republic's democracy. It was perhaps

15. See *Ergänzungsbericht über die polizeilichen Maßnahmen am 2.6.67 anläßlich des Berlin-Besuchs des iranischen Kaiserpaares, Berlin, den 4. Juni 1967*, pp. 11-13, file 127, Aktenbestand des Sozialistischen Anwaltskollektivs, HIfS.

16. Statement by POM Horst Geier, 6 June 1967, file 127, Aktenbestand des Sozialistischen Anwaltskollektivs, HIfS.

17. 'Kein Echo in der Bevölkerung', *Schwäbische Donauzeitung*, 8 June 1967, B166/1315, BK.

18. *Dokumentation: Zusammenstellung von Zeugenaussaugen [sic] anläßlich der Vorfälle während des Schahbesuchs in der Freien und Hansestadt Hamburg*, file 53, Aktenbestand des Sozialistischen Anwaltskollektivs, HIfS. This documents 55 eyewitness accounts. Small sections, including Oehrens's report, were reprinted in '"Das nächste mal wie in Berlin": Hamburger Studenten über Zusammenstöß mit der Polizei', *Der Spiegel*, 12 June 1967, p. 42.

understandable that among the most common chants and placard phrases used in the days following Ohnesorg's death was 'today Ohnesorg, tomorrow us?'[19]

The protests continued for some time after the shooting, particularly at the time of Ohnesorg's funeral on 10 June. On 9 June 5,000 FU students held a memorial march before Ohnesorg's body was driven for burial in his home town of Hanover.[20] More than 100 cars, most of them containing students expressing their sympathy, accompanied the procession, which was given permission by Walter Ulbricht to pass across East German territory. The convoy route was lined by thousands of people, and on 10 June around 10,000 students from all over Germany took part in a memorial march through Hanover that stretched for seven kilometres through the city. Indeed, the 2 June events had let the genie out of the bottle in terms of support for protest activity. Before 2 June, support for protests had been growing but was still limited: at the FU Berlin, with a student population of more than 10,000, only 600 students were members of political organizations in the period just before June 1967, of whom around 200 were SDS members and 167 were from the SHB.[21] Even the most liberal calculation puts SDS membership in 1967 at around 2,500 SDS members nationally.[22] Yet *Der Spiegel* estimated that around 100,000 students took part in the demonstrations around West Germany in the days immediately following 2 June. In light of the estimates of attendance for individual demonstrations a figure of perhaps twice this may be more realistic.[23] Although two-thirds of students in the period before the shooting declared themselves to be apolitical, in the immediate aftermath of the shooting a survey found that 65 per cent of students had been politicized by Ohnesorg's death.[24]

19. See for instance *Sachverhalt: Plakate und Gegenstände, die mit dem Tode des Studenten Benno Ohnesorg in Zusammenhang stehen*, 4.6.67, file 127, Aktenbestand des Sozialistischen Anwaltskollektivs, HIfS. This is a police report into a demonstration in Berlin on 4 June 1967.

20. 'Berliner Polizeipräsident beurlaubt', *Flensburger Tageblatt*, 9 June 1967, B/166/1316, BK.

21. 'Berlin, Studenten', *Der Spiegel*, 5 June 1967, p. 59.

22. See the evidence of Dr René Ahlberg to *1. Untersuchungsausschuß (V. Wahlperiode), 66 (Öffentliche) Sitzung, Dienstag, den 13. Februar 1968*, p. 44, Rep 014/842, LB. Ahlberg says this figure is taken from the student journal *Colloquium*. His estimate seems to have been accurate: a government report published in 1969 found that in 1968 there were around 2,500 SDS members based in 38 cities. See 'Zunahme des Linksradikalismus', *Der Tagesspiegel*, 11 September 1969, file Zeitungs Auschnitte 1968/69, Aktenbestand des Sozialistischen Anwaltskollektivs, HIfS.

23. 'Studenten: Protest', *Der Spiegel*, 19 June 1967, p. 25.

24. Schnibben, C., 'Vollstrecker des Weltgewissens', *Der Spiegel*, 2 June 1997, p. 111.

Such a clear turning point was partly a response to the attitude of the authorities. Mayor Albertz displayed a striking lack of remorse for Ohnesorg's death and the day after the shooting he announced

the patience of this city is at an end. A few dozen demonstrators, including students, have made the sad contribution not only of insulting and offending a guest of the Federal Republic of Germany in the German capital, but a death and numerous injuries – police and demonstrators – are also charged to their account . . . I say explicitly and with vigour that I approve of the restraint shown by the police.[25]

In a speech on 8 June he described Ohnesorg as the victim of an extremist minority 'who have abused freedom, in order to reach their final goal of overthrowing our democratic rule of law'.[26] Albertz was given widespread support in the city government. As early as 3 June the Berlin Senate had defied the Basic Law and banned demonstrations in the city. Albertz revoked this on 12 June when the details of the shooting had become clearer and he was no longer so sure of his ground. The Senate also passed a motion promising to bring disciplinary charges against students who had taken part in the 2 June demonstrations, thereby undermining the independence of university government. In a press conference Police Chief Duensing compared his tactics to dealing with a liver sausage where 'the left end stinks' so 'we had to cut into the middle to take off the end'.[27] The police appealed to the people of Berlin, saying they were opposed to 'the minority of radicals who have terrorized the people of Berlin for months through the abuse of freedoms of demonstration and opinion'.[28]

Students roundly rejected this demonization of protesters as troublemakers or gullible followers of an extremist minority. The storm of outrage that poured forth from German universities in the days after the shooting produced an overwhelming mass of written evidence that documented the disgust and anguish of the mass of students. The FU Berlin AStA asked 'is Albertz now oppressing serious political opposition to his policies with the help of the police through murder?'[29] The FU *Konvent* claimed that

25. Quoted in 'Berlin: Albertz', *Der Spiegel*, 19 June 1967, p. 41.

26. 'Albertz erklärt Unruhen mit Unbehageb an der Gesellschaft', *Frankfurter Allgemeine Zeitung*, 9 June 1967, B/166/1316, VDS, BK.

27. 'Kurras und die Folgen', *Süddeutsche Zeitung*, 24 November 1967, Rep 014/1021, LB.

28. Untitled flyer by the Gewerkshaft der Polizei Landesbezirk Berlin, 16 June 1967, file 53, Aktenbestand des Sozialistischen Anwaltskollektivs, HIfS.

29. *Berlinerinnen und Berliner!*, file 53, Aktenbestand des Sozialistischen Anwaltskollektivs, HIfS. Dated 5 June 1967, this flyer is an appeal for support from the Berlin population.

Ohnesorg had been shot by the 'Berlin Executive' and demanded the resignations of Albertz, Duensing and Büsch as well as the 'denazification of the Berlin police, especially its leadership'.[30] The VDS described the shooting as 'an act of police terrorism' and the National Executive of the SDS claimed that Ohnesorg's death was 'the first political murder of the post-war period'.[31]

Yet to a great extent the police and the city government were supported by the press and the public. Students at the FU Berlin felt so strongly that their role on 2 June was being misrepresented in the press that they established a committee to look into the problem. The final report provided overwhelming evidence of bias, particularly from Springer publications. Protesters were described as 'rowdies' in *Bild*, 'communist street fighters' in *Berliner Morgenpost*, and 'hordes, who shout Ho Ho Ho and throw bottles, who use hooliganism as an argument' in *Die Welt*. *Bild* even suggested on 3 June that 'in Berlin until now there was only terror to the east of the Wall. Yesterday malicious and stupid muddle-heads attempted for the first time to carry terror to the free section of the world.'[32] Press reports in the immediate aftermath of 2 June tended to concentrate on the riots, which were blamed on demonstrators, and there was a consistent lack of remorse for Ohnesorg's death, which at most was described as 'tragic'. Above all, the majority of newspapers failed to understand the implications of the shooting for a democratic state.

It is clear that these views reflected the concerns of the general public throughout West Germany. The survey of Berlin public opinion quoted at the start of this volume showed an overwhelming opposition to the protesters rather than sorrow at the fatality, and this was repeated in a survey by the Hamburg University AStA just after the Ohnesorg shooting.[33] This received 108 replies, only 15 of which were positive in their attitudes toward students, who were attacked for having long hair and beards, and were blamed for undermining social values because 'students used to be, or wanted to become, an elite'. Complaints about students wasting taxpayers' money were included in 50 per cent of all letters. One person wrote

30. *Resolution der a. o. Sitzung des XIX. Konvents vom 5. Juni 1967, Vorlage des AStA und des Konventsvorsitzenden*, Berlin file 00113, BfZS.

31. 'VDS protestiert gegen den "Polizeiterror"', *Bayerische Rundschau*, 6 June 1967, B/166/1315, BK, and *Pressemitteilung*, 3.6.1967, file 53, Aktenbestand des Sozialistischen Anwaltskollektivs, HIfS.

32. All quoted in Doyé, W.G., Nevelling, U., Schmidt H. and Wersig G. (eds), *Dokumentation zum gegenwärtigen verhältnis der Berliner Presse zur Studentenschaft*, 8 June 1967, Berlin file 00113, BfZS.

33. Schübel, R., 'Rowdies, Gammler und Schmarotzer', *Auditorium*, July 1967, pp. 9–10, ZA 745, HIfS.

'we tax-payers demand 1. that all students who take part in demonstrations on the occasion of a state visit should be immediately thrown out of their universities, 2. that in future in all demonstrations that are hostile to the state will be beaten down with armed might if necessary'. The old phrase 'quiet, discipline and order' appeared in almost all letters. Accusations that demonstrators were funded by East Germany and were communists were particularly common and 10 per cent of people felt police had not been harsh enough. Again direct and startlingly casual references were made to the Nazi past with the clear assumption that such views were consistent with democracy.

It is possible to go too far, though, and opposition to the demonstrators should be balanced against evidence of widespread disgust both with the shooting and the reaction to it from the authorities, the press and the public. Whereas after Philipp Müller's shooting in Essen in 1952 the only outcry had been against the demonstrators, Ohnesorg's death prompted vociferous, if minority, opposition from all sections of German society. The leaders of the Berlin postal workers' union called for the resignation of Albertz and Duensing 'as well as the cleansing of former SS and SA members from the West Berlin police', and although expressions of concern for German democracy were not particularly common in the press, they were made.[34] Rudolf Augstein, the owner of *Der Spiegel*, argued 'there are enough photos and eyewitness accounts, both close-ups and from a distance, that recall the killer instinct of the concentration-camp period'.[35] The *Frankfurter Rundschau* complained that 'the spirit of democracy, as it is known in other west European countries, scarcely exists in West Berlin'. It attacked Albertz directly, saying 'his first declaration after the death of the student Ohnesorg was so cynical that one doubted whether he was serious'.[36]

On 8 June the Berlin *Abgeordnetenhaus* (House of Representatives) held a heated seven-hour debate on the 2 June events, the most important result of which was the establishment of a committee of investigation, which published its report on 18 September. This took the surprisingly balanced approach of criticizing the protesters for the use of missiles and provocative behaviour, and reprimanding the police for employing tactics

---

34. Deutsche Post, *Die Notstandsverordnungen in der Praxis – Schießbefehl für die westberliner Polizei, 6. Juni 1967*, file 51, Aktenbestand des Sozialistischen Anwaltskollektivs, HIfS.

35. Augstein, R., 'Warum sie demonstrieren', *Der Spiegel*, 19 June 1967, Nr. 26, p. 18.

36. Granz, R., 'Langjäriger Haß hat sich blutig entladen', *Sonderdruck Frankfurter Rundschau*, p. 1, Sammlung Schlemper, ED 328/1, IfZM. This special edition is undated but was produced within a few days of 2 June 1967.

that made violent clashes more likely and for viewing all protests as 'wild demonstrations' that should be broken up.[37] In response Interior Minister Wolfgang Büsch resigned on 19 September, Duensing did the same on 22 September and Albertz followed them on 26 September, to be replaced as Mayor by Klaus Schütz (SPD). The report had made it clear that their support for the police tactics on 2 June had been both misguided and in contradiction of their role as protectors of the freedoms enshrined in the constitution. Albertz's popularity with the people of Berlin had shrunk from 60 per cent in March to 34 per cent in August.[38] After the publication of the 2 June report Albertz's enemies went on the offensive, describing him as a 'village idiot', and his position became untenable.[39]

The release of details about the Ohnesorg shooting had particularly weakened Albertz's position. In the aftermath of the shooting, varied and often contradictory information was released to the public by both the police and the press. It was widely reported that Kurras had fired in self-defence even though Ohnesorg had been shot in the back of the head. The *Frankfurter Rundschau* lamented that 'within three days the authorities have disseminated five different versions of the circumstances of the death', adding to the air of conspiracy.[40] First the authorities said Kurras had fired in self-defence against Ohnesorg, then that Ohnesorg had been hit by a warning shot, and in a third version he was said to have been attacked by people with knives. In a fourth version Kurras himself announced that he had fired two shots. Finally, in an interview with *BZ* Kurras stated that one of the people attacking him with knives had cut his hand 'and the shot went off'.[41] The contradictory evidence given by Kurras himself and others makes it impossible to establish the exact details of what happened, but a reconstruction goes some way to putting the conspiracy theories into perspective.

It should be established first and foremost that despite police claims that Ohnesorg was 'one of the greatest rowdies' in the demonstration, Ohnesorg was anything but a leader of student radicals.[42] He was a student of German literature at the Free University, and a letter to the *Rektor* from

---

37. See particularly 'Empfehlung des Untersuchungsausschusses', in *1. Beschlußempfehlung des 1. Untersuchungsausschusses*, p. 101.

38. 'Berlin: Regierungskrise', *Der Spiegel*, 25 September 1967, pp. 69–70.

39. 'Berlin: Regierungskrise', *Der Spiegel*, 2 October 1967, pp. 27–9

40. '"In Notwehr" wurde Benno Ohnesorg von hinten erschossen', *Sonderdruch Frankfurter Rundschau*, p. 1, Sammlung Schlemper, ED 328/1, IfZM.

41. See 'Knüppel frei', *Der Spiegel*, 12 June 1967, p. 44.

42. *Vermerk*, Berlin, den 3.6.67, signed by *Kriminalmeister* Zepernick, file 127, Aktenbestand des Sozialistischen Anwaltskollektivs, HIfS.

his tutor, Dr Werner Schlotthaus, states that he was a quiet, 'outstandingly gifted, conscientious, responsible and self-controlled student'.[43] Ohnesorg was 26 years old, and a month before his death he had married a fellow student, Christa Hahnke, who on 2 June was five months pregnant with their first child. He was not a member of any political organization, and had never taken part in any demonstration before. A statement to the police by a Herr Bering, a friend of Ohnesorg's who was with him on 2 June, states that Benno and Christa had been in Krumme Strasse as bystanders, observing from a distance.[44] Ohnesorg's son stated in an interview in *Der Spiegel* in 1997 that 'my father did not stand with the flags at the front, but only went to the Opera in order to see what was happening there. He was an interested citizen, nothing more.'[45]

It seems Ohnesorg had crossed the road to Krumme Strasse 66 to 67 to get a better view. He got caught up in the police clearing action in the car park, and during this he was attacked by three policemen, who repeatedly hit him with their truncheons. This was confirmed by the injuries highlighted in the autopsy and by numerous witnesses. At this point a shot was fired that hit him from behind, entering the side of his head, just above and to the rear of his right ear.[46] Eventually a nurse who happened to be at the scene treated him, and someone called an ambulance. This eventually got to the Moabit hospital 40 minutes after their arrival in Krumme Strasse.[47] The fact that this was not the nearest hospital, and that the ambulance had continued to pick up casualties even though they were already dealing with a potentially fatal injury, fuelled speculation that there had been a conspiracy to make sure Ohnesorg died.

Kurras paints a different picture. According to his confused statements he had been cornered at the back of the car park by two youths with knives,

43. Letter from Dr Werner Schlotthaus to the *Rektor* of the Free University, 4 June 1967, B/166/1318, BK.

44. *Aussage Bering,* in *Informationsveranstaltung am 22.6.1967,* p. 22, file 53, Aktenbestand des Sozialistischen Anwaltskollektivs, HIfS. This is a collection of eye-witness accounts from AStA interviews and statements received by Horst Mahler.

45. *Der Spiegel,* 2 June 1997, p. 118.

46. See report *Benno Ohnesorg* by Prof. Dr med. Krauland and Prof. Dr med. Bischof, 3.6.1967, as well as *Leichensache,* 3.6.1967 and *Tatbefundsbericht,* 3.6.1967, both by *Kriminalmeister* Schwinzer and *Kriminalmeister* Ulrich, all from file 127, Aktenbestand des Sozialistischen Anwaltskollektivs, HIfS. These give details about Ohnesorg, his injuries, and the way he was treated in hospital. The first document is an autopsy report that indicates extensive injuries all over Ohnesorg's body.

47. Statements to the police by Gerhard Gritzka and Günter Quast, File 127, Aktenbestand des Sozialistischen Anwaltkollektivs, HIfS. Gritzka was the paramedic and Quast the driver of the ambulance.

who threatened to kill him.[48] He took his service pistol from its holster to warn them off, to no effect, so he fired a shot in the air. When they ran away he stood with his finger still on the trigger and the pistol went off accidentally, hitting Ohnesorg. There are several problems with this story. Although the police interviewed scores of witnesses, including fellow police officers, only a handful heard any threats against the police, and not one saw any youths with knives. By the time the shot was fired, the police had gained control of the car park, making it almost impossible for Kurras to have been at risk. The overwhelming majority of witnesses heard only one shot, and among the seven people who said they heard more than one shot, all but one were on the street outside.[49] Many of them stated that at first they thought the shot was one of the numerous fireworks being let off and even the one witness who was in the car park to hear more than one shot, journalist Günter Lahmann, thought they were fireworks.[50] Only one shell casing was found at the scene, and only one bullet was recovered; this came from Ohnesorg's body.[51] The shot was fired from a distance of about 1½ metres, in a dark and confined space, and into a crowd of people, including fellow officers. Officer Horst Geier, the key witness in the trial, was stood next to Kurras when the shot was fired, and shouted to Kurras, 'are you crazy to be shooting here?'. Geier, who did not know Kurras, recalled 'I heard a gunshot to the right of me . . . I saw a person in civilian clothing stood with a pistol in his right hand. He was stood at close quarters to the three police officers and the man in the red shirt [Ohnesorg]'.[52] In order to avoid hitting fellow officers who were scuffling with Ohnesorg, Kurras would have needed a very careful aim. Whatever happened, it

48. See statement by KOM Karl-Heinz Kurras, 9 June 1967, file 127, Aktenbestand des Sozialistischen Anwaltskollektivs, HIfS. See also *Strafsache gegen den Kriminalobermeister Karl-Heinz Kurras, 3. November 1967*, file 24 of the same archive. This contains a different statement by Kurras, as well as summaries of statements by other witnesses. See also *Anklageschrift*, 10 July 1967, file 43, in the same archive. This gives a full list of witnesses to be used in the trial, as well as the Defence version of Kurras' story.

49. See the statements by Werner Kowenick, 8 June 1967, Wilfried Berkefeld, 9 June 1967, and by Lothar A. Binger, 9 June 1967 in file 127, Aktenbestand des Sozialistischen Anwaltskollektivs, HIfS. See also the statements by Wolfgang Tumler, 19 June 1967, Klaus Hirschfeld, 21 June 1967, Edith Merchert, 21 June 1967, and Günter Lahmann, 26 June 1967 in file 24, Aktenbestand des Sozialistischen Anwaltskollektivs, HIfS. Lahmann is the witness who heard 2 or 3 shots.

50. Statement to the police by Günter Lahmann, 26 June 1967, file 24, Aktenbestand des Sozialistischen Anwaltskollektivs, HIfS.

51. See *Betrifft: Pistolen-, Hülsen- und Geschoßuntersuchung in Sachen Benno Ohnesorg, 3. Juni 1967*, file 127, Aktenbestand des Sozialistischen Anwaltskollektivs, HIfS.

52. Statement by POM Horst Geier, 6 June 1967, file 127, Aktenbestand des Sozialistischen Anwaltskollektivs, HIfS.

seems clear that Kurras's testimony was nonsense. Even the wound he supposedly received from the knife-wielding protesters was, according to the doctor who examined him, almost certainly an older wound that was not caused by a knife.[53]

This leads to the question of Kurras's motivation. His Defence argued that Kurras was in such a traumatized state he could have been convinced he was being attacked by youths with knives, even though they weren't actually there. The psychologist who examined Kurras, Dr Heinz Spengler, pronounced at the trial that 'at the time of the act he was in a state of overwhelmed psychogenic alarm'.[54] This may have been accurate, but all evidence of Kurras looking panicked and shocked refers exclusively to his condition after the shooting. While the idea of psychological trauma cannot be dismissed, it is worth noting a few other facts about Kurras's life. After service in the Wehrmacht, from 1946 to 1949 he was interned by the Soviets in Sachsenhausen concentration camp in northern Berlin for distributing anti-Soviet propaganda, and upon his release he went to West Berlin and joined the police.[55] His role in *Abteilung I*, which dealt with 'political crime', was again closely connected with anti-communism: one eyewitness on 2 June had been investigated by Kurras on suspicion of being a member of the KPD or the SED.[56] Kurras viewed the use of a firearm against protesters, even in a confined space, as perfectly normal, just as other police officers presented the use of truncheons against dissenters.[57] In his statements he described himself as a hunted man, and viewed demonstrators collectively as 'rowdies' or 'thugs'. At best, then, he may have been prompted by trauma to give vent to underlying prejudices. Claims by protesters that Kurras was taking a common police attitude a step further, and that the shooting was an extension of his previous anti-communism, would therefore seem to have had some justification.

53. Zylka, H., '13 Zeugen hörten nur einen Schuß!', *Bild*, 8 November 1967, p. 2. See also *Arztbericht*, 3.6.1967 and *Untersuchung auf Verletzungsspuren*, 5.6.1967, both in file 127, Aktenbestand des Sozialistischen Anwaltskollektivs, HlfS.

54. Trial testimony given by Dr med. Heinz Spengler, *6. Verhandlungstag, 15. November 1967, Fortsetzung der Hauptverhandlung in der Strafsache gegen Kurras wegen fahrlässiger Tötung*, pp. 93–4, file 24, Aktenbestand des Sozialistischen Anwaltskollektivs, HlfS.

55. 'Mord ohne Mörder', *Der Spiegel*, 2 June 1997, pp. 114–15. This article gives valuable information about Kurras's life.

56. See Statement to the police by Alfred Alexander Mentschel, 10 July 1967, file 127, Aktenbestand des Sozialistischen Anwaltskollektivs, HlfS.

57. See Statement to police by Karl-Heinz Kurras, 9 June 1967, p. 10, file 127, Aktenbestand des Sozialistischen Anwaltskollektivs, HlfS.

In the period after the shooting, Kurras's colleagues even aided him. He was relieved from duty rather than imprisoned on remand, even though he was under investigation for a fatal shooting. The criminal investigation only started on 5 June, and although the initial police reports stated there had been only one shot fired, they later took at face value Kurras's version of two shots.[58] As a result he was not charged with murder, or manslaughter, but with causing death through negligence. While it is possible that these mistakes were made through police favouritism toward one of their own, human error or just plain incompetence, they undoubtedly added to the atmosphere of conspiracy surrounding the case.

This was further compounded by the fact that Kurras was acquitted in November 1967 even though the judge at his trial accused him of lying under oath. It was established that Kurras had fired the shot, that Kurras had not been at risk and that firing the shot had been an illegal act. Nonetheless, the judge felt he could not find Kurras guilty because of the possibility that his judgement had been impaired by psychological trauma. It was also not possible to decide which part of Kurras's testimony was true, and again, according to the judge this may have been due to psychological trauma. The judge therefore felt he had to acquit Kurras of the charges, even though he was unhappy to do so.[59] The press, even Springer titles, reacted with disbelief: *Bild-Zeitung* declared Kurras guilty and asked 'can the freeing of the man who fired the fatal shot be satisfactory?'[60] The FU Berlin AStA called it 'support for police terrorism and a direct threat to democratic opposition. This verdict is in fact a free invitation for the police to go ahead with further brutality against demonstrators.'[61] An important footnote, however, is that Kurras was later convicted by the same judge in a second trial in 1970, and was sentenced to 2½ years in prison. During this trial a recording of the shooting, made by a radio journalist, was used to show that only one shot was fired.

There is no evidence that Ohnesorg's death was the start of a police-or state-sponsored campaign to shoot demonstrators. The fact that so many police officers gave evidence that directly contradicted Kurras's testimony adds to the picture of Kurras as a rogue officer who was working alone. Above all, if there was an attempted cover-up it was incompetent to say the least: Kurras was eventually convicted and his reputation was in tatters

58. See *Vermerk: Ermittlungsverfahren wegen Tötung des Studenten Ohnesorg, Berlin, den 8. Juni 1967*, file 127, Aktenbestand des Sozialistischen Anwaltskollektivs, HIfS.

59. See 'Polizist Kurras freigesprochen', *Süddeutsche Zeitung*, 22 November 1967, p. 2 and Zylka, H., 'Freispruch', *Bild-Zeitung*, 23 November 1967, p. 2.

60. Zylka, H., 'Freispruch', *Bild-Zeitung*, 23 November 1967, p. 2.

61. *Information für die Studentenschaft der Freien Universität Berlin*, Berlin file 00121, BfZS.

after lying at his trial in 1967. There can be no doubt, however, that a great deal was done to make Kurras's life easier, both before and after his conviction. It is significant that Kurras was released as early as March 1971 after just four months in prison, and that in the summer of 1971 he was found drunk in a Berlin park with an illegal service pistol in his briefcase. Despite this, in 1975 he was allowed back into the police service as a member of uniformed search units, although he was never again allowed to carry a firearm. He retired in 1987 as a Detective Inspector (*Kriminal-oberkommissar*).

These events all added to feelings of outrage among protesters and fears that there was an establishment conspiracy to protect Kurras, that the police and legal system were colluding to pervert the course of justice to protect one of their own, and even that this was the first death in a secret campaign to eliminate protesters. On the day after the shooting a mass meeting was held in the SDS headquarters in Berlin. Gudrun Ensslin was in tears, saying 'this is the generation of Auschwitz. At that time they attacked the Jews, now they are trying to destroy us. We must protect ourselves. We must arm ourselves.'[62] On 11 June Ensslin took part in a small protest against Albertz on the Kurfürstendamm. It was the first time she had taken part in a demonstration, and it was a direct response to Ohnesorg's death. She was later a core member of the Red Army Faction (RAF) terrorist group, one of whose units was the *Kommando 2. Juni*. The *Bewegung 2. Juni* (2 June Movement) terrorist organization was also named after the date of the Ohnesorg shooting, and one member, Bommi Baumann, has said he became involved in the terrorism 'because 2 June 1967 came along'. Another *Bewegung 2. Juni* member, Anne Reiche, has said that she felt 'they are shooting at us now. They are shooting at us all.'[63] For many people this would have been an overreaction, and most of those who took part in demonstrations against the shooting seem to have been expressing concern at the future of West German democracy, rather than interpreting the shooting as the death knell of that democracy. Nonetheless, the shooting, and the reaction of both sides, increased the sense of alienation and distrust between protesters and the state to a new and unprecedented level. Baumann says the name *Bewegung 2. Juni* was chosen 'so that everything was clear: the state shot first'. For a small minority, then, the Ohnesorg shooting permanently undermined the legitimacy and democratic credentials of the Federal Republic and provided the justification for an escalation of violence that resulted in a full-blown terrorist campaign in the 1970s.

---

62. Quoted in Becker, J., *Hitler's Children*, p. 41.
63. 'Die Schießen auf uns alle', *Der Spiegel*, 23 June 1997, Nr. 26, p. 106.

Part III
1967–1969

–7–

University Reform

The period after 2 June was marked by a hardening of lines, ever more melodramatic rhetoric, and a more frequent resort to violence by both sides. The issue of university reform helped to fuel these developments, with many of the students who had been shocked by Ohnesorg's death demonstrating a greater willingness to support protests to win democratic rights within universities. Although the FU Berlin remained the focus for the most radical activities, universities around West Germany experienced a wave of outrage from students that prompted incursions on university autonomy by incensed *Land* governments. University authorities consistently equated the politicization of institutions proposed by the SDS with the experience of Nazi rule, and determined to prevent a repetition of past mistakes while maintaining the existing model of higher education in essence. Having been outmanoeuvred in the period before 2 June, universities sought to seize the initiative. Student accusations of exclusive government were blunted through limited reform that mollified moderates and limited direct intervention by *Länder* to new draconian disciplinary measures that made it easier for universities to target activists. In parallel with a governmental rethink on higher education, the reform of the relationship between universities and students, academics, *Land* governments, and society in general left activists isolated. By 1969 the far left was struggling to maintain the momentum of its campaign, its use of ever more extreme measures was alienating moderate students, sectarian rivalries were tearing it apart, and its supporters were becoming increasingly frustrated. From the euphoric high points that followed 2 June, the far-left campaign had all but disintegrated just two years later.

Protests dramatically increased in scale and frequency after 2 June and only one student in nine believed at the end of June 1967 that university reform would threaten academic freedom.[1] Reform of university study was deemed 'absolutely necessary' by 64 per cent of students. The Left

---

1. 'Was denken die Studenten?', *Der Spiegel*, 19 June 1967, pp. 29–33.

remained a small minority (around 3 per cent), the majority of students supported the main political parties (around two-thirds were SPD supporters), and many continued to hold conservative views: it was even found that 44 per cent agreed there had been positive aspects of Nazism. The trend toward greater radicalism is nonetheless confirmed by a survey of students in February 1968 in which 74 per cent of students said demonstrations by young people were a good thing, and 67 per cent said they were prepared to take part.[2] According to another survey by *Der Spiegel*, 92 per cent of students were prepared to attend demonstrations and 71 per cent would support strikes at universities. If students were undoubtedly more amenable to participation in protest, the majority remained interested in non-violent activities that sought reform rather than revolution. Only 24 per cent were willing to get involved in violence toward the police, 25 per cent would use violence to resist police violence, and only 5 per cent would turn cars over or break windows.[3] The niceties of these distinctions were often lost on academics for whom challenges to their privileges were the work of revolutionary minorities who needed to be rooted out.

As with student opinion, academic attitudes to reform were varied. Many, but by no means all, junior members of staff seem to have supported reform along with some senior academics. Some senior academics remained implacable in their opposition: sociologist Eduard Baumgarten told *Der Spiegel* that academics should defend their monopoly of power 'with every resource under the sun: religion, morals, legends, fiction'. Others warned of 'anarchy and chaos' and one Göttingen University staff member even stated 'a university cannot be democratic'. *Der Spiegel*'s survey of 41 Göttingen professors found only 17 who agreed with the need for reform and 19 who would not hear of the use of the term 'crisis', preferring 'unrest' instead and blaming unruly students for recent disturbances. Around half of professors described student demands for inclusion in government as 'abstruse', 'too radical' or 'not realizable'. The idea of 'one-third parity', put forward by the Hamburg AStA in July 1967, and referring to equal government between professors, junior staff and students, was opposed by almost all professors. Perhaps political scientist Professor Peter von Oertzen presented an accurate picture when he suggested that a small percentage of professors agreed with student demands for representation in principle, with a slightly larger liberal minority who genuinely wanted some reform. In contrast, according to von Oertzen,

2. 'Zwei drittel zum Protest bereit', *Der Spiegel*, 19 February 1968, p. 40.
3. 'Bereit, auf die Strasse zu gehen', *Der Spiegel*, 12 February 1968, p. 31.

there was a large 'middle group' who would only consider reform in order to regain peace in universities once again.[4]

Pragmatism and expediency combined with a desire to preserve the existing system certainly informed the attitudes of the *Westdeutsche Rektorenkonferenz* (WRK). In January 1968 the WRK made its stance on university reform clear in a declaration by the representatives of 25 universities. The document was a clear attempt to limit incursions upon the privileges of academics by both students and *Land* authorities. Although it described universities as 'a community of teachers and students' and acknowledged the need for reform in courses, admissions, and governmental structures, it gave no details of what this should entail. It reasserted the necessity to preserve freedom of research and teaching while accepting that universities had an undefined social role to play, and attempted to fend off state interference by insisting that the 'critical function of academia in society requires the autonomy of universities'.[5] The document tried to please everyone in an effort to resolve the crisis while conceding as little ground as possible. It was a major change in outlook, but it was not sufficient to please its target audiences, for many of whom it went either too far or not far enough. More was to come, though, and the WRK declaration was only the start of a concerted effort by universities to regain the initiative from the Left.

In an interview with *Der Spiegel* shortly after this declaration Walter Rüegg, *Rektor* of Frankfurt University and head of the WRK, presented a model for reform that centred on the need to prevent the politicization of universities. For Rüegg the reform hinted at in the declaration was 'not a capitulation before hooligans' but was a proposal for unified 'reform of the internal structure of universities' in general. He condemned the 'systematic provocation' tactics used by the SDS and defended the right of students of all political persuasions to take part in critical debate. On the political role of professors he reaffirmed the view that they had a duty to take part in politics as citizens but felt that in lectures 'we as professors have no right to take any position on current affairs. We have our very particular lectureships and we have to fulfil them'. Indeed, he described the 'discussion of personal political opinions' as a 'misuse of professorial authority'. He dismissed accusations that academics were *Fachidioten*

4. 'Gesellschaft: Professoren', *Der Spiegel*, 19 February 1968, p. 46.
5. 'Godesberger Rektoren Erklärung zur Hochschulreform vom 6. Januar 1968', reprinted in Lönnendonker, S., Fichter, T. and Staadt, J., *Dokumentation FU Berlin*, Teil V, pp. 269-271, Archiv "APO und soziale Bewegungen", Fachbereich Politische Wissenschaft der Freien Universität Berlin (ehem. ZI 6) (henceforth APOusB). This unpublished multi-volume work, produced in 1983, reprints documents from the archive.

with the retort 'was Max Plank a *Fachidiot*?' and warned that a 'risky politicization of universities' would put academic freedom at the mercy of party politics. He even warned that the SDS wanted academic staff to attend hearings before their appointment to assess their political suitability, and described this as the same as in 'the time of National Socialism'.[6] Ultimately, through limited reform and ruthless disciplinary measures, academic staff undertook a successful rearguard action against the reduction of their privileges and power, and universities remained autonomous non-political institutions.

Of course, the SDS was unlikely to remain passive, and what followed was a bitter and sometimes violent struggle. On 9 June 1967 Jürgen Habermas, the Frankfurt School academic whose work had informed the SDS's view of capitalism, addressed the 'Universities and Democracy Congress' in Hanover. He famously accused the anti-authoritarians within the SDS of 'left fascism' and said

> in so far as you mean by 'provocation' the practice of demonstrational force, it is entirely legitimate. Demonstrational force is that with which we force attention to arguments and so establish conditions for a discussion where it is needed. But if I am to understand provocation in the sense of provoking violence hidden in the institutions into declared and manifest violence, then systematically undertaken provocation by students is a game with terror, with fascistic implications.[7]

Naturally, the SDS wholeheartedly rejected this interpretation. Even though Bernd Rabehl has since admitted that 'he had hit upon something that was correct', for Rabehl this meant 'our lack of political analysis'.[8] This misunderstands Habermas's point by resorting to the stock solution of the Left in the 1960s: 'we need better theory'. In Habermas's interpretation, the SDS' tactics were an end in themselves which could only lead to further escalation, with no understanding of the mechanisms by which this would bring a revolution about. At no point did the SDS propose anything other than vague ideas about *Rätedemokratie* as their ultimate goal. Although this undoubtedly betrayed a 'lack of political analysis', Habermas went further by suggesting that the means could not be at odds with the ends. The evidence of SDS tactics so far indicated that it was unable to countenance alternatives to its own view, in conformity with

6. 'War Max Plank ein Fachidiot?', *Der Spiegel*, 12 February 1968, pp. 36–42.

7. Quoted in Becker, J., *Hitler's Children*, p. 43. Becker is uncompromisingly opposed to the protests of the late 1960s and provides a good example of overly judgmental and ill-informed history.

8. Quoted in Fraser, *1968*, p. 146.

Leninist theory that there can only be one true revolutionary party. Its manipulative behaviour within the KfA, in numerous AStAs, and in mass assemblies, along with its adoption of Marcuse's theory that liberalism was merely counter-revolutionary 'repressive tolerance', suggested that the attitudes which informed the means would inform SDS behaviour when *Rätedemokratie* was achieved. Instead of encouraging a democratic multiplicity of views, *Rätedemokratie* would instead represent a rubber stamp lending the legitimizing veneer of popular approval to decisions made by SDS members among themselves. For Habermas, then, neither the methods nor the goal being aimed at could be described as democratic.[9] In a strikingly accurate prediction, the 50 signatories of a declaration by left-liberal FU Berlin staff supporting reform warned of 'a hardening of extreme positions, that isolate both sides and finally must lead to the use of force'.[10]

By this stage, universities across West Germany were experiencing student unrest. Students had engaged in protests at various institutions before the Ohnesorg shooting, but after 2 June the trickle became a flood. Hardly a day went by without some form of protest at a university somewhere in the country. Taking some examples at random gives some idea of the scope of this activity: on 20 November 1967, the SDS disrupted a lecture by Professor Carlo Schmidt at Frankfurt University. The *Rektor*, Heinrich Rüegg, describing the action as 'fascist terrorist methods', brought charges of breach of the peace against the leaders, and suspended the Frankfurt SDS from its membership of the student body.[11] The following month students at Technischen Hochschule Bochum held a Go-in against the appointment of a Dr Kesting as Professor of Sociology.[12] In April 1968, 1,500 students at the same institution attended a mass-protest meeting that attacked the *Rektor*'s failure to condemn the shooting of Rudi Dutschke. This took place as part of wider protests by Ruhr Universität Bochum students in reaction to the shooting, including barricading the entrance to the Springer building in Essen.[13] In December 1968, 1,000

9. Habermas later expanded upon his ideas in Habermas, J., 'Scheinrevolution unter handlungszwang', *Der Spiegel*, 10 June 1968, pp. 57–9, and in Habermas, J., *Toward a Rational Society*.

10. *Zwölf-Punkte-Erklärung von Professoren der Freien Universität*, Berlin file 00114, BfZS.

11. 'Professoren: Rektoren', *Der Spiegel*, 26 February 1968, pp. 30–1.

12. Described in 'Go-in', *Spots*, January 1968, p. 2, AFAS. *Spots* was the student journal at the Rheinisch-Westfalischen Technischen Hochschule Aachen, from which Kesting came.

13. 'Fast 1500 Studenten waren dabei!', *BSZ: Bochumer Studenten Zeitung*, 2 May 1968, p. 1.

Bochum students invaded a sitting of the academic Senate and held a teach-in on university democratization.[14] Later the same month police were used to remove around 300 students from a sit-in at Bochum University.[15] At the Technischen Hochschule Aachen on 18 October 1968, SDS students disrupted the *Rektor*'s speech during the opening ceremony for the new academic year and police were used to remove them forcibly from the building. Although junior staff attacked this as 'falling back on the methods of an authoritarian police state' the *Rektor* remained unrepentant, and the following month the academic Senate suspended the SDS from participation in student politics.[16]

Examples of events at Hamburg and Munich universities are particularly interesting for combining challenges to traditional forms of deference with concerns over the Nazi past. On 9 November 1967, Hamburg University students disrupted the new *Rektor*'s installation ceremony, demanding a discussion of student problems 'instead of academic ritual'. In a much-publicized incident, SDS members preceded the academic procession with a banner saying 'under the academic gowns, the mildew of 1000 years'. The phrase succinctly encapsulated the student position, but the irreverence of the protest caused outrage in the press and several students were injured during the subsequent heavy-handed police intervention. Bags and coats were searched and some students were even forced off the campus because they were distributing political leaflets.[17] A Professor Bertold Spuler, who had been a Nazi Party and SA member, even told students 'you all belong in concentration camps'.[18] The AStA demanded that the University distance itself from this remark, which was quickly agreed to by a horrified *Rektor*. A few days later, though, *Rektor* Ehrlicher gave a press conference in which he condemned those students who wanted 'to destroy our society', those who had 'an aversion to the Establishment and any other authority', and those who had 'skilfully manipulated' other students.[19] He also announced Spuler's suspension pending disciplinary

14. *BSZ*, 5 December 1968, p. 1. It is difficult to pin down the exact differences in the usage of the term 'go-in' compared to 'sit-in'. 'Go-in' is peculiar to Germany and seems to refer to disruption tactics and the occupation of rooms or buildings on a temporary basis. 'Sit-in' on the other hand appears to be applied to long-term occupations, particularly those that continued overnight.

15. 'Extrablatt: Polizeieinsatz', *BSZ*, 19 December 1968, p. 3.

16. 'Studenten: SDS', *Der Spiegel*, 18 November 1968, pp. 80–2.

17. *Hochschulkonzeption und Wahlprogramm des SDS*, file 46, Sammlung Jürgen Klein, HIfS. SDS called for the banning of political police from the campus.

18. 'Hoschschulen: Hamburg', *Der Spiegel*, 20 November 1967, p. 84.

19. Quoted in 'Zehn Tage . . . chronologisch', *Auditorium*, November 1967, p. 5, ZA 745, HIfS.

measures. Later that month Reinhold Oberlercher (SDS) criticized former SA man Dr Hans Wenke as authoritarian and was banned from the latter's course. Early in December, when Oberlercher insisted on attending anyway, Wenke was forced to leave his lecture, the first time this had happened at a West German university. The challenge to traditional deference was so great that these events, despite seeming relatively minor, were given their own article in *Der Spiegel*.[20] Conflicts of this kind rumbled on over the next year.

The confrontation at Munich University was just as controversial. Along with the Nazi legacy, the relationship between students and the police, already strained before 2 June, was particularly tense in Munich. A police raid on the SDS offices in Schwabing during the demonstrations against the Ohnesorg shooting, as a result of which 50 flyers were confiscated because they were 'not in accordance with legal requirements', only worsened matters.[21] Members of the SDS and the LSD followed this up in the Autumn term by disrupting the new *Rektor*'s installation ceremony, as had recently happened in Hamburg. The Bavarian Minister President Alfons Goppel, who had been state prosecutor for Kaiserslautern from 1934 to 1938, attended the ceremony with Culture Minister Huber. Students in the balcony of the University assembly hall threw confetti and paper streamers, as well as blowing soap bubbles onto the dignitaries below. The speech of the departing *Rektor*, Ludwig Kotter, was interrupted by shouts of 'Huber out! Goppel out! Fascists out!' as well as 'Ohnesorg! Ohnesorg!'.[22]

Later in the month students held a teach-in during which it was suggested that secret service personnel were monitoring protest activity at the University. A Go-in during a lecture by *Rektor* Becker produced no further information on this issue, but in another teach-in the next day, 19 December, students realized they were being observed by a plain-clothes police officer from the political police. On 10 January 1968 six students, including Reinhard Wetter and Heinz Koderer (both SDS), protested against this police deployment on university land by dressing in Munich police uniforms and entering a lecture by Professor Kuhn, formerly a supporter of the Nazi regime. They told him they were there to protect him from 'Left radical elements', but when Kuhn realized they were actually students he ended his lecture and left the hall. The students were ordered by the University authorities to leave University land, but instead they

---

20. 'Studenten: Hamburger Universität', *Der Spiegel*, 18 December 1967, pp. 60–1.

21. 'Polizeiaktion gegen Sozialistischen Studentenbund in München', *Abendzeitung*, 4 June 1967, Sammlung Werner Röder, ED 387/3, IfZM.

22. 'Aufgeblickt, himmlische Heerscharen!', *Der Spiegel*, 4 December 1967, p. 72.

went into Prof. Reinhart Maurach's lectures, where they repeated the performance. Maurach had been an associate of senior Nazi Alfred Rosenberg and had published the anti-Semitic book *Russian Jewish Policy* in 1939. The students then left the University and returned later that day without the uniforms, ignoring demands that they leave University land until eventually they were forcibly removed. The *Rektor* banned them from the University for a month with immediate effect, but Koderer and Wetter regularly flouted this ruling over the following weeks. They were eventually tried and convicted of breach of the peace.[23] As at Hamburg, protests at Munich continued throughout the next year.

It was at the FU Berlin, however, that the most radical and sustained campaign for university reform took place, continuing on from developments before 2 June. The appointment of a new *Rektor* on 15 October 1967, former Nazi party and SA member Professor Ewald Harndt, would have added to tensions by definition, but Harndt was a disciplinarian who used the University statutes and Federal laws to challenge the Left in an increasingly vicious conflict. The *Kritische Universität* (Critical University or KU), proposed by SDS member Wolfgang Nitsch in June 1967, provided the first source of conflict. The founders of the KU, mostly SDS members, saw it as an alternative to existing universities 'in which professorial *Fachidioten* train student *Fachidioten*'; its highly politicized structure and events, run for and by students, conformed entirely to anti-authoritarian SDS ideas on higher education.[24] The FU *Rektor* gave provisional approval to the creation of a KU at the FU on the condition that it provided the university with a written outline of its aims, but this simply reprinted much of the *Fachidioten* flyer handed out on 26 November 1966.[25] Perhaps not surprisingly this was rejected at an academic Senate meeting on 18 September which decided the University could no longer support a KU that was 'not a contribution to university and course reform, but a contribution to the political actions of the extra-parliamentary opposition'. In an outright rejection of the APO influence at the FU, the Senate identified the AStA, which had helped draw up the KU aims, as representing 'political powers from outside the university'.[26] The *FU*

23. See *Rechtshilfe der APO München 1968–1969*, pp. 6–8, ED 713, IfZM.

24. 'Hochschulen: Gegen-Universität', *Der Spiegel*, 24 July 1967, p. 36.

25. 'Reformationszeit: Kritische Universität', *FU Spiegel*, November 1967, p. 5 gives an excellent outline of the course of events at the FU on the KU. It also details the Byzantine constitutional and committee structure of the KU in which the mass assembly was nominally the ruling organ. The KU was actually run by separate working groups and committees.

26. *Beschluß des Akademischen Senats zu Thema 'Kritische Universität'*, Rep 014/1017, LB.

Spiegel saw this as 'the politics of repression' and an 'ultimatum to the AStA' to distance itself from the KU if it wanted to take part in reform discussions. The AStA refused to be cowed: in defiance of the Senate decision a meeting on 24 September established the constitution of the KU and determined that it should meet at the FU and TU Berlin. The FU authorities acquiesced for the moment and the new *Rektor* allowed FU rooms to be used as long as the discussion was limited to university issues, making it possible for the founding assembly of the new KU to take place at the FU on 1 November 1967. The idea was later copied directly at Hamburg University, in the 'Karl Marx University' created at Frankfurt University the following May, at universities in France and Italy (notably Turin), and in the 'Free University' established in London. At the FU the episode added to student frustration at the pace and methods of reform: the *FU Spiegel* expressed concern that 'reform will be replaced by regimentation, critical debate by discipline'.[27]

This frustration expressed itself most clearly in the results of the *Konvent* elections at the start of December. Having fought a negative election campaign based on the appeal not to vote for the Left, a right-wing coalition of independent candidates, 'Aktion 20. Konvent', comprising members of the RCDS, NPD-backed groups and others, gained only two seats.[28] The RCDS itself gained seven but the *Burschenschaften* failed to win a single seat. The election was an undoubted victory for the Left, with the SDS gaining an unprecedented 15 seats. The HSU and SHB won 4 seats apiece and a Left coalition of 'United Working Societies' or *Vereinigte Arbeitsgemeinshaften* won 22 seats, so in a *Konvent* with 76 representatives, many of whom were independent candidates sympathetic to the Left, the election result was a landslide victory for the Left. The SDS interpreted this as a mandate for even more extreme actions which, by alienating much of the student body, played into the hands of university authorities.

The first months of 1968 were marked by almost continuous confrontations between students and the University authorities. This centred particularly on individual faculties where the pace of change had been limited or even non-existent, especially the Philosophy Faculty, where students at the Department of Romance Studies refused to take part in the basic course in January in an attempt to force the pace of reform. The Faculty had opted out of many of the reform measures recommended by the reform commission established after the 1966 sit-in, and had consistently

---

27. 'Reformationszeit: Kritische Universität', *FU Spiegel*, November 1967, p. 5.
28. *HSU-SDS-Wahlkurtorium*, Berlin file 03793, BfZS. This is a flyer by *Aktion 20. Konvent*.

resisted student attempts to criticize courses, let alone take part in their alteration. On 20 January staff resolved that the protest, and the debate it hoped to generate, aimed to 'destroy and fundamentally alter the teaching programme', leading them to cancel the teaching programme for a week starting on 24 January.[29] Romance Studies students held a mass meeting on 26 January in which they demanded the immediate cessation of the staff action, and the opening of courses to 'public opinion and criticism'. They also wanted the creation of a Working Committee to reassess the 'premises and methods and the social function' of the department.[30] Of course, students were hardly in a strong position to dictate to academics on what, when and to whom they should teach. On 31 January a mass meeting of all faculties demanded public discussions on events in Romance Studies, but staff sitting in a simultaneous Faculty meeting in the Deanery simply rejected this and instead proposed a special meeting of the Faculty Committee to look into the issues behind closed doors.

At this point a group of SDS supporters declared their intention to hold a sit-in and attempted to smash doors in the Deanery open to gain access to the Faculty meeting, although they succeeded in breaking down just one door.[31] When students blocked the entrances to doors using passive resistance the SDS occupiers used violence against them. The RCDS attacked the events as 'repressive democracy' and alleged that one of their *Konvent* representatives had been assaulted when he criticized SDS tactics as 'fascist methods'. The RCDS even accused one SDS member of shouting 'Professors into concentration camps!'.[32] The violence was widely condemned, with representatives of the Maths and Natural Sciences Faculty describing it as inconsistent with 'rational discussion and argument' and saying it had put reform at risk.[33] For the *Rektor* the events provoked memories of 'the worst times in Germany' because 'in this way SA men gained entry to the houses of Jews, and by the same methods and ways communist groups stormed the Berlin Rathaus in 1948'.[34]

The Berlin City authorities then exacerbated tensions. On 6 February, after intervention by Mayor Schütz, the *Rektor* of the TU told the KU that

29. *Zur Dokumentation*, and *Romanischen Seminar: Hilflose Dozenten ohne Argumente*, both Berlin file 03795, BfZS.

30. *Romanistik Studium*, Berlin file 03795, BfZS. This AStA flyer includes the resolution of the mass meeting on 26 January.

31. 'Studenten: Berlin', *Der Spiegel*, 5 February 1968, p. 56.

32. Grasser, U., *Repressive Demokratie*, Berlin file 03795, BfZS. Grasser was the RCDS leader at the FU Berlin.

33. *Zur Information*, Berlin file 03796, BfZS.

34. 'Rektor der Freien Universität verurteilt "brutalen Terror"', *Tagesspiegel*, 2 February 1968, p. 2. It is worth remembering that Harndt was himself a former member of the SA.

he would no longer allow it to hold its meetings in TU rooms. During the first session of the KU Springer Tribunal at the TU on 1 February Holger Meins, a future leader of the RAF, had shown a film on how to make Molotov cocktails, and the same evening the windows of the *Berliner Morgenpost* offices in Berlin had been smashed.[35] The KU argued that 'stones against American Embassies and *Morgenpost* offices are not violent in comparison with carpet bombing in Vietnam; films on Molotov cocktails are a parody of violence in comparison with the permanent muzzling of the masses'.[36] The ban remained, however, and thereafter the FU played reluctant host to the KU, while on 14 February the Berlin Interior Ministry discussed the possibility of banning SDS.

In response, on 20 February SDS members refused to answer questions put to them by the Berlin City Governments' Committee of Investigation into the disturbances at the FU. Three SDS members were each fined 200 DM by the Committee for refusing to answer questions. Rudi Dutschke then took the stand and like his comrades he also refused to cooperate. In common with the other SDS witnesses Dutschke attempted to turn the sitting into a political debate and protest. At one point the hall had to be emptied because SDS supporters were making such a disturbance. He called one committee member a 'fascist' and told the Chairman, Gerd Löffler, an SPD member with an anti-Nazi background, 'your liberalism disappeared a long time ago under the authoritarian state apparatus of fascism'. He was fined 400 DM, and two further SDS witnesses who refused to cooperate were also fined.[37] There were of course two sides to this situation: the SDS had legitimate objections to the attempted ban, but at the same time the Committee unwittingly gave them the opportunity to engage in their tried and tested provocation tactics. In response to the City government's activities the various AStAs of the universities and colleges in Berlin protested that the APO had been 'denounced as terrorists' when in fact it was the City authorities who were using tactics of 'systematic escalation that produce terror'.[38]

---

35. *Springer schlägt zurück!*, Berlin file 00131, BfZS. This document by the FU AStA and TU student representatives gives useful details on these events. Also see 'TU-Rektor: Keine Räume für das "Springer Hearing"', *Der Tagesspiegel*, 6 February 1968, Zeitungen 1968, Aktenbestand des Sozialistischen Anwaltskollektivs, HIfS.

36. *Resolution zur Vollversammlung der KU eingebracht von Initiativausschuß*, Berlin file 03796, BfZS.

37. Evidence of Rudi Dutschke, *1. Untersuchungsausschuß (V. Wahlperiode), 67 (Öffentliche) Sitzung, Dienstag, den 20. Februar 1968*, Rep 014/842, LB, pp. 16–20. Also reproduced in Dutschke, R., *Mein Lange Marsch*, pp. 111–15.

38. *Nicht unsere Demonstration*, Berlin file 03796, BfZS.

The confrontation at the FU Berlin continued to expand to departments beyond the Romance Studies throughout Spring and Summer 1968. On 22 April, Journalism students launched a lecture strike in favour of course reform and representation. This was followed by a lecture strike at the East Asian Seminar that started on 15 May and lasted for several weeks. On 22 May, simultaneously with the third reading of the new Emergency Laws in the *Bundestag*, students held a lecture strike throughout the University in response to the refusal of some staff to cancel their lectures. At the Otto-Suhr Institute a staff–student debate on the Emergency Laws came to blows in which RCDS leader Ulrich Grasser and CDU Berlin representative Jürgen Wohlrabe were attacked. From 27 to 31 May students followed an SDS recommendation, passed at a series of Faculty mass meetings, to occupy the FU buildings in protest at the Emergency Laws. The damage to furniture, buildings and books resulting from this occupation was estimated at 30,000 DM and, although undoubtedly provocative, it hardly proved Habermas or opponents of the protests wrong.[39] Mass meetings and minor acts of disruption continued over the next month with particular emphasis on the Otto-Suhr Institute. A mass meeting of students and staff at the Institute on 13 June heard student proposals for reform that repeated the demand for 'one-third parity' in government, the decentralization of institutes and departments allowing for open discussion of teaching and research, public meetings of Institute committees, and government through referenda in each department. The academic Senate rejected these proposals as unworkable, with Faculty Dean Horst Sanmann declaring 'the existence of the University, the existence of teaching and research, are at stake. We are standing at a turning point.'[40]

These events may have created outrage but it is striking that the students were so singularly unsuccessful. Protests either were simply ignored, were dealt with by the police, or became bogged down in the intractable committee structure of the University. At the East Asian Seminar for instance, students faced resolute staff opposition to the reform of courses, especially by the Head of Department, former Nazi Hans Eckardt. Their frustration boiled over on 25 June when 17 students occupied the East Asian Seminar building, demanding Eckardt's resignation.[41] In the early hours of 27 June 1968 the *Rektor* deployed 100 police to remove the students by force in order 'to allow the proper organs of the Free University

---

39. *2. (abschließende) Beschlußempfehlung des 1. Untersuchungsausschusses – V. Wahlperiode – vom 3. Juli 1968*, pp. 7–8, Rep 014/845, LB, gives details of all these events.

40. 'Studenten: Freie Universität', *Der Spiegel*, 8 July 1968, p. 47.

41. *Das ist die Antwort des Rektorats: Polizei*, Berlin file 03802, BfZS.

to resolve the problems that need to be dealt with'.[42] In parallel with another mass meeting of all faculties a group of 100 students occupied the Rectorate in an attempt to force the *Rektor* to explain his actions. Having failed to find him, the students entered into a debate on reform with journalists, professors, and members of the Berlin city government who were present.[43] Once again the police were used to remove the students from the building. The AStA called a mass meeting of all faculties on 28 June in which its representatives argued that further discussions with the *Rektor* on reform were now pointless because 'in order to protect the *Rektor* from discussion, the police had to clear the Rectorate of students who were willing to hold discussions'.[44] When the academic Senate threw out reform proposals for the Otto-Suhr Institute for a second time, on 10 July students occupied the Rectorate again, demanding 'the resignation of the reactionary *Rektor* Harndt, the dissolution of the academic Senate, and the democratization of all Institutes of the Free University'.[45] This time they threw documents out of the windows and declared Fritz Teufel the new *Rektor* of a 'Socialist University', complete with robes and a certificate of office. Teufel's comedic installation as *Rektor* was another step in the ongoing attack on the mystique of professorial authority, but by this time the shock effect of such provocation was wearing off. Once more the *Rektor* deployed police, this time using 600 officers against barricades of tables and cupboards. The police used axes and crowbars against the barriers, and the students tried unsuccessfully to defend themselves using fire-extinguisher foam and water.

At the start of the next term SDS members at the FU took stock of their situation. In an interesting document from October 1968 they lamented that the AStA only became involved in protest after a confrontation had already developed.[46] At no point was university reform mentioned or even implied, but rather vague plans were suggested for widening the 'uni revolt'. The documents makes it clear once again that the campaign within universities was, for the SDS, only a part of a much wider programme of revolutionary activity: the 'strategic purpose for the Winter Semester' included 'the integration of the KU in the University, universal struggle

42. Flyer *Der Rektor der Freien Universität Berlin hat heute folgende Erklärung der Öffentlichkeit übergeben*, Berlin file 03802, BfZS. The flyer and the announcement by the *Rektor* date from 27 June.

43. *Rektoratsbesetzung*, Berlin file 03802, BfZS.

44. *Antrag an die Vollversammlung aller Fakultäten am 28.6.68*, Berlin file 03802, BfZS.

45. 'Berlin: Studenten', *Der Spiegel* 15 July 1968, pp. 29–30.

46. *Strategische SDS-Gruppe an der FU*, Berlin file 00135, BfZS.

against the University authorities, centrally and from Institute to Institute' and also the agitation and education of schoolchildren and young workers. This latter was a typical attempt by a 1960s far-left organization to link the student revolt with the labour movement, in line with classic Leninist thinking that only the working class can be the true agent of revolutionary struggle. Such attempts were made in almost all Western countries that experienced student revolts, and they almost always failed. The document as a whole gives the impression of a campaign that had lost its way, and the assertion that they 'must consider the value of illegal actions' speaks of the SDS's growing frustration.

By this stage the University authorities were going on the offensive. During the Summer vacation the FU authorities removed the subscription to the AStA that all students had previously been required to pay, leading to a financial crisis for the AStA that emasculated it as a political body, and neutralized the impact of the SDS take-over. Amid regular disruption of lectures by the far left, the *Rektor* removed leading SDS member and FU student Bernd Rabehl from his post as a research assistant because, in May 1968, he had opposed 'free democracy' by calling for 'permanent revolution' at the FU Berlin.[47] Staff and students went on strike on 29 October in reaction to the *Rektor*'s actions and the next day several hundred students held a Go-in that disrupted the sitting of the academic Senate. They demanded a discussion of the Rabehl case, as well as the publication of a blacklist they suspected had been drawn up by the FU authorities.[48] They succeeded in gaining neither, and although junior staff attacked the decision to sack Rabehl as an 'administrative intervention in the self-government of academic work and the subject competence of the Institute', they were unsuccessful in reversing the decision.[49]

In the New Year the University authorities continued their successful offensive against the Left. At the Film and Television Academy, 18 students were expelled and disciplinary charges with the threat of expulsion were brought against 14 others from a variety of faculties, including the Otto-Suhr Institute and the Philosophy Faculty, for various protest activities. On 10 January 1969 the *Konvent* announced plans for another referendum, to be carried out from 15 to 17 January, on whether students

47. Statement by *Rektor* Harndt quoted in the flyer *Studienreform und Karies*, Berlin file 03804, BfZS. The reference to 'karies' or tooth decay was aimed at Harndt, who was a dental surgeon.
48. *Vollversammlung aller Fakultäten Heute, 31.10, 12.00, audimax, Harndt zieht Zahne*, Berlin file 03804, BfZS.
49. *Resolution*, Berlin file 03804, BfZS. This resolution was passed on 1 November 1968 by the non-professorial teaching staff of the *Germanischen Seminar*.

wanted to reverse a *Konvent* resolution that 'the *Konvent* rejects the politically disciplinary student house rules'.[50] The referendum was accompanied by a wave of strikes, mass meetings and Go-ins across the FU, including the construction of barricades. The referendum, which was narrowly won by the *Konvent*, exposed deep divisions within the student body: in the Maths and Natural Science Faculty the resolution was defeated by just one vote, 506 to 505.[51] Nevertheless, having been given what they felt was a mandate to oppose the *Rektor*, the Left attempted to expand support for the strikes through votes in each faculty. The University maintained its implacable stance, and on 20 January two of the 14 students facing charges were expelled from the University, while a third was given a 'sharp reprimand with a threat of expulsion'.[52] Two days later, after students in Romance Studies had smashed down Professor Baader's door to force him to discuss the situation, the police were called and students were dragged forcibly from the building.[53] The University simply sat out the worst of the disturbances and resolutely pressed on with the disciplinary proceedings. Having played their only card and failed to change University policy, students had nothing left with which to oppose the *Rektor* and the strikes petered out.

It is clear that the Left enjoyed substantial but by no means overwhelming support. Ohnesorg's death had made many more students receptive to the arguments in favour of reform, more distrustful of authorities and more willing to take part in protests. It has been shown, though, that most were moderates, and many, including large numbers of students who supported reform, were appalled by the activities of the Left. On 27 January, 160 staff members and students of the Maths and Natural Science Faculty signed a declaration attacking the tactics of both the Left and the university authorities. For these people 'democratization of the University through undemocratic methods is impossible', although it was also 'undemocratic to use house rules as political disciplinary measures'. The signatories rejected the SDS's methods, saying that 'in the long run provocation cannot replace constructive criticism', while the SDS actions on 31 January 1968 in which other students were attacked was seen as going against the wishes of the majority.[54] Moderate reformism does indeed seem to have been the aim of the majority and, as the actions of the Left became more

50. *Nachrichten aus dem Konvent*, Berlin file 03807, BfZS.

51. *Urabstimmung Math-Nat: Senatspolitik gescheitert!*, Berlin file 03808, BfZS.

52. *Was soll noch geschehen?*, Berlin file 03808, BfZS.

53. *Information zu den Vorfällen am Romanischen Seminar*, Berlin file 03808, BfZS.

54. *Erklärung von Dozenten, Assistenten und Studenten der Math.-Nat. Fakultät*, dated 27 January 1968, Berlin file 03894, BfZS.

extreme, so the far left became more isolated from the main body of students.

In March 1969 the Federal Culture Minister announced plans for the unification of university government into a single code common to all universities. A new stage in the protest campaign at the FU Berlin therefore began with proposals for a new *Hochschulgesetz* (University Law), to be introduced in the Summer of 1969. This beefed up the disciplinary powers of the university authorities, including the right to censor student political flyers and documents, allowed for more student representation, and restructured the university government, including the liquidation of the *Konvent* and AStA, to be replaced by a *Präkonzil* and a *Konzil* in which students attained one-third parity with senior and junior academics. The title of the *Rektor* was altered to that of *Präsident*. Those opposed to the changes accurately interpreted the loss of the 'political mandate of the *Konvent* and AStA' as a ploy with which to bypass the Left and impose reform from above.[55] Students at the Economics and Social Science Faculty felt the University Law put the reforms they had fought hard to achieve at risk and in a mass meeting on 18 June they voted 210 to 180 to start a lecture strike in protest. The next day police occupied their building and a confrontation with protesting students descended into violence in which stones were thrown and windows were broken. Students eventually occupied the building on 20 June and constructed barricades, although they left the same evening after further clashes with police. Although the strikes continued, and on 2 July the Faculty announced that a referendum of students had voted by 1009 to 724 to reject the new Law, such efforts were in vain, and the new structures were introduced on 10 July 1969.

This was far from the end of the struggle, however. By this stage the Left was fragmenting into tiny factions, both at the FU Berlin and throughout Germany, as the SDS lost its way and finally disappeared in 1970. These groups not only hung on to the dream of a politicized university, but spent as much time attacking each other as concentrating on the themes of their campaigns. In June the *Rote Zelle Germanistik* (German Studies Red Cell) was created at the FU, the first such 'red cell' to be formed. It was quickly followed by an alphabet-soup of *Rote Zellen* from other departments and faculties as well as newly formed Leninist and Maoist organizations. In his exhaustive study of the post-1968 Left in Germany, Gerd Langguth quotes a 1971 report by Interior Minister Hans-Dietrich Genscher which stated that there were at that time around 250 Left radical (Maoist, Trotskyist, anarchist, etc.) groups in Germany, including West

55. See flyer *Teach-in*, Berlin file 03810, BfZS.

Berlin, with around 84,300 members. There were a further 130 'orthodox' communist groups with 81,000 members.[56] Many of these were tiny and short-lived factions of only twenty or so members, often the remnants of an earlier organization that had then split.

It was these groups that took on the challenge of continuing the battle for university reform that, for many students, had already been won or lost. Autumn 1969 was dominated by attempts to discredit the reforms as the work of former Nazis. Further expulsions prompted strikes, and student representatives at the Economics and Social Sciences and Philosophy Faculties at the FU described the University tactics as an 'attempt by the Nazi faction' and 'reactionary professors' to kill off student radicalism and then to hand the expelled students over to the police to face further charges.[57] A few days later various *Rote Zellen* called the new *Konzil* 'rogues', describing its first sitting as 'an assembly of comedians' because State Prosecutor Blaesing, a former Nazi, was pressing on with even more expulsions.[58] Vocal opposition, accompanied by irregular outbreaks of protest activity, rumbled on, and in Autumn 1970 far-left students attempted to impose a political university by default by setting up their own politically motivated courses. In November 1970 students in German Studies announced plans for a 'Socialist Course by the *Rote Zelle Germanistik*'. The University opposed this vehemently: the new *Präsident*, Rolf Kreibich requested the course's withdrawal because it was 'directed at the destruction of the organizational constitution' of the University and was not consistent with critical analysis allowing for all political viewpoints.[59] In January 1971 the *Präsident* banned the course saying it would have created a 'party University'.[60] Such desperate attempts by the Left to retain the momentum of a protest movement that was almost dead could not hide the fact that they had been almost completely outmanoeuvred by university authorities.

This is not to say that protest activity at universities suddenly ceased. As in many other countries, sporadic protests took place on campuses throughout the following decade: in May 1976 several hundred police

56. Langguth, G., *Die Protestbewegung in der Bundesrepublik Deutschland, 1968–1976*, p. 50.

57. *Relegationsflugblatt Nr. 1*, Berlin file 00139, BfZS. This flyer is dated 1 November 1969.

58. *Setzt den Spitzbuben die Spitzenhüte auf!*, Berlin file 03812, BfZS. The flyer is dated 10 November 1969.

59. Letter from *Präsident* Rolf Kreibich to the *Fachbereichsrat Germanistik*, 18 November 1970, Berlin file 00149, BfZS.

60. Letter from *Präsident* Kreibich to all members of the FU, 20 January 1970, Berlin file 00149, BfZS.

were used to break up a mass assembly of left-wing students at Munich University.[61] The following year, amid renewed political activity by students, *Der Spiegel* was able to ask 'will there be a new APO?', although so much had been done to reform higher education that it's answer was an emphatic 'no'. By that stage there were more than half a million university and college lecturers, an increase of 200,000 since 1967, and 300,000 students were attending universities alone, representing 13 per cent of school leavers, compared to just seven per cent in 1967.[62] The proportion of students from working-class families attending universities increased from seven to 13 per cent over the same time period. This was far short of the proportions achieved elsewhere (nearly a third of all students in Britain, for instance), but it did highlight a willingness to address the problems of limited access. In September 1969 the Federal government had passed laws allowing for the creation of a central planning committee to oversee university expansion, including the construction of new universities, and in February of the following year it announced the results of a four-year investigation into the needs of the higher education sector. This resulted in a ten-year plan for the expansion of student num- bers and resources that involved the allocation of 100 billion DM by *Länder* and central governments. Throughout the 1970s the Federal Government set about imposing a standard system of higher education for the country as a whole, culminating in the *Hochschulrahmengesetz* (Framework Law for Higher Education) of 1976. This gave new regulation to the comprehensive universities that had grown since the 1960s, and committed the whole sector to a national comprehensive system. Although the *Hochschulrahmengesetz* confirmed many of the essentials of the exist- ing system, and even returned governmental power to professors in those universities where 'one-third parity' had been achieved, in many ways it imposed reforms that had been delayed since the late 1940s. Most notably, by creating a unified system of higher education, it confirmed that univers- ities had a social educational function that had to be recognized in the comprehensive and interdisciplinary nature of courses and research.[63]

Above all, universities had defended themselves against a concerted attempt at their politicization by the Left. Students had forced a debate on the role of universities in which academics had had no choice but to reassess the Nazi past and conclude that reform was essential if academic

61. 'Zeimlich üppig', *Der Spiegel*, 31 May 1976, p. 123.

62. 'Revolte von Stadtindianern und Spontis', *Der Spiegel*, 20 June 1977, pp. 62–5.

63. Pritchard, *The End of Elitism?*, pp. 97–102 gives an excellent description of these reforms.

freedom of thought and expression was to be retained or attained, even if this meant an academic environment that was more socially engaged. Universities had successfully resisted the demands made by the SDS, and unlike practice during the Nazi period had opposed political encroachment, but at a cost: the one-sided politicization represented by the anti-communism of the 1950s was no longer acceptable or possible and students had forced a re-evaluation of the nature of academic political engagement, though with varying degrees of success. Although reform meant greater inclusion of students in university government, the new disciplinary powers enjoyed by universities, including in some instances the ability to censor student literature, often contradicted the demands of democratic and critical freedom. As in so many areas of life in post-war Germany, university reform entailed a negotiation of the meaning of democracy, and particularly of the need to defend democracy without undermining it.

–8–

The Vietnam Campaign

In his 1968 May Day speech Günter Grass perceptively went straight to the heart of one of the key issues that terrorist groups would later return to again and again. At the evening family meal, he said, parents were confronted with awkward questions from their children: "tell me, when the Americans deploy Napalm as a weapon, that is a war crime isn't it?"[1] As protesters turned their backs on the Federal Republic, and the reactions and violence of both sides became more extreme, opponents of the War slid toward acceptance of the proposition that only by waging a genuine war against Western capitalism could they make a meaningful contribution to the Vietnamese efforts. By the end of the decade the rhetoric of armed struggle against perceived fascism and imperialism which had previously been the stuff of abstract debate was being translated into concrete actions.

Ohnesorg's death had an immediate impact upon the Vietnam campaign. On 3 June the SHB and the SJD held in Berlin a Vietnam demonstration 'against genocide' and supporting 'the right of self-determination' that had been planned some time in advance.[2] The protest turned into a demonstration against both the shooting and Vietnam, presenting them as related acts of violence. The following day 600 SJD members were prevented from building a memorial cross to Ohnesorg on Krumme Strasse and had to content themselves with setting it up outside an FU Berlin student residence, in defiance of the ban on demonstrations.[3] On 16 July the widespread hatred of demonstrators that was commonly expressed in Berlin after the Ohnesorg shooting poured forth during a small Vietnam demonstration at Tempelhof airport. The US Air Force was holding an open day that was attended by around 220,000 people. About 20 women, along with around 15 of their children, held a protest march through the displays

---

1. "'Gewalttätigkeit ist wieder gesellschaftsfähig": Günter Graß zum 1. Mai über Staat, Springer und Studenten', *Der Spiegel*, 6 May 1968, p. 52.
2. *Demonstration gegen Völkermord*, and *Aufruf zur Vietnam-Demonstration*, both Sammlung Schwiedrzik zur Studentenbewegung, ZSg 153/7, BK. The former is an SHB flyer, the latter is by the SJD.
3. 'Ein Kreuz für Ohnesorg', *Der Abend*, 5 June 1967, B166/1315, BK.

carrying placards with messages such as 'bombs, bullets and Napalm are not for small children'. Onlookers objected to both the inclusion of children in the demonstration and the assertion that American tactics were killing Vietnamese children, saying 'that is an abuse of innocent children' and 'you are ruining your children for the communist cause'. Others shouted that 'all students should be locked up', 'go back over to Ulbricht, you belong there', and incredibly 'you have forgotten about the gassing'.[4]

The strength of feeling among protesters finally boiled over on 21 October when around 10,000 people took part in a Vietnam demonstration in Berlin. The demonstration took place in parallel with demonstrations around the world, including those in Washington, Paris, Copenhagen, Ottawa, and Sydney.[5] Flyers produced in advance of the Berlin demonstration by the FU AStA, proclaimed 'solidarity with the NLF' and urged people to join 'the international opposition to the American war of extermination'.[6] This acceptance of the SDS position was repeated in another flyer by the SDS, LSD, SHB, SJD, KfA and various AStAs which presented 'the example of Vietnam' as 'highlighting the political, economic and ideological manipulation of our society'. It continued 'as in all of the large cities of the West, we are demonstrating on 21 October against the USA's War in Vietnam. For us this is not only a moral protest. At the same time we oppose a social order that makes this War possible, aids it, and justifies it.'[7] The demonstration was dominated, therefore, by a larger militant core of support, with greater approval given by a greater number of participants to openly revolutionary aims and tactics, than had been possible prior to Ohnesorg's death.

There can be little doubt that some protesters were determined to provoke the police, or that the police actively sought a confrontation. The demonstration took place along the Kurfürstendamm but this time the police tried to direct it along a route that had been cleared of onlookers. Since the aim of the protest was to make people aware of the issues and convert them to the cause, the police tactics meant that, as one observer in the *FU Spiegel* concluded, 'the Vietnam protest could not remain the

4. See *Vietnam – Demonstration auf dem Tempelhofer Feld*, as well as *Aktenvermerk über die Spaziergangsdemonstration mit Kindern am 16.7.1967 zum Tag der Offenen Tür der US-Luftwaffe auf dem Flughafengelände in Tempelhof*, file Diverses Demonstration I, Aktenbestand des Sozialistischen Anwaltskollektivs, HIfS.

5. *The Times*, 23 October 1967, p. 1.

6. Untitled flyer by the FU Berlin AStA dated 17. October 1967, Sammlung Schwiedrzik zur Studentenbewegung, ZSg/153/17, BK.

7. *Vietnam 6. Information*, Berlin file 00122, BfZS.

only purpose of the demonstration'.[8] A number of marchers demanded that assembled protesters should try to force their way out of the police cordon and follow the route of their choice. When this was attempted the police lashed out indiscriminately at protesters, and the rest of the evening was marked by violent confrontations, the deployment of water cannon, and once again the sight of officers hitting defenceless protesters as they lay on the ground. With a notable change of tone Ulrike Meinhof responded to the violence by saying that the Vietnam War was not about a choice between 'communism and "freedom"', but rather had an 'imperialist character'. For Meinhof 'whoever leads discussions with rubber truncheons, whoever refuses to report differences of opinion, whoever withholds from people details of the character of American management of the War, so that in the eyes of the people, of the Bild-Zeitung readers, demonstrators are idiots, makes a police state out of democracy'. Questioning the use of demonstrations as effective tools, she also acknowledged that the alternatives, such as calling for US military personnel to desert, was 'risky' and that it had the 'smell of illegality'. This was not an expression of disapproval, however, and Meinhof continued that 'it is women and children, harvests and industries, it is people, whose lives are saved through this. Those who have the courage to grasp such methods of oppositional work intend to be effective. It must be considered.'[9]

In raising the issue of illegality Meinhof was entering a debate that was already exercising members of the SDS, and it is worth considering the details of the debate. Rudi Dutschke's pronouncements on the use of violence and illegality were the most widely covered, in horrified tones, by the press, although his statements were by no means consistent. In September 1967, at the annual SDS Conference in Frankfurt, Dutschke made a joint statement with the SDS Frankfurt leader and theorist Hans-Jürgen Krahl in which they proposed 'the propaganda of gunfire in the Third World must be completed by the propaganda of action in the Metropole, which historically makes the urbanization of rural guerrilla tactics possible. The urban guerrilla is the quintessential organizer of irregularity for the destruction of the system of repressive institutions.'[10] Dutschke's wife claims that Dutschke's views had 'nothing to do' with the terrorism of the RAF, and suggests that he had not understood the boundaries of

---

8. 'Fetischismus: Zur Demonstration am 21. Oktober 1967', *FU Spiegel*, November 1967, p. 18. See also 'Russen Raus: Nachwehen der Vietnam-Demonstration', *FU Spiegel*, November 1967, p. 19.

9. Meinhof, U. M., 'Vietnam und Deutschland', *Konkret*, November 1967, pp. 2-3.

10. Quoted in Dutschke, G., *Rudi Dutschke*, p. 151.

such calls to violence. She talks of a desire to support actions that challenged legal tolerance, and says that blockades of Springer offices were what Dutschke had in mind. Yet she also acknowledges that at this time he had links with ETA and the IRA that Bernd Rabehl eventually persuaded him to drop.[11] Dutschke was playing with fire and his statements show him to have been aware of what he was doing. In an interview with *Konkret* in March 1968 Dutschke refused to condemn violence by protesters and insisted that 'the limit of our opposing violence is decided by the violent measures of those in power.'[12] In another interview conducted at around the same time, when asked whether his revolutionary aims meant carrying weapons was necessary, Dutschke replied 'a clear answer: if I was in Latin America, I would fight with weapons. I am not in Latin America, I am in the *Bundesrepublik*. We are fighting so that it is never necessary for us to carry weapons. But that is not up to us. We are not in power'. He went on to say, 'it is certain we will use weapons if German troops fight in Vietnam or Bolivia or elsewhere'.[13] Further insight was provided by a public discussion in which Dutschke took part along with other luminaries of the Left in February 1968. Arguing that violence by the state took place both physically and in the form of manipulation he continued

> I think in late capitalism under our present conditions violence against people is no longer legitimate as revolutionary violence . . . I can imagine in today's circumstances only terrorism against independent inhuman machinery, but no longer against people . . . I would say an assassination, also the murder of a tyrant, is always legitimate. But against Kiesinger, Brandt and other character masks, employing such tactics I take to be mistaken, inhuman and counter-revolutionary.[14]

Dutschke's position was far from clear, and was seemingly subject to considerable change over time. He seems not to have supported individual acts of terrorism against (most) people because they were not effective revolutionary tools in bringing about the collapse of a governmental system. Yet he was clear that attacks on property were appropriate, and above all he accepted implicitly that at the time of any revolution violence would probably be necessary.

11. Ibid., pp. 177–8.
12. "Der SDS läßt sich nicht verbieten", *Konkret*, March 1968, pp. 5–6.
13. Interview with Günter Gaus, quoted in Dutschke, *Mein langer Marsch*, p. 51.
14. 'Heiterkeit in die Revolution bringen', *Der Spiegel*, 4 March 1968, p. 49.

Some members of the SDS probably shared Dutschke's views, but they were certainly not representative of the attitudes of large numbers of people both within the SDS and on the Left in general, whether by going too far or not far enough. In fact, Dutschke's indecision on what form of illegality was legitimate when facing a 'fascist' regime echoed intense debates by the Left. Those who accepted that violence was necessary asked whether provocation of the police and the disruption of events should be the limit of such activity, or whether it should involve the destruction of property, attacks on police or politicians, or even acts of terrorism in which lives were put at risk? Should attacks on property be confined to acts of vandalism such as window-breaking, or should they involve arson or bombings? Should attacks on the police be limited to egg-throwing, stone throwing, hitting them with clubs, or shooting them? To the disgust of the Springer press, *Kommune I* member Ulrich Enzensberger told the investigation into the 2 June events that 'smoke bombs and eggs are permissible methods of demonstration. I have also nothing against equipping the police with such missiles.'[15] Although these discussions were initially confined to abstract theory, they were soon given practical expression: in February 1968, the *Liberale Studentenzeitung*, the LSD journal, published an article in which it gave instructions and illustrations on the construction of Molotov Cocktails.[16] Two months later police in Munich found 12 Molotov cocktails during a house search and on the same day senior Munich SDS member Rainer Jendis told the press 'we will employ further violence against property, and we will continue to break the law'.[17]

The journal of the *Republikanischer Club* provides a representative example of the debate on violence and illegality. The Club was created in April 1967, opening its doors on Wielandstrasse in Berlin on 20 May with a fanfare of publicity.[18] It was intended as a social club for the Left, 'to be a meeting place, discussions forum and information centre of a not really defined Left, that has not been represented in Berlin's institutions for some time'.[19] In the first month Gabriel Kolko talked on Vietnam at the Club,

15. 'Zeugen vorgeführt', *BZ*, 12 July 1967, Rep B014/1024, LB.

16. 'Studenten: LSD', *Der Spiegel*, 19 February 1968, p. 28.

17. 'Polizei fand 12 Molotow-Cocktails', *Bild*, 20 April 1968, and 'Gewalt muß sein!', *Bild*, 20.3.68, both file Zeitungen April 1968, Aktenbestand des Sozialistischen Anwaltskollektivs, HIfS.

18. 'Berlin: Opposition', *Der Spiegel*, 29 May 1967, pp. 44–5 made much of the fact that copies of *Isvestija* and the *Peking Review*, as well as copies of works by Marx and Mao, were lying around in the Club.

19. Marianne Regensburger, *Jahresbericht*, 25 May 1968, file 152, RC (Allg) Republikanischer Clubgesellschaft Bd 1, 2, Aktenbestand des Sozialistischen Anwaltskollektivs, HIfS.

and other speakers in a series of organized lectures included Herbert Marcuse and members of the International War Crimes Tribunal.[20] After 2 June the Club also acted as an information centre for the Left, a focus for the organization of protest activity, and the location for press conferences. This was made all the more possible by the fact that left-wing lawyer Horst Mahler, a key figure in the foundation of the Club and a member of its Executive Committee, represented the Ohnesorg family and helped present the Prosecution case in the Kurras trial. By May 1968 the Club had around 200 members and 800 other regular visitors, including students, academics, trade unionists, professionals and so on, and had organized itself into a series of Working Groups, each concentrating on issues such as 'action', 'emancipation', and 'political theory'.[21] It would continue to be an important venue for the Berlin Left in the organization of protests and discussions on theory through to the early 1970s, and its journal, *RC-Bulletin*, was one of a number of key texts in the ongoing discussion on the use of violence.

The journal was launched in the autumn of 1968, amid a rising tide of violence in demonstrations. Debates about illegality and violence were already tearing Left apart and dominated *RC-Bulletin* from an early stage, often occupying the majority of the space in the journal. Violence was the cover story of the third edition, for instance. This was released three days after the massive and unprecedentedly violent demonstration on 4 November 1968 on Tegeler Weg, outside the court where Mahler was being tried for his part in violent protests the previous April. Far from being the passive victims of police attempts to break them up, demonstrators who arrived armed with clubs, stones and helmets executed a successful assault on the police lines, pushing them back down the road in disorder.[22] *RC-Bulletin* described this as a 'new dimension' because 'for

20. Circular to members dated 17.5.67, and *Der Republikanische Club in Westberlin*, both in file 153, Republikanischer Clubgesellschaft m.b.H. 1967, Aktenbestand des Sozialistischen Anwaltskollektivs, HIfS.

21. *Selbstdarstellung aller im RC tagenden Arbeitskreise*, file 152, RC (Allg) Republikanischer Clubgesellschaft Bd 1, 2, Aktenbestand des Sozialistischen Anwaltskollektivs, HIfS.

22. 'Berlin: APO', *Der Spiegel*, 11 November 1968, pp. 67–72 is an excellent account of the riot. Scheuch, E., 'Pflasterstein statt Argumente', *Die Zeit*, 8 November 1968, p. 3, typifies the fear the riot provoked, especially the assertion that 'the new Left have taken up the methods of the old Right'. Tegeler Weg, which left 131 officers injured, forced a rethink in police tactics and equipment, leading to the abandonment of the old shako helmet and the introduction of purpose-designed riot gear. See 'Polizei: Demonstrationen', *Der Spiegel*, 16 December 1968, pp. 62–3 for the shocked police reaction and calls for better protection.

the first time student demonstrators have not only been hit and arrested but they have themselves hit back . . . more police than demonstrators were injured' and 'demonstrators beat the police into retreat'. It acknowledged that a tactic of provocation could not, by definition, rely on peaceful protest in the long run but would necessarily escalate into violence. It called the demonstration a 'liberation from the trauma of 2 June' and an 'escape from powerlessness and isolation through actions of solidarity'. It balked at an outright call to violence, though, saying that tactically the use of violence was an error because the public was willing 'to identify with the victims of violence, but not with opposing violence, so they are indignant about napalm in Vietnam, but don't want to identify with the revolutionary struggle of the Viet Cong'.[23]

By the next edition the journal had received a barrage of criticism for its stance. One letter-writer called violent demonstrations in general 'counter-revolutionary' while another, Kurt Fabian, did not discount violence as a possible tactic but said 'the use of violence is only useful if the demonstrators are powerful enough at least to shake the existing power structure. That was the case in the Spring in Paris, it is not the case in the *Bundesrepublik* and still less in West Berlin'. He warned that police had much better weapons than demonstrators, and would use these weapons if pushed too far. Helmut Gollwitzer wrote that the article had disappointed him: he had expected the Club to distance itself from the violence and added that the Club had to decide whether it wanted to be 'an assembly of the radical-democratic Left or a Trotskyist or similarly titled sect'. Johann-Wolfgang Landsberg (SPD), a former FU Berlin AStA representative who had resigned earlier in the year in opposition to the violence of the demonstrations in April, talked of a 'brutalization and emotionalization of the APO' and a 'discrepancy between democratically inclined decisions and the tactics' of the APO. The journal was forced to print a declaration by its Executive Committee on the front page but, although this described the use of violence as 'risky' and took a much more defensive attitude, it did not condemn violence outright.[24] This response prompted an extraordinary meeting of members on 9 January 1969, for which the *RC-Bulletin's* December 1968 issue provided 18 pages of discussion by

23. Ehrler, S., 'Demonstration und Gewalt', *RC-Bulletin*, III/1968, 7 November 1968, pp. 1–3, file 151, RC Bulletin, Aktenbestand des Sozialistischen Anwaltskollektivs, HIfS. Ehrler was the editor of the journal at this point.

24. *RC-Bulletin*, IV/1968, 21 November 1968, pp. 1–7, file 151, RC Bulletin, Aktenbestand des Sozialistischen Anwaltskollektivs, HIfS. The Club clearly thought Ehrler could not be trusted after his article of the previous month, and so Elke Jung and Matthias Pfüller joined him as editors.

various members, for and against violent protest. Bernd Rabehl argued 'we should learn from the Viet Cong, from the Chinese and Cuban revolutions, then we will be victorious'.[25] The next edition, published two days before the mass meeting, included Roland Reichwein's '21 theses on the use of violence' in which he began by asserting that the APO could not use peaceful demonstrations as long as its aim was to bring about a revolution.[26] At the meeting the left-liberal majority tried and failed to get the membership to reject the pro-violence stance. Over the next year the struggle for control of the Club between left-liberals, the anti-authoritarian far-left, and the 'traditional' pro-Soviet Left, with the issue of violence as the core source of division, eclipsed almost all other issues.

Such debates were of crucial importance to the development of the Vietnam Campaign. On 24 December 1967, for instance, Rudi Dutschke and other SDS members carrying a Viet Cong flag and pro-Vietnamese placards attempted to disrupt the Midnight Mass at the Gedächtniskirche on the Kurfürstendamm. As they filed into the church, members of the congregation shouted 'shame on you' and 'get out you pigs', and when Dutschke took the pulpit with the words 'I want to say, it is really hypocritical to speak of peace here', he was dragged away. In the ensuing struggle Dutschke received a cut to the head; when the Sexton asked people to leave the church Dutschke shouted at him 'you are the servant of the Devil' and rubbed his blood-covered hand over the Sexton's face. By the time the police arrived the church had been cleared of protesters.[27] Spluttering opprobrium poured forth from the press over the next few days: *Der Spiegel* complained that 'all year long Berlin's recalcitrant students have attacked taboo after taboo'.[28] On 27 December the Gedächtniskirche issued a statement laying the blame for the disturbance squarely at the feet of the demonstrators, noting that the service had included a prayer for the ending of the War in Vietnam.

25. Speech by Bernd Rabehl on 9 November 1968, reprinted in *RC-Bulletin*, V/1968, 5 December 1968, p. 21, file 151, RC Bulletin, Aktenbestand des Sozialistischen Anwaltskollektivs, HIfS.

26. Reichwein, R., '21 Thesen zur Gewaltanwendung', *RC-Bulletin*, I/1969, 7 January 1969, p. 10, file 151, RC Bulletin, Aktenbestand des Sozialistischen Anwaltskollektivs, HIfS.

27. *Was ist geschehen? Dokumentation zu den Störungen der Gottesdienste in der Kaiser-Wilhelm-Gedächtniskirche in Berlin am Heiligen Abend und in der Silvesternacht 1967*, file % Gebbert u. a. Rathaus Go-in I, Aktenbestand des Sozialistischen Anwaltskollektivs, HIfS. This is the detailed and impressively balanced report by the Church Council of the Gedächtniskirche.

28. 'Berlin: Kirche', *Der Spiegel*, 1 January 1968, p. 38.

Reactions to the event from Christians were mixed. A telegram from a group of Bremen priests said that 'the student concern over the War in Vietnam is also the concern of our Church' and, attacked the use of violence against the students, arguing that Dutschke should be given an apology by the Church. Another Bremen priest, Father Pohl, asserted (correctly) that the disruption of religious ceremonies was a breach of the Basic Law, and in a swipe at the protesters stated 'whoever in such a tense situation uses provocation does not serve peace, whether in Vietnam or in Berlin'. For Pohl the idea of apologizing to Dutschke 'stands the case on its head'. Helmut Gollwitzer, whose services had previously been banned by the Nazis, talked of the 'unchristian congregation' at the Berlin church and felt that protesters had merely expressed the Christian desire for peace, which the violent reaction of the congregation had negated. This is to misunderstand the intention of the protest, which was to challenge religion, the Establishment, cosy conservatism, but above all pacifism. The violence provoked by the protest played into the hands of the protesters, who wanted to expose the violence underlying a seemingly benign system. The episode added to Dutschke's growing infamy in the press, provoking memories of Nazi attacks on the Church and prompting even more vilification, particularly from the Springer empire. The disruption was a perfect example of the use of illegality and provocation by the SDS, raising questions about the appropriateness of both the method and the target of the protest, while guaranteeing that it gained maximum publicity for its cause.[29]

Far from being an isolated incident, Dutschke's protest at the Gedächtniskirche was part of the build-up to the Berlin International Vietnam Conference planned for 17 and 18 February 1968. In advance of the Conference the Vietnam Campaign moved into a new phase of intensity. In the first week of December 1967 the SDS and the FU AStA held a Vietnam Week and in the New Year, particularly after the launch of the Têt Offensive by the North Vietnamese, a series of violent demonstrations took place throughout the country. In Frankfurt 1,000 people took part in an SDS demonstration that turned into a riot when protesters attempted to storm the American General Consulate, shouting 'weapons for the Viet Cong'. When water cannon were deployed, protesters threw fireworks. Later in the day protesters forcibly entered the Swiss General Consulate

29. In a trial in September 1968 three people were acquitted, but two of them were each given sentences of 4 days in prison for contempt of court. See 'Freispruch – aber Ordungsstrafen', *Die Welt*, 1 October 1968, file Zeitungs Ausschnitte 1968/69, Aktenbestand des Sozialistischen Anwaltskollektivs, HIfS.

where an American trade office was located, and replaced the *Bundes-republik* flag on the roof of the building with a Viet Cong flag before police dragged them from the building. Further violence occurred outside, in which windows in the American Consulate were broken with stones.[30] In Munich on 8 February 1968 around 40 SDS members disrupted the opening of an exhibition at the American Consulate. During a speech they rushed the stage, unfurled a Viet Cong flag, seized the microphone and began shouting 'Ho Chi Minh' and 'Johnson, murderer'. When security guards tried to remove them from the stage with truncheons, punches and kicks, smoke and stink bombs were thrown and a sit-down demonstration was begun.[31] Eventually the police used force to drag them from the building, with the *Abendzeitung* alleging that one female protester was dragged across the floor by her hair.[32] Another SDS demonstration, this time in Hamburg, called for 'solidarity with the Viet Cong' and took place on 9 February.[33] Because of a massive police presence, including horses and police dogs, protesters were unable to hold a planned teach-in in front of the American Consulate and so decided to hold a march through the city instead. The violence that followed was so extreme that armed members of the *Bundeswehr* were deployed on the streets, to the disgust of SDS Hamburg.[34]

The International Vietnam Conference itself was the high point of the Vietnam campaign in Germany and one of the key events for the movement internationally. The SDS were able to use the Conference to challenge the democratic credentials of the *Bundesrepublik* even before it took place. Rising to the bait, on 6 February 1968 Berlin Culture Minister Stein effectively attempted to ban the Conference by suggesting to the *Rektors* of the TU and FU Berlin that it should be barred from university rooms. This bid failed when the TU reluctantly agreed to the use of its main auditorium. The police then announced on that the application for permission to hold a demonstration after the Conference had been rejected because of fears of 'a risk to public security or order', and the

30. 'Dutschke provoziert in Frankfurt antiamerikanische Tumulte', *Der Tagesspiegel*, 6 February 1968, file Zeitungen 1968, Aktenbestand des Sozialistischen Anwaltskollektivs, HIfS.

31. See the details of the charges against Heinz Koderer and Reinhard Wetter in *Rechtshilfe der APO München 1968–1969*, ED 713, pp. 10–11, IfZM.

32. 'Demonstration gegen Vietnamkrieg im Amerikahaus', *Abendzeitung*, 9 February 1968, Sammlung Schlemper, ED 328/6, IfZM.

33. *Großdemonstration gegen den schmutzigen Krieg der USA in Vietnam*, Sammlung Jürgen Klein, file 14, HIfS. This is a Hamburg SDS flyer advertising the demonstration.

34. *Presse Erklärung: zum zweiten Mal Bundeswehreinsatz gegen den SDS Hamburg*, Sammlung Jürgen Klein, file 48, HIfS.

demonstration had been banned.[35] Just before the Conference, police even arrested 47 people for distributing flyers opposing the American policy in Vietnam, and Mayor Schütz announced 'what we are defending ourselves against are criminal actions, disorder, revolutionary rehearsals after foreign recipes, as is desired by muddle-heads'.[36] The SDS responded by calling on the people of Berlin 'to remember the numerous results of 2 June 1967 and to prevent their repetition'.[37] The Conference was a showcase for the anti-authoritarian wing of the SDS and just by organizing it they had created an act of provocation that raised fears of international revolutionary collusion and violent revolt. The city that the West presented as 'the outpost of the "free world"', surrounded by communist oppression, had taken actions that, far from defending democratic rights, fundament-ally undermined them, and all this was publicized on the international stage.[38] For the SDS then, the Conference was a success before it had even taken place.

The Conference was intended to bring revolutionaries together 'in order to express their solidarity with the War of Liberation of the Viet-namese people and to discuss common measures for the struggle against US imperialism'.[39] This was to lead to the formation of a 'United Front in order to achieve the final victory of the Vietnamese Revolution'.[40] It was attended by 3,000 to 4,000 people, most of whom were from across Germany, but also including delegates from 44 left-oriented organizations from all over the world. From outside Europe there were representatives from Ethiopia, the ANC in South Africa, Latin America, and Iran, as well as two members of the American SDS and Dale A. Smith, of the SNCC. Much larger numbers came from countries across Europe, including around 150 from Denmark, 100 from Italy and 300 from France.[41] Above

35. Letter from *Der Polizeipräsident in Berlin*, dated 15 February 1968, file 116, Vietnam Demonstration 17/18.2.68, Aktenbestand des Sozialistischen Anwaltskollektivs, HIfS. In this letter the Police Chief defended his decision following a letter of protest from Horst Mahler.

36. 'Vietnam-Demonstration bleibt verboten: Politiker appellieren an die Berliner', *Die Welt*, 17 February 1968, Zeitungen 1968, Aktenbestand des Sozialistischen Anwalts-kollektivs, HIfS.

37. *Wie wird Berlin reagiert*, Berlin file 00131, BfZS

38. Ibid.

39. *Schlußerklärung des SDS zum Vietnam-Kongress 17./18.II.68 in Berlin*, Sammlung Mehringer ED 308/10, IfZM.

40. *The Struggle of the Vietnamese People and the Global Strategy of Imperialism: A Call to the International Vietnam Conference in West Berlin on February 17–18, 1968*, Berlin file 00106, BfZS. This SDS flyer is in English in the original.

41. *An der internationalen Vietnamkonferenz teilnehmende Organisationen*, Berlin file 00131, BfZS

the podium a massive Viet Cong flag was draped, with the phrase 'Victory for the Vietnamese Revolution' emblazoned across it, followed by the Che Guevara quote 'the duty of every revolutionary is to create revolution'. The Conference was chaotic, tumultuous, and above all it wallowed in strident revolutionary rhetoric and grandiose gestures. Sessions explicitly made the link between the North Vietnamese struggle and the work of the revolutionary Left elsewhere.[42] The debates made it clear that for representatives from across the world the moral and material support that had been given to the North Vietnamese by the international Vietnam campaign so far was no longer sufficient. One Iranian delegate called for a 'global war of liberation' and SDS Federal representative Karl Dietrich Wolff claimed that the campaign had to move 'from mere protest against mass murder and the imperialist war . . . to resistance'.[43] Such comments, and calls by the Conference organizers for a 'second revolutionary front' could, and indeed would, be translated literally by some as a call for an international terrorist campaign.[44]

The Conference had only mixed success in creating a united front for action on Vietnam, however. The establishment of an International News and Research Institute known as INFI, to be run by SDS Berlin, was the only evidence of the creation of a co-ordinated campaign. This body was to be a collection and distribution point for information relevant to revolutionary groups, free from the taint and distortions of the capitalist media, as well as providing a focus point for debate and research on strategy and theory. From the start it was dominated by a clique of SDS members and was subject to the intense rivalries and sectarianism within the SDS. In terms of its role within Germany, let alone internationally, it was a marginal and, for most protesters, an obscure institution that suffered further from the fact that the SDS was itself gradually marginalized over the next two years. Perhaps in the atmosphere of sectarianism that informed the Left in general, and which was especially pronounced in a Conference involving people from such differing countries and circumstances, the vagueness of INFI and the declarations of support for the Vietnamese represented the best possible compromise.

42. *Programm der Internationalen Vietnamkonferenz – Westberlin 1968*, Berlin file 00127, BfZS.
43. Quoted respectively in 'Weiss ruft Genossen zur Sabotage auf', *Berliner Morgenpost*, 18 February 1968, 'Vietnam-Kongreß in Berlin, Vom Protest zum Widerstand, *Bild*, 18 February 1968, and, 'Vietnam-Kongreß in der TU: Vom bloßen Protest zum Widerstand', *Der Tagesspiegel*, 18 February 1968, all in file Zeitungen 1968, Aktenbestand des Sozialistischen Anwaltskollektivs, HIfS.
44. *Schlußerklärung des SDS*, ibid.

The march through Berlin the day after the Conference was not as violent as perhaps may have been expected, or as violent as had been planned. On the evening of 17 February it was announced to the Conference that a legal challenge to the ban had been successful after the personal intervention by the Bishop of Berlin and the writer Günter Grass who negotiated a compromise solution between Dutschke and the Mayor of Berlin. The original route ended at the American McNair military base, and Dutschke had planned to storm the barracks simultaneous to a mutiny by black GI's who supposedly had links with the Black Panthers. The plan became known to the Berlin authorities and the US military who made it clear that the military police had orders to fire on anyone attempting to force entry into the base. After these warnings Dutschke's friend Bernd Rabehl succeeded in persuading him to back down and the route was changed at the last minute.[45] The march involved between 15,000 and 20,000 people carrying Viet Cong flags and placards bearing images of Rosa Luxemburg, Karl Liebknecht, Che Guevara and Lenin. In a rare display of restraint the police wisely held back from the demonstration and there was no repeat of the violence of 2 June. While chanting 'Ho Ho Ho Chi Minh' and 'Weapons for the Viet Cong', marchers were subject to abuse and missiles from the crowds of onlookers throughout.[46] At the opera house, where the marchers assembled to hear speeches by various people, including Rudi Dutschke, the most serious disturbance of the day occurred when a group of construction workers started burning the demonstrators' flags and placards after protesters had tried to take over their scaffolding as platforms from which to listen to the speeches. When the protesters began to respond with violence, Dutschke told them over the microphone 'don't allow yourselves to be provoked by them, they don't know any better'.[47] The protesters backed off, and the demonstration remained largely peaceful. Ronald Fraser has quoted Tariq Ali making the rather ambitious claim that during the march 'you felt that the old revolutionary movement was being revived, that history was being re-made' while Robin Blackburn has said of the march 'it was there that I first really felt what you could call the spirit of '68'.[48] These comments seem rather far-fetched, especially as that evening several hundred people were

45. Fraser, *1968*, pp. 177–80. It is also referred to in Gretchen Dutschke, *Rudi Dutschke*, p. 182.

46. Eyewitness statement *Rexin*, file 116, Vietnam Demonstration, 17./18.2.68, Aktenbestand des Sozialistischen Anwaltskollektivs, HIfS. This detailed account is by a participant in the demonstration.

47. Quoted in Chaussy, *Die drei Leben des Rudi Dutschke*, p. 214.

48. Fraser, *1968*, p. 180.

involved in counter-demonstrations across the city 'against street terror and anarchy'.[49]

Such minor acts of opposition were dwarfed by the massive protest march through Berlin that took place on 21 February. In a demonstration outside Rathaus Schöneberg arranged by the curious alliance of the CDU, the SPD and the DGB, 150,000 Berliners assembled to maintain that 'Berlin stands for peace and freedom.'[50] Mayor Schütz told the crowd that 'a small radical group of extremists is attempting to make the free constitutional state unworkable. Our answer: stop it.'[51] Ominously, Rudi Dutschke was a particular target for the protesters. By this stage he appeared regularly on television and in newspapers, and was a household name, synonymous with student violence and SDS intolerance. Gretchen Dutschke tells of how one innocent participant was mistaken for Rudi Dutschke and was almost lynched. With shouts of 'beat him to death! String him up' they set upon the man who was able to get to a police officer before the crowd attacked both of them, shouting 'lynch the pig', 'castrate the Jewish swine' and 'Dutschke into the concentration camp'. Luckily the police officer was able to bundle the man onto a bus so that he could make his escape.[52]

The Vietnam campaign lost its way after the International Vietnam Conference. In April and May it was almost completely overshadowed by the shooting of Rudi Dutschke and the massive protests against the Emergency Laws in May. This was followed over the next few months by only sporadic activity on Vietnam as the Left concentrated on other things, including arguing among themselves. The occasional demonstration could not disguise the fact that the campaign was suffering as a result of the rapid fragmentation the Left was experiencing. Campaign events did continue, whether the occasional march, like that through Berlin on 3 April 1968, or the mass blood donation for the Viet Cong on 3 July at the FU, organized

49. 'Gegen Terror und Anarchie', *Der Abend*, 19 February 1968, p. 1, file Zeitungen 1968, Aktenbestand des Sozialistischen Anwaltskollektivs, HIfS.

50. 'Klare Absagen an den Radikalismus', *Der Abend*, 22 February 1968, file Zeitungen 1968, Aktenbestand des Sozialistischen Anwaltskollektivs, HIfS. The demonstration was organized by the umbrella group *Aktion Demokratisches Berlin*. As well as the main political parties this consisted of politicians, journalists, lawyers, teachers, lecturers and even actors who united under the motto 'peace is only possible in freedom'. They were against, among other things, 'Soviet dictatorship, Left fascism and Right fascism' and 'illusions and political suicide'. The flyer *Berlin demonstriert*, Berlin file 00124, BfZS, is a call to the 21 February demonstration that gives a list of signatories, including Walter Sickert and Peter Lorenz, the future head of the Berlin CDU.

51. '150,000 Berliner gaben die Antwort', *Berliner Morgenpost*, 22 February 1968, file Zeitungen 1968, Aktenbestand des Sozialistischen Anwaltskollektivs, HIfS.

52. Gretchen Dutschke, *Rudi Dutschke*, p. 189.

by the AStA and *Aktion Solidarität mit Vietnam.*[53] An International Vietnam Week at the *Republikanischer Club* took place from 21 October to 4 November and included collections of money for the Viet Cong, as well as 'Agitprop' performances, demonstrations on 21 October as well as 7 and 9 November, and several mass meetings and discussions.[54] These were in many respects exceptions: by this time protests against the War were becoming noticeably more irregular, less well supported, and failed to attract the attention of mass media who were becoming much more interested in the acts of violence against property that were becoming the preferred protest weapon of some on the Left.

Throughout 1969, as the Left disintegrated and the SDS destroyed itself, leadership of the Vietnam campaign devolved onto the newly formed far-left cells. It is impossible to give a detailed account here of the multitude of small (often tiny) demonstrations, marches, protest meetings, and so on that took place from 1969 until the end of the War in 1975. Such a task would not only be repetitive and take up an inordinate amount of space, but it would also concentrate on obscure protests at the expense of the bigger picture. For the whole of the period from 1969 to 1975 it is possible to make the general observation that the Left was increasingly talking to itself. Grandiose and often pompous statements, divorced from political realities, usually including sectarian abuse, and almost always involving strident declarations of solidarity with the Vietnamese revolution against American 'imperialism', were the dominant themes in the literature produced by the Vietnam campaign in these years. Some typical examples would perhaps be helpful.

The protests surrounding the My Lai massacre are a particularly useful focus point. The massacre took place in March 1968, but was not reported in the press until mid-November 1969, around the time of the second round of international protests in parallel with the US Moratorium (the first round had taken place in mid-October). The Vietnam campaign had already become a marginal force, since troops were being pulled out of Vietnam (after Nixon's announcement of phased withdrawal in May 1969) and the broad appeal to a wider populace through humanitarianism had been hijacked by revolutionary sentiments that most people could not support. In an advert for a demonstration in Berlin on 13 December a group of *Rote Zellen* complained inaccurately that the capitalist press had

53. *Aufruf zur Kundgebung und Demonstration gegen den Krieg der USA in Vietnam*, Berlin file 00131 and *Solidarität mit dem Vietnamesischen Volk*, Berlin file 00107, both BfZS. The SHB demonstration included a collection to support the North Vietnamese, illustrating its move toward the SDS. See *Demonstration gegen Völkermord*, Sammlung Schwiedrzik zur Studentenbewegung, ZSg 153/17, BK.

54. *Internationale Vietnamwoche 21.10–4.11.68*, Berlin file 03801, BfZS.

stopped covering the My Lai massacre because it confirmed anti-capitalist claims by protesters. They then proceeded to attack their rivals, the *Sozialistische Einheitspartei Westberlins* (SEW), arguing 'whoever – such as the SEW revisionists – wants to paste together a "socialist united front" from this [the Vietnam campaign], shows only where they stand themselves. They cut off the only strength of the struggle against imperialism that is able to lead them successfully: the mass of people under the leadership of the proletariat'.[55] Such sectarianism, coupled with esoteric statements like 'the people's war in Vietnam is the practical negation of the position of revisionism' was hardly going to attract mass support from a broad cross-section of society. This is not to underestimate the importance of the massacre in contributing to popular disgust at the War. It was widely condemned in the German press, and was the cover story for the 1 December edition of *Der Spiegel*, featuring an American soldier leading Viet Cong prisoners by a rope around their necks, with the headline 'American war crimes in Vietnam'. A large proportion of this edition was devoted to a detailed account of the massacre, including a cartoon that compared 'Song My' to war crimes at Lidice, Katyn, Badajoz (by Franco's troops), Malaysia (by the British), the Congo, Biafra, and Hue (by the Viet Cong).[56] Popular revulsion was undoubtedly indicative of a widespread lack of support for the War by this stage, but the Left had made it almost impossible to translate this into mass support for protest activity.

As the campaign developed in the early 1970s, it became even more limited to participation by squabbling factions of the revolutionary Left. The literature of the period was consistently preoccupied with American imperialism: 'Fight US Imperialism', 'fight imperialism', 'the US army – a weapon of US imperialism that will be blunted' are just some of the titles that referred to imperialism among the abundant flyers for demonstrations produced in the early 1970s.[57] This was a key aspect of the protest and the terrorist campaigns, and concerned both the physical occupation of Vietnam by American forces and cultural imperialism. Bernd Rabehl's recent claims that the student protests in general, and the Vietnam campaign in particular, were part of a struggle for national liberation for Germany

55. *Von der Revolution in Vietnam lernen*, Berlin file 00106, BfZS.

56. 'Vietnam: Kriegsverbrechen', *Der Spiegel*, 1 December 1969, p. 124. My Lai was variously referred to as Song My, Son My and Pinkville.

57. *Kampf dem US-Imperialismus, Kampf dem Imperialismus, Die US-Armee – eine Waffe des US-Imperialismus, die stumpfer wird*, all Berlin file 00106, BfZS. The first of these flyers advertises a demonstration in Berlin on 12 December 1971 by various *Rote Zellen*. The other two flyers are for a Berlin demonstration on 13 February 1971, again by *Rote Zellen* as well as the student committee of the *KPD-Aufbauorganisation*, the *Komitee Kampf dem Imperialismus*, and other groups.

are surely misguided.[58] The xenophobia that has accompanied his move to the Right, including claims that Germany is suffering from *Überfremdung* (too much foreign influence), is in direct contrast to the internationalism and anti-fascism of the Vietnam campaign. It is necessary to acknowledge the Left's contradictory opposition to nationalism while supporting a war of national liberation, but Rabehl has muddied the water for his own ends and it is easy to tie oneself in knots trying to disentangle the subtle but important differences between his position and that of the Vietnam campaign. Above all, although the campaign supported the Vietnamese struggle for national liberation, it was not concerned with the preservation of a cultural heritage, which the North Vietnamese authorities also attacked as inconsistent with communism. Rather, references to cultural imperialism were concerned with capitalism as a hegemonic force. West Germany, of course, was also occupied by American forces, and had manifestly embraced American culture. In this sense attacking capitalism in West Germany, especially American capitalist cultural imperialism, could be viewed as contributing to the international communist revolution of which the Vietnamese were a part. For some, albeit a tiny minority, protest against such things had become meaningless by the early 1970s and physically attacking American military bases and personnel, as well as the state and media institutions that, according to the Left, maintained capitalist hegemony, was identified as the only option.

Demands made in the past, notably at the International Vietnam Conference, for a continuation of the Vietnam War in West Germany would be taken literally and terrorists could claim that American violence in Vietnam would be met by violence in Europe. Most protesters did not cross this particular Rubicon, and however violent some demonstrations remained, the majority of political activists in the early 1970s were unconvinced that terrorism, especially terrorism against people, was the best method of bringing about a revolution, or ensuring the establishment of democratic systems. Despite these objections, terrorism had already taken over as the most visible method of protest against the Vietnam War. Ironically, from pacifist and humanitarian beginnings the campaign had been at the centre of debates on revolutionary violence that had eventually been taken literally and applied in practice.

58. The file Originale Dokumentation, 'Rabehl', APOusB, contains details of Rabehl's theories dating from 1998 and 1999. Kraushaar, W., 'Das Jahrhundert der Befreiung: 1968, das Jahr der Rebellion', *Der Spiegel*, 29 March 1999, pp. 186–8 refers to Rabehl's *überfremdung* ideas. The idea that the Left could exploit nationalism for seemingly internationalist ends that could be viewed simultaneously as imperialist is not new: see Seton-Watson, H., *The Imperialist Revolutionaries* for a more sophisticated and less polemical interpretation than that advanced by Rabehl.

The Dutschke Shooting

Weeks before the riots in Paris in May 1968 *Der Spiegel's* cover sombrely spoke of 'Students on the barricades', complete with a photograph of rioters silhouetted against the sky.[1] West Germany had just experienced the worst rioting of the post-war period after Rudi Dutschke was shot on 11 April, a mere seven days after the assassination of Martin Luther King. Dutschke's shooting could not be blamed directly on a representative of the state, unlike Ohnesorg's, but against the background of growing violence and hysterical press headlines attacking protesters it prompted greater violence and outrage than had ever been seen before. Protesters across West Germany spent several days laying siege to, and physically attacking, the offices of the Springer empire, which they accused of inciting the shooting by turning Dutschke into a national hate figure. The Springer group was certainly not alone among German media in vilifying protesters in general, and the SDS and Dutschke in particular. Yet the unashamedly vitriolic treatment of protests in Springer titles, as well as the sheer size of the empire, made it a natural target for protesters for whom it exemplified a state in which varied and open democratic debate was stifled.

The Springer publishing empire was undoubtedly powerful. Having been created with tiny resources in the British zone of occupation in 1946 by Axel Springer, in 1964 the group controlled 31 per cent of the daily newspaper market, along with 89 per cent of regional and 85 per cent of Sunday newspaper sales. In Berlin 67 per cent of daily newspapers, and in Hamburg 69 per cent, came from the Springer stable.[2] In 1968 the tabloid *Bild-Zeitung* had a circulation of 4,094,884 copies per day, with a further 2,319,192 copies of *Bild am Sonntag*, making it by far the largest newspaper in Germany. *Die Welt*, Springer's largest broadsheet title, with sales of 225,886 newspapers every day, was approximately equivalent in size to its main non-Springer rivals such as *Die Zeit, Frankfurter Allgemeine*

1. 'Studenten auf den Barrikaden', *Der Spiegel*, 22 April 1968, front cover.
2. 'Fernsehen: Springer', *Der Spiegel*, 3 February 1965, p. 44.

Zeitung, and *Süddeutsche Zeitung*. In Berlin, *BZ* and the *Berliner Morgen-post* sold more than half a million copies between them every day. The dominance even stretched to weekly magazines, with *Eltern* selling 1,175,736 copies per week, the women's magazine *Jasmin* achieving sales of 1,380,000, and the teen magazines *Bravo* and *Twen* accounting for sales of just under a million.[3] By 1966 the latter two titles, along with *OK*, represented 87.7 per cent of the market for magazines aimed at young people.[4] The group also included comics, specialist trade journals and magazines covering music, sport, and television. This colossus represented the largest single publishing house for newspapers and magazines in Germany, easily dwarfing its nearest rivals in sales, financial might, resources, and above all in the size and variety of its readership, whether in terms of age, social background, geographical location or even personal interests. Such domination of the press by one group, in the iron grip of Springer himself and consistently representing his views, had clear implications for German democracy.

Germany in the 1960s had perhaps more newspapers and magazines than any other western European country, expressing the full spectrum of political viewpoints and, in line with the Allied plan for a free decent-ralized and liberal press, many were small local independent newspapers. With the existence of newspapers and magazines such as *Frankfurter Allgemeine Zeitung*, *Die Zeit*, *Frankfurter Rundschau*, *Süddeutsche Zeitung*, *Stern*, *Konkret* and *Der Spiegel*, it is impossible to maintain that West Germans had access to only a limited range of viewpoints. Indeed, Peter J. Humphreys, in his study of the post-war West German press, has noted that according to many previous interpretations this Allied policy was completely successful, although Marxist commentators have sug-gested that the press in Germany in the post-war period rapidly returned to the pre-war situation of control by a small group of press barons.[5] Humphreys takes the middle road, with some justification, in saying that the existence of the Springer empire undermined the Allied policy of decentralization: the system that was established can 'stand positive comparison with any other media system in the Western liberal democratic world'.[6] He acknowledges, though, that the press in Germany was over-whelmingly conservative in nature, with a bias toward the CDU, and that

3. 'Presse: Springer-Verkauf', *Der Spiegel*, 1 July 1968, p. 53. The Federal Cartel Office produced these figures during its investigation of Springer for monopolistic practices.
4. 'Materialen 3: Springer: Eine Dokumentation zur publizistischen macht', *Stuttgarter Studentenzeitschrift*, December 1967, p. 1.
5. Humphreys, P.J., *Media and Media Policy in West Germany*, p. 3.
6. Ibid., p. xi.

the press concentration that occurred in the 1950s, and in which Springer led the way, 'stored up trouble for the future'.[7] This manifested itself particularly in the abuse of such concentration for political influence, in the limitation of freedom of expression, and in the unfettered extremism of press pronouncements.[8]

The rabid hatred of protesters that ran through the whole of the politically conservative Springer empire was informed by a particularly uncompromising brand of anti-communism. Whether Springer's attitudes reflected or helped to create popular anti-communism and attitudes to democracy is open to debate, for which there is no room here. There is no doubt, however, that the underlying anti-protester ethos of the Springer empire was shared with large sections of public opinion. Rudi Dutschke was the particular target for Springer's contempt, and he was represented as a demonic figure in consequence. He was after all the main theorist and most easily recognizable public face of the anti-authoritarian revolt, he was consistently in the thick of provocative events, he came from East Germany, and he regularly made comments that dared to criticize the *Bundesrepublik* and which, to Springer, sounded dangerously like communism.

The dangers presented by the Springer group had not gone unnoticed, though, and it was subject to attack even before the Dutschke shooting. In August 1967 *Konkret* lent its support to the *Enteignet Springer* (expropriate Springer) campaign which had been started by the SDS and the left-wing journal *Berliner Extra Dienst*, with the aim of forcing the Federal Cartel Office to break up the Springer empire. This was given a boost in January 1968 when the actor Wolfgang Kieling, who had received the Golden Camera award from the Springer television magazine *Hör zu* the previous year, returned his award in support of the *Enteignet Springer* action. In a startlingly prescient statement, Kieling explained that he felt Springer's coverage of student unrest 'has made it clear that it will shrink back from no kind of lies and defamation if it makes it possible to silence alternative thinking. It has not been afraid openly to incite the public, who have been misinformed by it, to a student pogrom, and as a result there is an immeasurable threat to freedom of opinion and democratization.'[9] The 'Springer hearings' conducted at the *Kritische Universität* in February 1968, with Rudi Dutschke as a member of their organization committee, were part of this campaign. When protesters smashed windows of the

7. Ibid., p. 67.
8. Ibid., pp. 89 and 97.
9. Quoted in Kraushaar, *1968: Das Jahr*, pp. 17–18.

Berliner Morgenpost on the night of 1 to 2 February 1968, following the first day of the hearings, Springer titles called it 'fascist terror', 'a second Kristallnacht' and 'SA methods'. The SDS responded by reminding the public that 'from 1933 Axel Springer wore the uniform of the Nazis'.[10]

Dutschke's shooting has to be seen in the context of what can only be described as mutual hatred between protesters and the Springer empire. The facts of the shooting and its aftermath only added to these prejudices. On the morning of 11 April the 23-year-old Josef Bachmann arrived in Berlin by train from Munich, where he worked as a house painter, a parallel with Hitler's life that was not lost on protesters. In his bag he carried an Armical 38 revolver along with 49 rounds of ammunition. Although he was not a member of any political organization, police later found posters of Hitler and Napoleon on the wall of his bedroom at his mother's house in Lower Saxony, as well as a copy of *Mein Kampf*. His stepfather had been a member of the SA, and Bachmann had a violent past that included a conviction for armed robbery which had resulted in a twelve-month prison sentence. He had been born in what became the Soviet sector, and only moved to West Germany as a small child, a forced move that seems to have fed his pathological hatred of communists.

Upon arriving in Berlin he eventually found his way to the SDS Berlin headquarters, at 140 Kurfürstendamm. When Bachmann enquired after Dutschke he was told that Dutschke had just left. A few minutes later Bachmann caught up with Dutschke sat on his bike outside 142 Kurfürstendamm, near the corner with Johann-Georg Strasse, just yards from the SDS building. Despite the fact that it was now dangerous for him to be seen in public, Dutschke was waiting for a chemist to open in order to buy medicine for his daughter. 'Are you Rudi Dutschke?' Bachmann asked. 'Yes'. Bachmann then drew his revolver and shot Dutschke in the head.[11] Bystander Klaus-Jürgen Ahrendts later told the police 'after the first shot a short wrestling match developed between Dutschke and the accused, during which Dutschke at least once, for a short moment, held a hand in protection over his face. At the same time two more shots were fired and the cyclist finally fell to the ground. Immediately after . . . the accused ran from the street on the pavement in the direction of Nestorstrasse'.[12] The

10. *Vietnam 10. Informationen*, Sammlung Schwiedrzik zur Studentenbewegung, ZSg 153/17, BK.

11. Quoted in Dutschke, G., *Rudi Dutschke*, p. 197.

12. Eyewitness statement by Klaus-Jürgen Ahrendts, in *Abschrift*, 3 March 1969, file Dutschke % Bachmann, Diverse Dokumentation, Dokumentation III (Ostern 1968), Aktenbestand des Sozialistischen Anwaltskollektivs, HIfS. This is a small collection of eyewitness statements, assembled for Bachmann's trial.

second and third shots had hit Dutschke in the neck and the right side of his chest. He staggered back toward the SDS building before two by-standers helped him to a bench, where he was laid down. According to witnesses various people passing the scene made comments of incredible callousness like 'one doesn't need to shoot, but it is very good that he has been given a lesson'.[13]

By the time the police arrived Bachmann was holed up in a building site around the corner at 54 Nestorstrasse. When the police investigated, Bachmann fired at them, shouting melodramatically 'you won't take me alive'. The police tried using tear gas to dislodge Bachmann, to no avail. At around 5.30 p.m. an officer managed to get into the building site and called on Bachmann to give himself up. Bachmann's response was to fire again, at which point the officer shot him in the chest and arm, seriously injuring him. In a shoot-out worthy of pulp fiction the police had fired 38 rounds to Bachmann's 15.[14] By this time Dutschke had been taken to hospital, where he underwent a series of operations, most critically to deal with the fact that his skull had been shattered above the left temple and a bullet had lodged itself in his brain. Bachmann was operated on successfully at the same hospital where the police, who had no idea who he was and had to search fingerprint records to establish his identity, had him under guard.

Bachmann's motivation was straightforward. Within days of the shooting it was widely known that he was a *Bild* reader, adding weight to the strongly held belief among protesters that the Springer group's campaign against Dutschke was responsible. As early as 13 April he was quoted in *Bild* saying 'I read about the murder of Dr Martin Luther King. I thought, you must do that too. Dutschke is a communist whom you must kill!'[15] It was only later, at his trial, that the direct link to Springer became absolutely clear. Although he lied on the first day of his trial, saying he never read Springer publications, he retracted this statement on the second day,

13. Quoted in 'Attentate: Dutschke', *Der Spiegel*, 22 April 1968, p. 61. The substance of this detailed account of the shooting seems to have come from police reports, as indicated by *Das Attentat auf Rudi Dutschke, Demonstrationen gegen den Springer Konzern: Dokumente, Herausgegeben vom Verband Deutscher Studentenschaften, Bonn, den 15. April 1968*, B/166/1311, BK.

14. *Verlaufs- und Erfahrungsbericht der Schutzpolizei über die polizeilichen Maßnahmen vom 11. Bis 15.4.1968 anläßlich der Aktionen der "außerparlamentarischen Opposition" in Zusammenhang mit den Schüssen auf Rudi Dutschke*, p. 2, file 106, Aktenauszüge Ostern 68, Aktenbestand des Sozialistischen Anwaltskollektivs, HIfS. This is a detailed 32-page police report on the weekend's events, starting with the shooting itself.

15. 'Er machte Hitler und Napoleon und schoß auf Rudi Dutschke', *Bild-Zeitung*, 13 April 1968, p. 1.

and admitted he had merely been trying to protect Springer from blame. He told the court, 'I have taken my daily information from the *Bild-Zeitung*' and felt that *Bild-Zeitung* reflected not just his views and but also 'what the masses think'. He continued 'very many are of my opinion. Or more correctly: I am of their opinion. That is better.' He shot Dutschke because he felt it was what *Bild*, and therefore the readers who sympathized with its pronouncements, wanted.[16]

In a bizarre exchange of letters between Bachmann and Dutschke just before the trial, the former again made constant reference to the wishes of others, usually in terms of abstract, generalized social groupings. He felt West Germany was so wealthy that he could not understand 'why there are demonstrations, against what are they demonstrating, why do they want our workers and our current system to play into the hands of the criminal Ulbricht and his comrades [*sic*]'. For this reason 'it is no wonder that I have directed my hatred at whatever is Bolshevist and Communist'. He understood that Dutschke and his allies felt they wanted a better system, but asked what this system would be and how it would be brought about, saying 'so long as things go well with the people . . . it is terrible to aim for something better'.[17] Bachmann felt he was acting in West Germany's interests and according to others' wishes in defence of democracy in the *Bundesrepublik*.

The shooting provoked the most violent protests yet seen. It was clear from the first that it was impossible to point to a direct state conspiracy: Bachmann was working alone and had been shot by police. Instead the Springer empire was the most obvious target for protesters: Göttingen University AStA asked 'what has Springer to do with the assassination attempt on Rudi Dutschke?' and answered that for years the Springer titles had 'systematically incited the people against the students'. Quoting a *Bild* article from February as saying 'one should not let the police and their water cannon do all the dirty work', the Göttingen students cut astutely to the heart of Bachmann's thinking: 'in the person of Josef Erwin Bachmann, Springer's demands have found their executor'.[18] Protesters were therefore called upon to blockade Springer offices and printing plants across West Germany, a tactic that necessarily prompted police intervention, and unsurprisingly led to widespread violence.

16. Quoted in '"Siebzig prozent reiben sich die Hände"', *Der Spiegel*, 10 March 1969, p. 78.

17. Letter from Josef Bachmann to Rudi Dutschke, dated 15.1.69, file 48, Dutschke % Bachmann, Diverse Dokumentation, Dokumentation III (Ostern 1968), Aktenbestand des Sozialistischen Anwaltskollektivs, HIfS. This is the original hand-written copy.

18. *Warum gegen Springer?*, Sammlung Schwiedrzik zur Studentenbewegung, ZSg 153/16, BK.

On the day after the shooting, Good Friday, Easter marches were quickly transformed into protests about the *Dutschke Attentat* (Dutschke assassination attempt). It is crucial to note that for the first day or so after the shooting protesters were under the impression that Dutschke was dead, and even when this was contradicted, his life remained in the balance for some time. Starting with skirmishes on 11 April, and building in size and violence as the weekend progressed, the various protests attracted huge support: Wolfgang Kraushaar estimates that 300,000 people participated in the Easter marches over the weekend, the largest figure achieved for demonstrations in West Germany in the 1960s.[19] Once again Berlin was the centre of the maelstrom and is worth looking at in detail as an exemplar of the prevailing polarization and intolerance. On the evening of 11 April a mass meeting at the TU placed the blame for the shooting squarely on the Springer newspapers, declaring them 'murderers', before deciding to hold a blockade of the Springer offices.[20] Around 500 people, many of them carrying red flags, then made their way through the city to the Springer offices on Kochstrasse, yards away from Check Point Charlie, where 2,000 to 3,000 people eventually assembled.[21] Missiles were thrown at the building amid choruses of 'Springer murderers' and 'Springer burn'. Police deployed two water cannon and used truncheons to break up the crowd, which had succeeded in blockading the entrance to the building, leading to a car park. Some protesters, led by Bernd Rabehl, charged the police line and succeeded, albeit temporarily, in storming the building, a pro-active and provocative action that was in sharp contrast to previous passive resistance. By 11.00 p.m. the car park was on fire, possibly as a result of molotov cocktails, or protesters setting light to cars. There can be little doubt that both sides actively engaged in violence, whether against people or against property. Photographer Konrad Giehr later told the police, 'I saw a person stood in the entrance [to the car park] preventing the fire service driving any further. I saw how another demonstrator smashed the window of a fire truck with a pole.'[22] Heinz Sadowski, in

19. Kraushaar, *1968: Das Jahr*, p. 108.

20. Eyewitness statement by Dieter Discher, file 106, Aktenauszüge Ostern 68, Aktenbestand des Sozialistischen Anwaltskollektivs, HIfS. Discher was a reporter for the *Berliner Morgenpost* who attended the meeting along with a number of other press representatives.

21. *Auszüge aus Erlebnisberichten eingesetzter Polizeieinheiten und einzelner Beamter*, p. 1, file 106, Aktenauszüge Ostern 68, Aktenbestand des Sozialistischen Anwaltskollektivs, HIfS, is another detailed police report that insists truncheons and water cannon were only used in self-defence after police lines were attacked. There may have been some truth to this, although once deployed police seem to have used them randomly.

22. Eyewitness statement by Georg Karl Konrad Giehr, file 106, Aktenauszüge Ostern 68, Aktenbestand des Sozialistischen Anwaltskollektivs, HIfS.

charge of the transportation of newspapers from the building recalled 'around 10.15 a number of demonstrators blocked the exit of the Kochstrasse car park with their cars, in which our distribution wagons stood. Of the 63 wagons 11 could not be dispatched in safety. Five of these wagons were set on fire during the evening by unknown culprits and completely burnt out.'[23] On the other hand, two protesters were run down by delivery wagons attempting to break out of the compound.

The following day protests took place throughout the city. A march by around 2,000 people in the afternoon quickly turned into a brawl on the Kurfürstendamm that created a scene described by *Bild* with justification as 'a battlefield'.[24] Demonstrators with stones and poles from placards clashed with truncheon-wielding police who also had the support of water cannon, and the violence continued throughout the day as the march moved through the city. The attempted blockade of the Springer offices in the evening produced even greater levels of violence. By around 10.45 p.m. demonstrators had succeeded in blocking the streets around the Springer building with perhaps as many as 500 vehicles. Police who tried to move protesters came under a hail of missiles, and one delivery wagon that managed to get outside the building was set alight. When the fire service arrived to try to remove the cars, protesters held a sit-down strike in the street. Over loudspeakers the police demanded that they move, and when they refused the police dragged them away. The police then told the car drivers to move their cars, which some did. Those cars that remained were rammed by fire trucks and often damaged beyond repair, while police again made use of truncheons and water cannon to clear the area of protesters who were again attempting to storm the building. The ferocious battle continued into the early hours of the morning and however much press reports blamed protesters for the violence, it was clearly not one-sided. Christa Boese, a secretary at the FU Berlin, reported 'police from the cordon in front of the entrance to the Springer building grabbed a demonstrator, beat him brutally (for instance heavy blows with truncheons on the shins) before throwing him into a police car. When I asked after his service number, a police officer fell on me with raised truncheon. Demonstrators who were fleeing were hit indiscriminately.'[25]

23. Eyewitness statement by Heinz Sadowski, file 106, Aktenauszüge Ostern 68, Aktenbestand des Sozialistischen Anwaltskollektivs, HIfS.

24. 'Ku'damm wurde zum Schlachtfeld', *Bild*, 13 April 1968, p. 6, Sammlung Schwiedrzik zur Studentenbewegung, ZSg/153/31, BK.

25. Statement by Christa Boese, file 48, Dutschke % Bachmann, Diverse Dokumentation, Dokumentation III (Ostern 1968), Aktenbestand des Sozialistischen Anwaltskollektivs, HIfS.

The following day, Saturday 13 April, protesters held a series of mass meetings at the TU Berlin. Speeches embraced the use of violence and Ulrike Meinhof's comment 'when a Springer car burns, that is arson, when all Springer cars burn, that is a political action' is of particular interest.[26] An SDS 'functionary' was quoted by *Bild* on the same day as saying 'Berlin must burn like the slums in American cities', a reference to the riots that had followed King's death.[27] From around 4.00 p.m. approximately 2,000 people assembled on several junctions of the Kurfürstendamm, clogging up the traffic, and prompting another massive police deployment accompanied by truncheons and water cannon: on this one day alone 12,200 litres of water were sprayed at demonstrators.[28] During the running battles 277 people were arrested, included Fritz Teufel and Willy Brandt's son Peter. Many protesters had come prepared for a physical confrontation, and the police made much of the fact that among the debris left behind after the clashes were a pistol complete with ammunition, a cudgel, a knuckleduster and a knife.[29] On the afternoon of the next day, Easter Sunday, the KfDA held its planned mass meeting on Wittenbergplatz which, along with the subsequent march down the Kurfürstendamm was attended by around 3,000 people. Once again the protesters blocked the road and the police used both water cannon and horses to break up a demonstration that had essentially been peaceful. The fact that the demonstration would block traffic had been entirely predictable when the police gave permission for it, but on the day itself this was used as justification for dispersing the protesters by force.

In many ways the events in Berlin were the tip of the iceberg. Large, sustained and violent protests took place throughout the weekend in at least 20 cities, with barricades being constructed outside Springer plants and offices in Hamburg, Essen, Esslingen, Frankfurt, Cologne and Munich. In all cities where blockades took place events followed a similar pattern: police cordoned off the Springer buildings, demanded that demonstrators disperse, and when they failed to do so used truncheons, water cannon and sometimes even horses and dogs to break up the protest. In every instance this meant indiscriminate and widespread violence that went beyond any claims of self-defence and which often included innocent bystanders,

26. Quoted in the eyewitness statement by Dieter Discher, file 106, Aktenauszüge Ostern 68, Aktenbestand des Sozialistischen Anwaltskollektivs, HIfS.

27. 'Zietungswagen in Flammen', *Bild*, 13 April 1968, p. 5, Sammlung Schwiedrzik zur Studentenbewegung, ZSg 153/31, BK.

28. Quoted in "Vor dem Knüppel sind alle gleich", *Der Spiegel*, 29 April 1968, p. 38. This figure was taken from a police report.

29. *Verlaufs- und Erfahrungsbericht der Schutzpolizei*, p. 8.

although it cannot be denied that some protesters arrived armed and prepared for violence, and that some actively sought it out. Above all, in Munich the violence claimed two lives. Surprisingly there has been very little coverage of these deaths in previous accounts of the Dutschke *Attentat* protests, despite the controversy surrounding them. This is a mistake, because the deaths, perhaps more than any other event of the Easter weekend, confirmed preconceptions for both sides.

In violent demonstrations over the weekend the *Bild* offices in Munich were smashed up and barricades were constructed.[30] Demonstrators re-assembled outside the Springer offices on the evening of Easter Monday, shouting 'Springer murderer' and 'yesterday Dutschke, tomorrow us' in chorus.[31] Approximately 1,000 police had used barriers to seal off the entrance on Barerstrasse in Schwabing and demanded that the crowd disperse. Events followed their familiar course when the protesters remained where they were, and the police fell on them with truncheons. Stones, bottles, and wooden poles were thrown and the police lashed out at random. In quick succession, at around 9.15 p.m., 32-year-old Associated Press photo journalist Klaus Frings and Economics student Rüdiger Schreck, aged 27, received fatal blows to their heads.

The battle spread to surrounding streets as groups of students, some carrying wooden poles or even steel bars from nearby building sites, broke and ran. Missiles continued to rain down, and fires broke out in several locations. In Schellingstrasse, just to the north of the TU, Ilona Drumm, a bystander, was attacked by a policeman who 'grabbed me by the hair, lifted me up and flung me over the people sitting in front of me, so that I landed on the street. Then I was – always by the hair – dragged through the line of riot police. From these I received a number of kicks in the side and the back.' When she was released the next day she found that the officer had pulled out a five-centimetre-long and two-centimetre-wide strip of hair from her head.[32] Protesters accused the police of using phrases such as 'communist pig', 'go back to Vietnam' or 'feel our strength you red pig'. One demonstrator was alleged to have said to a policeman 'it would be best if you put us straight into KZs [concentration camps] and

30. 'Demonstranten und Ordnungshüter ziehen Bilanz', *Süddeutsche Zeitung*, 29 April, p. 3, and 'Die Ereignisse der Ostertage', *Münchener Studenten Zeitung, Extra-Blatt, Sondernummer*, 2 May 1968, p. 1, both Sammlung Schlemper, ED 328/31, IfZM.

31. Quoted in 'Unruhen: Todesopfer', *Der Spiegel*, 29 April 1968, p. 77 and statement by Peter Hamm in *Dokumentation über die Demonstrationen in München, Ostern 1968, Heft I, Juni 1968*, p. 11, Broschure D1144, BfZS. This latter is a large collection of evidence in the Frings and Schreck cases, produced by *Rechtshilfe der APO München*.

32. Quoted in "Wir sind in einer Falle", *Der Spiegel*, 29 April 1968, p. 59.

gassed us'. This officer replied 'we should do that with you'.[33] The police did not regain control of the area until after midnight, by which time 110 demonstrators had been arrested and seven officers had been injured. Frings only regained consciousness once and died on Wednesday 17 April. Schreck died later the same day, after which mortified students held a memorial service on Königsplatz.

According to protesters Schreck had been struck by a wooden pole thrown by police when they destroyed barricades constructed from builder's material. *Rechtshilfe der APO München* (Legal Aid for the APO in Munich) produced witnesses who had seen the police throwing both stones and wooden poles at the crowds. One witness who gave evidence stated that when the barricade was stormed 'one of the riot police grabbed one of these poles – it was about 50 to 60 cm long – and threw it at this group [of protesters]. A demonstrator, who was dressed in a dark jacket and had his back to me, was hit by it and fell backward onto the road between the curb and the middle of the street.'[34] The doctor who treated Schreck stated that he could have been hit by either a wooden club or a truncheon.[35] Frings, they alleged, was hit by a stone thrown by police officers. Reiner Korbmann, a photographer who knew Frings, was stood just behind him when he was hit, and was the only witness produced by *Rechtshilfe* who actually saw what happened. Strangely, his evidence seems to undermine their position since the direction in which Frings's head recoiled upon impact meant the missile could have come from the police or, perhaps more probably, from the protesters.[36] In response the Criminal Director of the Police Presidium, Hermann Haering, insisted 'it is totally out of the question that Schreck was struck by a police officer' because officers had strict instructions only to use truncheons in self-defence and it was unthinkable that they would disobey. Instead the police pursued 'eyewitness reports' that a dark-haired young man with a beard had thrown the stone at Frings and that a 23-to-25-year-old dark-haired man with a brown jacket had hit Schreck with a wooden pole. Neither of these people was ever identified as the culprit, and no one was ever charged, despite a 17,000 DM reward.[37] Sympathies in the press were given overwhelmingly to the police interpretation. *Bild*, in a representative article, placed the blame for deaths squarely on protesters,

33. *Dokumentation über die Demonstrationen in München*, pp. 17–18. The document reproduces long and detailed accusations of police brutality from dozens of witnesses.

34. Ibid., p. 26a.

35. 'Steinwurf oder Gummiknüppel?', *Bild*, 19 April 1968, file Zeitungen April 1968, Aktenbestand des Sozialistischen Anwaltskollektivs, HIfS.

36. *Dokumentation über die Demonstrationen in München*, p. 23.

37. All quoted in 'Unruhen: Todesopfer', *Der Spiegel*, 29 April 1968, p. 77.

concluding 'despite the deaths small radical groups are still of the view: violence must be'.[38]

The numerous statistics of the weekend's events are instructive in showing the extremes to which both police and protesters were now willing to go. In total 21,000 police were deployed around the country to deal with demonstrations, and there were at least 400 injuries to police, protesters and bystanders, as well as the two deaths.[39] Springer property worth 250,000 DM was damaged or destroyed, including more than 100,000 DM worth of window panes.[40] In a special *Bundestag* debate, Interior Minister, Ernst Benda stated that police inquiries were being pursued against 827 people, of whom 286 were students, 92 were school pupils, 185 were public employees, and 150 were workers.[41] In Berlin alone 389 people had been arrested, 122 of whom were students, with 232 people from 'other trades'. Significantly, 346 of these people, the vast majority, were between 14 and 29 years of age. Among the 10,000 police officers deployed in Berlin, 63 had been injured, and 48 vehicles had been damaged or destroyed at a cost of 22,000 DM.[42] More than 200 demonstrators and bystanders were injured in Berlin during the weekend, although it is impossible to provide exact figures and the real number was probably much higher.[43] Benda estimated there had been demonstrations in 27 cities, in 26 of which there had been violence and law-breaking of various kinds.[44] These statistics, with all the human dramas that went with them, were the product of the largest, most widespread, and most violent protests in West Germany since the inter-war period; *Kristallnacht* in 1938 was probably the last event of an equivalent scale, although with very different aims.

The response from the press, the state and the general public, although conforming to previous trends, was perhaps even more outspoken in its opposition than ever before. A poisonous hate-filled atmosphere, marked by a lack of restraint by both sides, now left little room for moderation. Far from taking on board the arguments of the protesters about the Springer hate campaign against Dutschke, the press in general, and particularly the Springer titles, saw the events of Easter 1968 as yet more confirmation of

---

38. 'Gewalt muß sein!', *Bild*, 20 April 1968, file Zeitungen April 1968, Aktenbestand des Sozialistischen Anwaltskollektivs, HIfS.

39. 'Aufruhr: Studenten', *Der Spiegel*, 22 April 1968, p. 25.

40. 'Versicherungen: Demonstrations-schäden', *Der Spiegel*, 29 April 1968, p. 68.

41. Quoted in Kraushaar, *1968: Das Jahr*, p. 119.

42. *Auszüge aus Erlebnisberichten eingesetzter Polizeieinheiten und einzelner Beamter, Anlage 2, Zahlen und Statistiken*, pp. 2–3.

43. Quoted in 'Aufruhr: Studenten', *Der Spiegel*, 22 April 1968, p. 27.

44. Quoted in Langguth, *Die Protestbewegung*, p. 45.

their fears about the demonstrators and their intentions. Referring to the attacks on Springer buildings, *Bild* asked 'is that a demonstration? Is that discussion?' and answered the questions by calling the violence a 'naked destructive frenzy'. Above all it followed the standard Springer line by attempting to discredit protesters who 'want to destroy our whole society's order'.[45] *Die Welt* claimed the state was under attack 'from provocateurs, who declare that the laws of parliamentary democracy do not apply to them' and asked the main political parties to give reassurances that 'we will not be taken back to what happened in the Weimar Republic'.[46] As early as 12 April Springer brought charges against Horst Mahler for trespass and breach of peace, arguing that Mahler had been the ringleader of the attempt to blockade the Springer offices in Berlin and had incited the crowds to violence.[47]

The ramifications of the shooting for West German democracy were not lost on politicians, and initial responses to it, before the riots, were unusually contrite. Chancellor Kiesinger, hardly a supporter of the protesters, sent a telegram to Dutschke's wife on 11 April telling her 'I am deeply outraged by the assassination attempt on your husband. Whatever differences of political opinion separate us Germans, it cannot be the case in our country that they are settled through brutal violence.' He continued 'I hope from my heart that your husband will make a full recovery from his injuries.'[48] This was in contrast to his television broadcast on 13 April in which he warned ominously that the riots were the work of 'militant Left extremist powers, who have openly set about destroying our parliamentary democratic order' and would force 'a strengthening of the means for protecting the state'.[49] On 14 April Gustav Heinemann, the Federal Minister for Justice, and a rare calming voice of tolerance and mediation, made a television and radio speech in which he asked all sides, including the police and the demonstrators, to uphold the freedoms enshrined in the Basic Law. He reflected 'we must all ask ourselves what we contribution

---

45. 'Ist das Demonstration? Ist das Diskussion?', *Bild*, 16 April 1968, p. 1, Sammlung Schwiedrzik zur Studentenbewegung, ZSg 153/31, BK.

46. Georg Schröder, 'Die Standfestigkeit wird geprüft', *Die Welt*, 17 April 1968, file Zeitungen April 1968, Aktenbestand des Sozialistischen Anwaltskollektivs, HIfS.

47. See letter from Axel Springer & Sohn, Ullstein GmBH, Verlagshaus Berlin to the Generalstaatsanwaltschaft beim Landgericht Berlin, dated 12.4.1968, File 106, Aktenauszüge Ostern 68, Aktenbestand des Sozialistischen Anwaltskollektivs, HIfS.

48. Quoted in *Das Attentat auf Rudi Dutschke, Demonstrationen gegen den Springer Konzern: Dokumente, Herausgegeben vom Verband Deutscher Studentenschaften, Bonn, den 15. April 1968*, B/166/1311, BK.

49. '13. April 1968, Warnung an Gewalttäter: Fernseherklärung zu den Studentenunruhen, Bonn', quoted in full in Kiesinger, K.G., *Die Große Koalition 1966–1969*.

we could have made in the recent past to heighten anti-communism into attempted murder'.[50]

It soon became clear that Heinemann was expressing the views of a small minority. Berlin mayor Klaus Schütz ignored evidence that police had behaved with particular brutality in Berlin by thanking them because

> they have, when necessary, intervened hard and without hesitation, and not seldom they have been hindered by their circumspection. Whoever has looked and listened at how our officers were attacked and provoked, can not do anything else but express their esteem and respect.[51]

Interior Minister Benda even mooted the possibility of banning the SDS, having come to the conclusion that it was an 'anti-constitutional organization'.[52] He soon rejected this move during the special *Bundestag* debate on the Easter events on 30 April, deciding instead to monitor the SDS via the authorities responsible for defending the constitution.

Public opinion differed slightly, not in its overwhelming opposition to the protests but in its emphasis upon fears of a return to the chaos of the Weimar years, along with a conspicuous absence of concern about the Nazi past among opponents of the riots. In a representative letter Erna Graf from Berlin wrote to the *Telegraf* with the question 'do the students and the groups of the Extra-parliamentary Opposition want it to be the same as it was before 1933 again, where one could use truncheons and bullets against those who were not of the same opinion?'[53] Approval of the protests and concern at the behaviour of the police was a minority view-point: a *Der Spiegel* survey found that 92 per cent of Berliners disapproved of 'the use of violence by students'. The survey showed a genuine division in opinion between generations, with 67 per of over-50s, and 63 per cent of those between 30 and 50, disapproving of the protests in general, compared with 46 per cent of 16-to-30-year-olds. Indeed in this latter age group 50 per cent approved of the protests. A less distinct division occurred over the police actions, although the majority in all age groups approved of the measures used. Although 31 per cent of 16-to-30-year-olds felt the

50. *Abschrift: Fernsehsprache des Bundesministers der Justiz Herrn Dr Dr Gustav Heinemann,* B/166/1311, BK. This transcript was produced by the VDS.

51. "Vor dem Knüppel sind alle gleich", *Der Spiegel,* 29 April 1968, pp. 42–5.

52. 'Bonn: kein SDS verbot', *Der Abend,* 23 April 1968, file Zeitungen April 1968, Aktenbestand des Sozialistischen Anwaltskollektivs, HIfS.

53. 'Protest', *Telegraf,* 28 April 1968, p. 32, file Zeitungen April 1968, Aktenbestand des Sozialistischen Anwaltskollektivs, HIfS. Note that she says nothing against the post-1933 period.

police tactics were too harsh, only 14 per cent of 30-to-50-year-olds, and a mere 12 per cent of the over-50s agreed.[54] The measured judgement, composure and tolerance that might have dampened the flames were simply not welcome in this political environment, leaving black-and-white judgements, frustration and worsening violence as the natural responses for both sides.

Moderate opinion did exist but it was soon drowned out or alienated. The FU Berlin RCDS was an unlikely source of equanimity in the face of so much hysterical ranting, but it welcomed the protests against Springer while distancing itself from the use of violence.[55] The Munich University AStA issued a statement saying it 'sharply disapproved' of the 'uncontrolled actions of fanatical students and youths as a reaction to the insane attack on Dutschke', and in an act of public penitence the Munich LSD group declared itself 'answerable for the deaths of two people' while arguing in support of peaceful demonstrations, whether free from violent demonstrators or police for whom 'political demonstrators are seen as criminals'.[56] Such pronouncements were usually overshadowed by statements from the Left, which newspapers seized upon as proof of diabolical communist intentions. Horst Mahler's role in a debate on political violence at the TU Berlin on 17 April caused particular indignation. Presaging his future political career he said 'we want no agitation with peaceful methods', and on the deaths he felt 'we must reckon on such accidents from the start. There is no point in making humanitarian arguments.'[57]

Even more strikingly, Ulrike Meinhof, in a much-quoted watershed article entitled 'From Protest to Resistance', publicly expressed a change in her outlook. Having already moved incrementally toward a position where she questioned the validity of legal forms of protest, she now gave warning that during the Easter demonstrations 'the boundaries between protest and resistance were exceeded'. She acknowledged that the violence had been largely ineffective and that 'power relationships were not changed'. She also felt 'counter-violence' by protesters against the violence employed by the state would only turn shocked liberals against the APO and prompt yet more police violence. In turn 'the paramilitary

54. 'Was denken die Berliner über die Studenten?, *Der Spiegel*, 22 April 1968, p. 28.

55. *Politische Beirat des RCDS, Berlin, den 27. April 1968: Thesen zur Situation nach dem Attentat auf Rudi Dutschke*, Berlin file 03798, BfZS.

56. 'Zeugenvernehmen über den Tod des Studenten Rüdiger Schreck', *Tagesspiegel*, 20 April 1968, and 'Wir tragen Mitverantwortung', *Münchner Merkur*, 19. April 1968, both file Zeitungen April 1968, Aktenbestand des Sozialistischen Anwaltskollektivs, HIfS.

57. 'Wie wenn ich mich in ein Autos setze', *Die Welt*, 19 April 1968, file Zeitungen April 1968, Aktenbestand des Sozialistischen Anwaltskollektivs, HIfS.

deployment of the police will be answered with paramilitary methods'. For Meinhof the expropriation of the Springer empire was the only way to defuse the situation.[58] Meinhof did not explicitly reject peaceful protest in the article. Rather than simply representing a prediction, it can only be read as a threat that the state would force protesters to resort to terrorism.

Meinhof's demand for the destruction of the Springer empire by the state was never translated into reality. At the end of May the Federal Cartel Office declared that the size of the Springer organization was putting the press freedom guaranteed by the Basic Law at risk, but this was the result of a long-term investigation that predated the Easter events. It was found that Springer publications controlled twice the amount of the market as was deemed consistent with a free press.[59] There then followed one of many unsuccessful state attempts to challenge the Springer stranglehold on newspaper sales by breaking it up. A survey on public attitudes to Springer published in July is particularly interesting in showing the limited impact of the protests. This found that while only 22 per cent of people had a bad opinion of Springer, the same percentage had a good opinion of him. Only 10 per cent of those asked supported the break-up of the Springer group, and 49 per cent opposed it. Those who had never heard either of Springer or of the campaign against him accounted for 32 per cent of those questioned. Asked whether Springer had too much power, 34 per cent agreed that he had, and 28 per cent disagreed.[60] Far from being seen as a threat to democracy, Springer clearly enjoyed both popular support and widespread sympathy for his views.

If the ordeal and aftermath of Easter 1968 was fairly short-lived for the Springer group, this was not the case for Rudi Dutschke. At first his recovery was painfully slow: starting with the names of his immediate family he had to learn everything afresh while coping with the damage to his body and brain. After these early stages his recovery gathered pace, and within six weeks of the shooting he was already reading Marx.[61] After another operation to replace a piece of his skull that had been removed when he was shot, he left hospital in the middle of June. The following March, with Dutschke well on the way to recovery, Bachmann was convicted of attempted murder and sentenced to seven years in prison. He committed suicide in prison during the night of 23 to 24 February 1970.

58. Meinhof, U.M., 'Vom Protest zum Widerstand', *Konkret*, May 1968, p. 5.

59. 'Presse: Springer-Verkauf', *Der Spiegel*, 1 July 1968, p. 52.

60. 'Meinung: Springer-Umfrage', *Der Spiegel*, 15 July 1968, p. 30.

61. Dutschke, G., *Rudi Dutschke*, pp. 200–2 is a personal account of the early days of his recovery by Dutschke's wife.

After the shooting Dutschke was both physically and mentally scarred and, according to his wife, 'he saw the world with different eyes'.[62] Preferring to concentrate on his doctoral studies, and spending long periods abroad, notably in Denmark and Britain, he was never again the political figure, either on the Left or on the national stage, which he had been. He continued to be a demonic figure for the press even on the fringes of politics, although he did play a role in the creation of the environmental movement in the late 1970s. While he never returned to full health, he did recover sufficiently to complete his doctoral dissertation in 1974. The damage done to his body ultimately proved too great, however, and he eventually succumbed to his injuries, dying on Christmas Eve 1979 aged 39.

62. Ibid., p. 205.

–10–

Conspiracies and Counter-conspiracies?

A few weeks after the death of Benno Ohnesorg, Chancellor Kiesinger told the Federal Parliament 'the unrest among German students is a problem that deserves the greatest attention. It will not be solved with declarations or official measures'.[1] This short statement raises many of the conspiracy fears held by protesters: many on the Left believed that 'unofficial' measures were already being taken against them and against democracy, whether a secret state-sponsored policy of shooting demonstrators, a deliberate undermining of the legal system, the placing of Nazis in positions of power, or the ominous threat of the Emergency Laws. Such concerns continued in the period after Ohnesorg's death and were expanded upon by the legal persecution of *Kommune I* members and the Grand Coalition's continued determination to pass the *Notstandsgesetze*. Of course their opponents had their own deep-seated belief in conspiracies to destroy the *Bundesrepublik*. It is essential to note that by 1967 the press and television headlines were often dominated by the unrest, with an almost continuous stream of stories about some new protest or outrage to public sensibilities. Nearly every day there was a new demonstration, go-in, sit-in, or march. It should also not be forgotten that these events were also played out against a background of rapid and far-reaching social change that left many people confused and anxious for the future.

In this context the legal measures used against *Kommune I* members raised questions for both sides. For the public and the state authorities, the behaviour of *Kommune I* members during trials and protests, as well as their daily lifestyles, openly mocked authority and rejected established norms of behaviour. For protesters, on the other hand, the persecution of *Kommune I* by legal means exposed a biased justice system that was being used as a tool with which to silence dissent. In the period immediately following the Ohnesorg shooting, state measures against *Kommune I* centred on charges against Fritz Teufel and Rainer Langhans. Teufel was arrested on 2 June for throwing stones during the demonstrations at the Deutsche

---

1. 'Diese Unruhe ist ein Problem', *BZ*, 22 June 1967, Rep B 014/1024, LB.

Oper and 'on account of the compelling suspicion that he will commit this crime again, and on account of the risk of attempted escape' it was decided that he should remain in police custody.[2] He languished in prison, with short breaks, until the following March. A few days later charges were brought against both Teufel and Langhans for 'incitement to commit life-threatening arson' in the 'Burn, warehouse, burn' flyers they had distributed at the FU Berlin in May.

Both sets of charges proved to be controversial from the first, and allowed *Kommune I* to grab front-page headlines repeatedly over subsequent months. The trial on the arson charges, the *Flugblatt* (flyer) trial, began in Berlin on 6 July. It immediately descended into farce as both defendants refused to take the prosecution seriously and used the trial to provoke and laugh at the legal system while making political statements about Vietnam. Teufel insisted 'we did not want to commit the aggressive acts we are accused of, but only to call for the moral outrage of self-satisfied citizens through provocative acts'.[3] The trial gave them another chance to do just that. Wearing jeans and sandals, and sporting abundant long hair, as well a bushy Ginsberg-like beard in Teufel's case, their mocking, openly political, and provocative responses were a new experience for the Berlin courts. Faced with such eccentricity the judge suspended the trial while the defendants were sent for psychological analysis.

Teufel remained in prison, of course, and over the summer his case developed into a cause célèbre. Not only was he being kept in prison indefinitely on dubious grounds, but the case against him for throwing stones was based upon flimsy evidence that prompted suspicions of an attempt to frame him. Teufel's brother Alfred wrote to *Der Spiegel* in July saying he believed the state was trying to 'establish an example' and noted that while his brother languished in prison 'Herr *Kriminalobermeister* Kurras now sits in his favourite bar with a beer.'[4] At first glance the case against Teufel seemed straightforward. It was alleged that on 2 June Teufel was on Krumme Strasse when 'he drew his arm far back and hurled an object in the direction of the police officers, that, according to the account of the witnesses, *Polizeioberwachtmeisters* [Dieter] Heßler and [Peter] Mertin, was a stone'.[5] Both officers stated categorically that they had 'seen that the

2. *Beschluß*, dated 7 July 1967, file 66, Kommune I III Landesfriedensbruch Band 1, Aktenbestand des Sozialistischen Anwaltskollektivs, HIfS.

3. Quoted in 'Provokation oder Aufruf zur Brandstiftung?', *Stuttgarter Zeitung*, 7 July 1967, p. 2.

4. *Der Spiegel*, 10 July 1967, p. 10.

5. *Anklageschrift*, 13 July 1967, p. 7, file 66, Kommune I III Landesfriedensbruch Band 1, Aktenbestand des Sozialistischen Anwaltskollektivs, HIfS. This is the detailed description of the charges against Teufel produced by the Prosecutor.

above-named Teufel also threw a stone himself'.[6] According to Heßler a fellow officer, Helmut Heilscher, had been seriously injured by a stone at this time, although he could not say whether this had been thrown by Teufel.

The case was not as routine as initial appearances suggested. Heßler and Mertin's statements contradicted each other in crucial areas and often bore little resemblance to the facts of the demonstration. On 19 June these officers gave evidence to the State Prosecutor in which, according to Teufel's lawyer Horst Mahler, they 'described a crime scene that either never happened or in which Fritz Teufel certainty never participated'.[7] Heßler stated categorically that Teufel 'was one of the throwers' and flatly rejected claims that Teufel was assaulted by officers during and after his arrest.[8] Mertin was even able to describe the missile thrown by Teufel as 'a small paving stone'.[9] Despite the fact that on 21 June there were 24 witnesses presented to the State Prosecutor refuting the testimony of the two officers, Teufel was not released. Instead bail was set at the prohibitively high level of 10,000 DM. The *Oberbaum Blatt*, a left-wing Berlin weekly, in a characteristic example of the questions that were being asked about the state's motivations, queried the decision to press charges against only two of the many people involved in distributing the flyers. Further, it asked 'why does the Prosecutor assume a risk of escape by Fritz Teufel, but not by the Persians who attacked and injured the demonstrators with cudgels and poles in unison and so committed serious breach of the peace?' An arguably more serious question was whether 'the Prosecutor is clear on the inevitable political consequences should it be established that Fritz Teufel has been detained for a month on the basis of false accusations by the police?'[10] In the circumstances it was difficult for the Left not to conclude that Teufel was the subject of a state conspiracy of persecution, whether against him or against the Left in general.

6. Statement by Dieter Heßler, 2 June 1967, and statement by Peter Mertin, 2 June 1967, both file 67, Kommune I III Landesfriedensbruch Band 2, Aktenbestand des Sozialistischen Anwaltskollektivs, HIfS.

7. Erklärung zum Fall Fritz Teufel, 25.6.67, file 66, Kommune I III Landesfriedensbruch Band 1, Aktenbestand des Sozialistischen Anwaltskollektivs, HIfS.

8. Interview with Dieter Heßler on 19 June 1967, file 67, Kommune I III Landesfriedensbruch Band 2, Aktenbestand des Sozialistischen Anwaltskollektivs, HIfS. This document gives a transcript of Heßler's testimony.

9. Interview with Peter Mertin on 19 June 1967, file 67, Kommune I III Landesfriedensbruch Band 2, Aktenbestand des Sozialistischen Anwaltskollektivs, HIfS. This is also a transcript of the testimony.

10. 'Fragen zum Fall Fritz Teufel', *Oberbaum Blatt*, 5 July 1967, A–ZO 1507, HIfS.

In response a much publicized 'freedom for Teufel' campaign was launched within days of his imprisonment. On 19 June Teufel went on a short-lived hunger strike to protest against his imprisonment and Mahler produced a 25-page document questioning almost every aspect of the police statements.[11] The officers had said, for instance, that the stone had been thrown at 7.45 p.m., after the police clearing action, when in fact the clearing action had not even started until 8.00 p.m. Helmut Heilscher was not injured until 8.10 p.m. The statements included serious inaccuracies that were shown to be incorrect through photographic and eyewitness evidence, suggesting the officers were either making up their accusations or that they were exceptionally poor witnesses. By mid-July Mahler had even applied to the newly created European Human Rights Commission for intervention in Teufel's case in an attempt to get him released, and later in the year Amnesty International (founded in 1962), also looked into the case.[12]

Such international support was also evident in the reaction from protesters. A document was signed by AStA's from across West Germany, as well as student organizations in France (UNEF), Switzerland, Belgium and Holland, demanding Teufel's immediate release. This described the case as a 'political misuse of justice' and lamented that 'once again in Germany the dismantling of the constitutional state is beginning'.[13] Student representatives from these countries took part in a demonstration outside the Gedächtniskirche in Berlin at the beginning of August in which each held a placard bearing a letter, so spelling out the phrase 'Freiheit für Teufel'. The campaign was so widespread that *Die Welt* complained 'not a day passes in which a political organization doesn't demand the Teufel's [the Devil's] release'.[14] Teufel remained a hate figure for the press, who could not forgive his lifestyle, the way he looked, or their humiliation after the *Pudding Bomben Attentat*, but by this point even Springer titles were expressing concern. *BZ* questioned the need to keep Teufel in

---

11. Letter to Landgericht Berlin, 26 July 1967, file 66, Kommune I III Landesfriedensbruch Band 1, Aktenbestand des Sozialistischen Anwaltskollektivs, HIfS.

12. 'Schwere Vorwürfe gegen Berliner Justiz', *Abendzeitung*, 13 July 1967, p. 2; letter from Christel Marsh of Amnesty International to Horst Mahler, 28 November 1967, file 66, Kommune I III Landesfriedensbruch Band 1, Aktenbestand des Sozialistischen Anwaltskollektivs, HIfS.

13. *Westeuropäische Studenten fordern Freiheit für Teufel*, file 66, Kommune I III Landesfriedensbruch Band 1, Aktenbestand des Sozialistischen Anwaltskollektivs, HIfS.

14. 'Studenten fordern Rücktritt des Justizsenators', *Die Welt*, 2 August 1968, file 66, Kommune I III Landesfriedensbruch Band 1, Aktenbestand des Sozialistischen Anwaltskollektivs, HIfS. The headline refers to demands that the Berlin Justice Senator, Hans Günter Hoppe (FDP), resign over the Teufel affair.

prison, arguing he was 'perhaps a muddle-head. But he is certainly not a professional criminal who puts the lives and limbs of citizens at risk.' The idea that Teufel might escape was treated with scorn since 'he and his commune friends have proved through countless provocations and self-denunciations that they are interested in nothing more than a public trial. They yearn to assemble for their great show in court. Why would Teufel flee?'[15]

The case was becoming an embarrassment for the Berlin legal authorities, and so on 10 August Teufel was released. In return he was to give up his identification papers and report to a police station twice a week.[16] Two days later several hundred of Teufel's supporters celebrated by holding a hippie 'happening' on the Kurfürstendamm, to the consternation of passers-by.[17] Arguing that he was a free and innocent man, Teufel was not able to resist to temptation to provoke the authorities further, and he refused to report to a police station. When he left Berlin to attend the SDS Congress in Frankfurt, on 8 September the Berlin District Court deemed it necessary to place Teufel in custody yet again.[18] He immediately disappeared and did not resurface again until 15 September when he attended a Go-in protest at Rathaus Schöneberg during a debate on the Ohnesorg shooting by the City Government. Around 200 students held a sit-down demonstration in the Rathaus demanding 'freedom for Teufel' before they were forcibly thrown out of the building by the police. Teufel was arrested outside the building and remained in prison until his trial, which started on 27 November.[19] The opening day was accompanied by riots outside the Moabit court against what protesters perceived as state persecution.[20] In typically heavy-handed fashion the police tried to bludgeon the protesters

---

15. 'Warum sollte Teufel flüchten', *BZ*, 5 August 1967, p. 4.

16. *Beschluß*, dated 11 August 1967, file 66, Kommune I III Landesfriedensbruch Band 1, Aktenbestand des Sozialistischen Anwaltskollektivs, HIfS.

17. 'Narreteien à las Kommune', *Berliner Morgenpost*, 13 August 1967, file % Gebbert u.a., Rathaus Go-in I, Aktenbestand des Sozialistischen Anwaltskollektivs, HIfS.

18. *Beschluß*, dated 21 September 1967, file 66, Kommune I III Landesfriedensbruch Band 1, Aktenbestand des Sozialistischen Anwaltskollektivs, HIfS, is on a later decision to reject Teufel's request for release that gives details of the earlier decisions.

19. 'Berlin: Teufel', *Der Spiegel*, 18 September 1967, p. 82. The document *Abschrift*, dated 14 March 1968, file , file % Gebbert u.a., Rathaus Go-in I, Aktenbestand des Sozialistischen Anwaltskollektivs, HIfS gives details of various charges, transcripts of various SDS flyers advertising the Go-in which was ostensibly about 2 June, and details of what happened, from the Prosecution perspective.

20. The article 'Warum demonstrieren wir heute gegen die Moabiter Justiz', *Berliner Extra Dienst*, 27.11.67, AFAS, argued that the persecution of Teufel was 'an attack on all citizens of this city, who take constitutional rights seriously'.

into submission and sprayed 33,000 litres of water at them from water cannon.[21] The trial itself was predictably chaotic with Teufel again refusing to take the proceedings seriously while using the occasion to pour scorn on the legal system. On the opening day he stated clearly 'I can say with certainty that I have not thrown stones, let alone encouraged it.'[22] On the second day of the trial, when Teufel was told by the Judge to stand up, he answered 'only if it serves the search for the truth'. The case had generated a media frenzy and Teufel's quick-witted defiance of such rules of deference was even broadcast that evening to the whole country on the premiere daily news programme, the *Tagesschau*.[23] Far from displaying measured judgement, the court rose to his provocation: on 30 November Teufel told the Prosecutor 'you have the chance to move from the course of law-breaking to the course of law-giving'. For this minor contempt of court he was given four days in prison.[24]

Amidst this clowning the case against Teufel crumbled as the trial progressed. Not a single witness had seen Teufel throwing stones, and the police officers were forced to admit under cross-examination that they had not actually seen Teufel throwing anything. Heßler may actually have been transporting another arrested student away from the area when the stone-throwing incident was supposed to have taken place. When Court Director Pahl expressed his disgust at the fact that Heßler could not give any clear account, Heßler could only reply 'I had stomach-ache'.[25] Teufel was also the victim of a serious assault by officers during his arrest. Jan-Carl Raspe, at that time a member of *Kommune II* and later a leading figure in the RAF, remembered that while Teufel was being taken away by police who had just beaten him 'I could see that in one of his hands he carried his glasses.'[26] It was hardly a picture of a hardened and dangerous criminal, and eyewitness evidence that an officer had shouted 'That is the Teufel! He was already part of the assassination attempt against Humphrey!' just before his arrest suggests that Teufel was deliberately targeted.[27] On 1 December the Prosecutor had to drop the charges of 'serious' breach of the peace.

21. 'Berlin: Studenten', *Der Spiegel*, 4 December 1967, p. 68.

22. Quoted in 'Fürs Vaterland hingesetzt', *Der Spiegel*, 4 December 1968, p. 45.

23. Quoted in 'Einer, der gern saß', *Der Spiegel*, 9 June 1996, p. 78. This is a retrospective on Teufel.

24. Quoted in 'Einer, der gern saß', *Der Spiegel*, 9 June 1996, p. 78.

25. 'Teuflische Betrachtungen', *Berliner Stimme*, 16 December 1967, file % Gebbert u.a. Rathaus Go-in I, Aktenbestand des Sozialistischen Anwaltskollektivs, HIfS.

26. Statement by Jan-Carl Raspe, dated 5.6.67, file 66, Kommune I III Landesfriedensbruch Band 1, Aktenbestand des Sozialistischen Anwaltskollektivs, HIfS.

27. Quoted in 'Einer, der gern saß', *Der Spiegel*, 9 June 1996, p. 78.

Teufel was released after 148 days in prison and later in the month he was found not guilty of all charges.

Perhaps understandably the reaction to the trial from various quarters was one of disgust, but for very different reasons. For the *FU Spiegel* the trial, and particularly the arbitrary imprisonment, exposed the 'political methods of recent years: if a policeman reports an arrested demonstrator, he is as good as sentenced'.[28] In the *Republikanischer Club*'s view, Teufel had been considered guilty by the court until the time of his release, and the legal system had done everything in its power to convict him.[29] This misses the point that the legal system had actually done its job and released him, though there was clear evidence of a bias. The case had humiliated the justice system and brought the honesty of the police into question, just months after the *Pudding Attentat* and simultaneous with the Kurras case. As such the disastrous prosecution was seen as a victory for the Left for by all sides.

The *Kommune I* campaign of provocation continued almost immediately after Teufel's release, and he did not enjoy his freedom for long. On 19 December *Kommune I* members carrying placards reading 'such idiots govern us' shouted choruses of abuse during a speech by Mayor Schütz at the FU Berlin.[30] Teufel and others followed this on 31 December with the disruption of a service at the Gedächtniskirche, just a week after Dutschke's protest in the same church.[31] On 23 January 1968 Teufel was arrested for throwing a firework and shouting 'shit, shit' during a trial that was overseen by an ex-Nazi Judge. He returned to police custody and was sentenced to two months in prison at a trial on 23 February.[32] The *Flugblatt* trial then resumed on 4 March and lived up to expectations that it would be an unpredictable, tumultuous, and irreverent spectacle. Teufel and Langhans arrived in court dressed in psychedelic clothes and within five minutes of starting the trial the Judge warned that any impudence would be punished arbitrarily with a fine. Of course the two defendants did all they could to try his patience: after two days they had already been

28. 'Kein Alibi', *FU Spiegel*, January 1968, p. 5.

29. Presseerklärung, file % Gebbert u.a. Rathaus Go-in I, Aktenbestand des Sozialistischen Anwaltskollektivs, HIfS.

30. *Kommune I, Quellen zur Kommune Forschung*, Signatur D 0895, BfZS. This is an extensive collection of documents by and relating to *Kommune I*. It includes a photograph of the 19 December protest above a poem attacking Schütz.

31. *Anklageschrift*, dated 5 June 1868, file % Gebbert u.a. Rathaus Go-in I, Aktenbestand des Sozialistischen Anwaltskollektivs, HIfS.

32. *Strafsache*, file Kommune I, Justiz B, Aktenbestand des Sozialistischen Anwaltskollektivs, HIfS.

given three sentences of 24 hours in prison for contempt of court. Minor acts of rebellion like sitting on the defendants' table when they were supposed to be standing were sufficient to provoke the Judge.[33] On another occasion the Prosecutor tried to bait Langhans by telling him 'I thought you heard badly under your hair'. When the Prosecutor was invited to come closer he replied 'rather not'. 'Because I stink?' asked Langhans. 'Exactly'.[34] The Defence case went well beyond the remit of the charges, and instead turned the hearing into a political tribunal in which the legal system was on trial. As well as constant interruptions from the defendants, there were complaints about almost every aspect of the conduct of the trial, including the presence of plain-clothes police officers, the fact that only two people were on trial rather than the eight responsible for the flyers, and assertions that the testimony of the psychiatrist was unreliable. The Judge emptied the court regularly in response to a series of chaotic scenes. At one stage, after a return from one such break, Teufel questioned the wisdom of these tactics: 'exceptional reactions by the authorities provoke exceptional defensive measures by their victims'. He accused the Judge of being authoritarian and questioned a previous fine against Langhans. He was then fined on the spot.[35] Teufel and Langhans consistently maintained that the flyers were meant to be satirical and that they had not thought they would be interpreted as an incitement. They were confirmed in this interpretation by expert testimony from a host of experts, including numerous academics from the FU Berlin.[36] Against such evidence the court had no choice but to find the defendants not guilty on 22 March and Teufel was released from custody once again. The behaviour of the Judge and Prosecutor during the proceedings was hardly evidence of measured judgement, but the 'not guilty' verdict further undermines the view that the legal system was the corrupt weapon of a fascist state, although this was not how Teufel's supporters interpreted the case.

As one might expect, Teufel did not remain at liberty for long. By this stage he was a household name but with the series of prison sentences he faced on various charges in both Berlin and Munich he disappeared

33. Mauz, G., 'Sie kommen mir so bekannt vor' *Der Spiegel*, 11 March 1968, pp. 68–71.

34. 'Deutsche Justizkomodie', *Konkret*, 23 September 1968, p. 34. Also reprinted in 'Beiträge zur Strafprozessunordnung', *Der Spiegel*, 23 September 1968, pp. 74–6.

35. *Menschen und Paragraphen: Szenen aus dem Flugblattprozess gegen die Kommune I, 14. März 1968*, p. 16, file 17, Prozeßberichte Procontra, Aktenbestand des Sozialistischen Anwaltskollektivs, HIfS. This is a transcript of the hearing on 14 March.

36. *Auszüge aus den gutachtlichen Äußerungen zum Prozeß gegen Langhans/Teufel wegen Aufforderung zur Brandstiftung*, Berlin file 00135, BfZS.

from the limelight and his days as a political clown quickly came to an end. By the time of his release from prison in 1970 he had spent more than three years behind bars since 1967. In 1970 his frustration boiled over: in March he threw two incendiary devices in the Munich District Court, and two months later threw two Molotov-Cocktails inside the Bavarian *Land* Criminal Court.[37] By now considered to be highly dangerous, after six months on remand he was tried in January 1971 and after conviction he was kept in solitary confinement until his release in the Summer of 1972. In September 1975 he was arrested for allegedly playing a part in the murder of Günter von Drenkmann by the *Bewegung 2. Juni* terrorist group in November 1974 and the kidnapping of Peter Lorenz in February 1975. He remained in prison during an investigation and trial that lasted until May 1980, when he finally proved his innocence. There is no doubt that Teufel was the victim of unnecessarily harsh sentences for minor infractions and a degree of persecution by the legal authorities who were regularly humiliated at his hands. It is impossible to be unequivocal though, and there can be no question that he also paid the price for provocative behaviour that often flouted the law. He later cut a rather sad figure as an anonymous motorcycle courier in Berlin.[38]

Suspicions of state conspiracies were of course based, in part at least, on the presence of former Nazis in positions of power, and this still occupied protesters in a number of ways. A 1968 flyer from the Kirchlichen Hochschule Berlin advertised discussions on the presence of former Nazis in the Federal Interior Ministry, including former SS members Friedrich Lippich and Wolf Dreising. Heinrich Küppenbender was named in this flyer as a former colleague of Albert Speer who was involved in the deployment of foreign slave labourers in concentration camps, while Dr. Josef Kölble was identified as having worked with Goebbels.[39] Naming them as former Nazis was deemed sufficient to bring their integrity into question, in direct opposition to the assumptions of reconciliation upon which the *Bundesrepublik* was based. A demonstration in Berlin in January 1968 against Hans-Ulrich Werner, the commander of the Berlin uniformed police, is particularly interesting in this respect. Until 1943 he was a senior police officer in Germany, after which he held positions in the eastern territories with the *Gendarmerie*. In 1944, as commander of *Gendarmerie-Einsatzkommando Bürger* (Police Task Force Bürger) he

---

37. 'Prozeß gegen Fritz Teufel begann', *Tagesspiegel*, 6 January 1971, p. 7.

38. 'Einer, der gern saß', *Der Spiegel*, 9 June 1997, pp. 79–81 gives a brief summary of Teufel's post-*Kommune I* career.

39. *Jeden hat eine Chance!*, Berlin file 00132, BfZS.

was posted to Italy where, it was alleged, he was in charge of police operations against the civil population of northern Italy.[40] Werner strenuously denied any connections with the SS or similar organizations such as 'special commando' execution squads, and claimed he had nothing to do with concentration camps. Nevertheless, while attending the Lawyer's Ball at the Palais am Funkturm on the evening of 6 January he was the subject of a demonstration by a small group holding placards emblazoned with Swastikas and SS runes. When he arrived the protesters shouted 'SS murderer' and told police officers 'that is your commander. Your leadership comes from this SS swine.' The demonstrators resisted police attempts to break the protest up, and shouted abuse such as 'smash the police in the face'.[41] Protesters threw fireworks before dispersing, and later re-assembled at Hammarskjöldplatz along with reinforcements. Hand-to-hand fighting between protesters and police ensued, and again protesters waved placards with swastikas and the messages 'SS-swine' or 'Nazi murderer'.[42] One of the protesters, Bernd Kramer, was later fined for carrying one of the placards (displaying Nazi symbols was illegal) and taking part in the chants against Werner.[43] These events are perfect examples of the unequivocal stances adopted by both sides, with no ability to understand the perspective of their increasingly intolerant opponents. Werner had embraced the post-war settlement, and any attempts to take issue with his Nazi past were seen not only as insulting and hurtful, but identified those responsible as enemies of the *Bundesrepublik*. For protesters, the protection afforded him pointed at best to a desire to whitewash over the past, or at worst to a deeply sinister conspiracy.

Chancellor Kiesinger became a particular target after the Dutschke assassination attempt blurred the already limited differentiation made by the Left between the far right and the Grand Coalition. At the end of April, during an election tour of his native Baden-Württemberg, Kiesinger met with vocal far-left opposition, especially in Biberach an der Riß, where his open-air speech on 23 April was interrupted by choruses of abuse from crowds of student protesters who had travelled to the city. Placards 'against

40. *Auszug aus dem sog. 'Braunbuch'*, and *Dienstliche Erklärung* by Hans-Ulrich Werner, dated 2 December 1964, both file Diverses Demonstrationen I, Aktenbestand des Sozialistischen Anwaltskollektivs, HIfS.

41. Statement by police officer Peter Fehlberg, dated 6 January 1968, and statements by Bernd Kramer, dated 29 January 1968 and 28 February 1968, all file Diverses Demonstrationen I, Aktenbestand des Sozialistischen Anwaltskollektivs, HIfS.

42. Statement by police officer Klaus Ruby, dated 11 January 1968, file Diverses Demonstrationen I, Aktenbestand des Sozialistischen Anwaltskollektivs, HIfS.

43. *Strafbefehl*, dated 15 March 1968, file Diverses Demonstrationen I, Aktenbestand des Sozialistischen Anwaltskollektivs, HIfS.

the political misuse of the police' were carried by an angry crowd hurling abuse throughout, including the phrase 'kill us, we are the new Jews'.[44] At the start of April Kiesinger had been heckled from the public gallery of the *Bundestag* by activist Beate Klarsfeld, who had been dragged from the building. Klarsfeld carried out a sustained campaign against Kiesinger throughout the year, emphasizing his Nazi past in press conferences, in meetings, and in the 30,000 flyers she distributed around the country.[45] On 7 November she interrupted his speech to the CDU party conference in Berlin and hit him in the face, while shouting 'Nazi, Nazi'. She was dragged away and within two hours had been found guilty of assault in a Berlin court and sentenced to a year in prison. Klarsfeld's defence lawyer, Horst Mahler, had only been able to speak to her for 27 minutes before sentence was passed, and was given no opportunity to prepare a case. *Der Spiegel* expressed reservations not only about such summary dispensation of justice, but also about the excessively harsh sentence, comparing it with the 200 DM fine imposed on the 60-year-old man who had attacked and seriously injured Rudi Dutschke during the Gedächtniskirche disruption the previous December. It noted that there was no precedent for such a long sentence, and that 'twelve months imprisonment for a smack in the ear is a cruel step backwards'.[46]

Klarsfeld's campaign took place at the same time as the renewed attempt to pass the Emergency Laws that intensified fears of a return to openly Nazi government. The controversial nature of the news laws were such that the opposition to them attracted support from people with varying political views, most of whom would not have subscribed to the idea that the government was already fascistic, but who feared for the future. Opinion was certainly split on the issue. A survey by *Der Spiegel* in June 1967 found that only 6 per cent of students felt the *Bundesrepublik* did not need the *Notstandsgesetze*, whereas 35 per cent of the general population said they were unnecessary. Perhaps even more strikingly, 55 per cent of students, but only 37 per cent of ordinary citizens, were in favour of the laws. Those who were outright opponents, however, represented 39 per cent of students, and 28 per cent of the general public.[47]

44. 'Stürmisches Wiedersehen im Oberland', *Stuttgarter Zeitung*, 24 April 1968, p. 3; and 'Da sind Dämonen am Werk', *Der Spiegel*, 29 April 1968, p. 30.

45. "Die Ohrfeige war ein politischer Akt", *Der Spiegel*, 18 November 1968, p. 34. This is an interview with Klarsfeld. Particularly interesting is Klarsfeld, B., *Die Geschichte des PG 2633930: Kiesinger* in which Klarsfeld went into exhaustive detail about Kiesinger's Nazi past, including the reproduction of original documents.

46. "Den Bundeskanzler misshandelt", *Der Spiegel*, 11 November 1968, p. 32.

47. 'Was denken die Studenten?', *Der Spiegel*, 19 June 1967, p. 38.

Protests against the *Notstandsgesetze* reached a peak in May, at the time the new laws were being read in the *Bundestag*. Trade unions, the KfDA, student organizations, and members of the main political parties, including the SPD, took part in a massive and sustained series of protests. On 11 May, between 60,000 and 80,000 people from across the country converged for the KfDA *Sternmarsch* (Star march) on Bonn, just four days before the next reading of the law in the *Bundestag*.[48] Describing this as the 'decisive phase' of the campaign, the KfDA was by this time employing language that belied its domination by far-left groups. It called the new laws a contest between the 'profit-seeking of the monopolies and concerns' and the 'social interests of working people' and warned that the *Notstandsgesetze* would be 'an instrument in the hands of the rulers to oppress every form of political opposition'. It had not abandoned its pacifist roots, though, and was concerned that 'the demonstration against the *Notstandsgesetze* may in no case become a battle with the police'.[49] A repetition of the violence over Easter would certainly have denied the protest the support from a wide cross-section of society that the organizers were keen to attract. They appealed to the citizens of Bonn to ignore the abuse from *Bild*, which was calling them communists and terrorists, and find out for themselves that the 'radicals' were 'workers, professors, civil servants, schoolchildren, priests, students, housewives, and so on'.[50] This did not prevent newspapers from attempting to discredit the protest by predicting that 'the communist-led' march aimed to 'cause trouble'.[51]

In the event the protest passed peacefully, and seems to have been one of the least confrontational, as well as one of the largest protests of the period. Writing in *Konkret* one witness, Frank Werner, recalled the party atmosphere of the over-night train ride from Berlin to the march. The march was a massive event, one of the high-points of the 1968 protests in West Germany, and as such it was able to attract international attention: Werner talks of the presence of film crews from the BBC and the German broadcaster WDR on his train.[52] Three separate marches converged on the city for a mass meeting in the Hofgarten, where street theatre and cabaret groups were used alongside the usual speeches by people such as Heinrich

48. Bauß, *Die Studentenbewegung*, p. 152, estimates that only 15,000 were students.
49. *Aktionsbrief Marsch auf Bonn am 11. Mai*, dated 7 May 68, Berlin file 00124, BfZS. This was produced by KfDA Berlin.
50. *Die Terroristen kommen – Bonner Bürger paßt auf!*, Berlin file 00131, BfZS.
51. 'Am 11. Mai: Bannmeile um das Bundeshaus polizeilich abgesperrt', *Rhein Zeitung*, 10 May 1968, Sammlung Schlemper, ED 328/33, IfZM.
52. Werner, F., 'Die Revolution verschickt ihre Kinder', *Konkret*, p. 21.

Böll.[53] In one such speech SDS Federal representative Karl-Dietrich Wolff told the assembled thousands that 'the civil war plans [the *Notstands-gesetze*] have themselves thrown the Basic Law onto the scrap heap; now they exhort us to trust in the constitution. But the emergency strategists have made their calculations without us all. We will not look on in silence, as a parliament makes itself superfluous for the second time in German history and presents us with the new dictatorship.'[54]

In the weeks after the *Sternmarsch* tens of thousands of people took part in protests against the *Notstandsgesetze* in almost every West German city. The FU Berlin was paralysed throughout May by mass debates and lecture strikes in almost all departments and faculties, and in several instances staff called the police. The fear engendered by the new laws even among the politically inactive prompted students of the Biology department to hold their first mass political assembly.[55] On 15 May, the day on which the new laws had their second reading in the *Bundestag*, protests took place in 31 cities, including marches, mass meetings, lecture strikes, and even short strikes by thousands of workers. On 24 May students at Frankfurt University blockaded the entrance to the University and shortly after declared a 'Karl-Marx University' in opposition to the *Notstands-gesetze*. Three days later the *Bundestag* began the third and final reading of the new laws and from 27 to 30 May protests took place at every university in the country. In Marburg four SDS members went on hunger strike for 48 hours, in which 30 students at Bonn University soon joined them.[56] In Frankfurt 20,000 workers took part in a strike on 27 May and at a mass protest meeting in the Alten Botanischen Garten in Munich demonstrators unfurled a banner over the park gates saying 'no second 1933'.[57]

53. *Brief an die Teilnehmer des Sternmarsches auf Bonn*, file 50, Aktenbestand des Sozialistischen Anwaltskollektivs, HIfS. This letter to participants from the organizers gave practical information on assembly points, behaviour during the protests, and details of the planned events.

54. *Rede beim Sternmarsch gegen die Notsandsgesetze, Karl-Dietrich Wolff, Bundes-vorsitzender des Sozialistischen Deutschen Studentenbundes (SDS), Bonn, 11. Mai 1968*, Sammlung Mehringer, ED 308/10, IfZM.

55. 'Streiks', *FU-Spiegel*, June 1968, p. 7.

56. 'Protest in den Universitätsstäten', *Süddeutsche Zeitung*, 30 May 1968, p. 2, lists a number of the protests around the country on 29 May, while 'Bonn: Geschlossene Gesellschaft', *Der Spiegel*, 3 June 1968, pp. 21–4 provides information on protests throughout May.

57. *Information IV*, dated 28 May 1968, file 50, Aktenbestand des Sozialistischen Anwaltskollektivs, HifS; also Sittner G. and Ude, C., 'Großangriff auf die Notstands-verfassung', *Süddeutsche Zeitung*, 28 May 1968, p. 9.

On 29 May, the day of the final debate in the *Bundestag*, the protests reached their peak. In Munich 2,000 striking students and schoolchildren held a sit-down demonstration outside the Culture Ministry and succeeded in blocking the city centre. Students in Erlangen held a sit-in at Nuremburg University; all but three *Gymnasien* (high schools) in Frankfurt were closed in opposition to the *Notstandsgesetze*; and 10,000 people signed a petition in Freiburg, where students blocked the entrance to the University. Lectures at Würzburg University were cancelled so that staff and students could attend a teach-in on the *Notstandsgesetze*, and at Tübingen University 80 to 90 per cent of students supported a strike.[58] This is just a small representative cross-section of the total protest activity, all of which was to no avail. In the final *Bundestag* vote the CDU tactic of including the SPD in government paid off, with 384 votes in favour of the *Notstandsgesetze* and only 100 against, including a mere 53 of the 202 SPD members. It became the 17th amendment to the Basic Law on 24 June. Significantly, Ulrike Meinhof condemned the campaign against the *Notstandsgesetze* as having failed to change a thing after ten years of struggle because it had not attempted to create a fundamental social change through 'class war'. She warned 'the democratization of state and society are the aims. The fight against the Emergency Laws is one means among others to achieve those aims, which means depriving the dictators in state and society of power. That doesn't work if one only fights against the change from a large to a small prison cell, and forgets to prepare in advance for a break-out.'[59] Meinhof was not alone in reaching such conclusions, and violence as a solution became even more attractive to those on the Left frustrated with debate and protests that had such little effect.

By the end of the 1960s, then, the conditions were in place for a rapid descent into organized violence against the state. Attitudes among the public and authorities, which allowed little room for dissent even in the early 1960s, had hardened to the point where harsh measures were seen as the only solution to worsening violence and perceived threats to the future of the *Bundesrepublik*. Both sides cited evidence to support their belief in conspiracies to overthrow democracy, however much these suspicions may have been exaggerated. Simultaneously, or in quick succession, protesters experienced violent Vietnam demonstrations, Emergency laws, police violence, street battles, shootings, undermining of the legal process, sit-ins, go-ins, conferences, counter-demonstrations,

---

58. *Süddeutsche Zeitung*, 30 May 1968, p. 11, Sammlung Schlemper, ED 328/33, IfZM.

59. Meinhof, U.M., 'Notstand-Klassenkampf', *Konkret*, June 1968, p. 2.

fire-bombings, claim and counter-claim, court hearings, public and press vilification, sectarian divisions and hatreds on the Left, and so on. This was a fluid situation, in which hardly a day went by without some new controversy, protest or outrage to inflame the indignation of demonstrators or their opponents. These and other social changes which, for good or bad, have been used for the vilification or glorification of the 1960s, challenged assumptions in almost every aspect of life in West Germany. Previously cherished expectations, whether deference to age and authority, the honesty and authority of the police, of the legal system and of the government, the accuracy of the press, the inferiority of youth, women, and so on, sexual mores, the nature of popular culture, of family relationships, of attitudes to leisure and consumption, patriotism, anti-communism, the nature of democracy, the Nazi past or the recovery from it were all stripped of their certainties. For some this was the beginning of a new age of possibilities, for others the collapse of everything they held dear. People on both sides were left confused and worried for the future, though for very different reasons. Frustration, intransigence, and deepening mutual distrust created the foundations for a remorseless, vicious, and relentless terrorist campaign that would challenge the fundamentals of democracy in West Germany and would place that democracy at risk of destruction.

Part IV
The 1970s

–11–

The Descent into Terrorism

Terrorism was undoubtedly one of the negative legacies of the 1960s, and it certainly evolved from 1960s protest movements, but the hysterical reactions of authorities, a resistance to reform, state violence and so on all made their contributions to its creation. Protests in the late 1960s had raised questions for the state about how best to defend democracy while preserving its essential liberties. The terrorist campaigns took this debate to its logical conclusion, putting the fundamentals of democracy at risk from both terrorism and the state as entrenched positions prompted actions and reactions that continued to confirm suspicions and hatreds for both sides, locking the country into a destructive cycle of violence.

In seeking to understand the terrorist groups, the role of revolutionary politics has to be given centre stage. The rigid inability to countenance alternatives that was so manifest in the SDS has to be considered alongside the kind of strident rhetoric that informed their protest tactics and theoretical discussions. Resorting to terrorism was a logical development from fierce debates on violence, although it must be emphasized that the small terrorist groups were always tiny minorities even on the far left. The *Republikanischer Club* told the RAF in 1972 that its 'politics of bombs . . . does not clarify the question of a long-term revolutionary strategy, because it [the RAF] doesn't ask how the masses learn to defend themselves. Bombs do not bring capitalism into danger, it is only in danger when the masses don't want it any more and see a practical alternative.'[1] Most people on the Left, including many who were sympathetic to the terrorists' cause, were actively concerned with other things, whether the nascent women's or environmental movements, agitation within the labour movement, or simply the attacking of other far-left groups. Nevertheless, the terrorists

---

1. *Papier von Genossen aus dem RK zur RAF*, p. 4, Sammlung Mehringer, ED 308/10, IfZM. Willy Brandt's view is interesting here. For him 'the very gulf between young student activists and the working class . . . led to an arrogant intensification of extremist attitudes on the part of the spurned suitors: if the "masses" failed to realize where their duty and earthly bliss lay, they had to be coerced into that realization'. See Brandt, W., *People and Politics: The Years 1960–1975*, p. 199.

were clearly taking widely used slogans promising international revolutionary struggle at their word and felt justified in continuing the armed North Vietnamese revolutionary struggle in Europe against regimes they perceived as morally bankrupt accomplices in an international fascist capitalist conspiracy.

Andreas Baader and Gudrun Ensslin announced their intentions to the world with just such a pro-Vietnamese display of violence on 2 April 1968. Along with Horst Sohnlein and Thorwald Proll, they set off incendiary devices in the Schneider department store and a Kaufhof in Frankfurt, causing around two million DM of damage. Following their arrest the next day they were brought to trial in October on arson charges. Ensslin, an FU Berlin Germanistik student like Ohnesorg, admitted that she and Baader had carried out the attack 'in protest against the indifference with which people view the genocide in Vietnam'. She told the court 'We have learnt that speech without action is wrong.'[2] They were each eventually sentenced to three years in prison.[3] For Ulrike Meinhof, who had been sent by *Konkret* to report on the case, 'the progressive moment of department store arson does not lie in the destruction of goods, it lies in the criminality of the act, in breaking the law'.[4] She viewed this law as defending the spirit of trade rather than people, making an attack on the law a simultaneous attack on the fundamentals of capitalism. The SDS, on the other hand, distanced itself from this new form of protest, prompting Baader to declare 'the revolutionary movement in the *Bundesrepublik* is dead'.[5]

The SDS was at this time in the midst of destroying itself, a process that left a vacuum in the leadership of the Left that the RAF later attempted to fill. It would be wrong to claim that SDS members formed the core of the future terrorist groups: membership came from a variety of groups such as the LSD, SHB and SJD, as well as 'fellow travellers' like Baader and Ensslin. Others were recruited in a haphazard way, through personal contacts or through the *Sozialistische Patienten Kollektiv* (SPK), the strange Stuttgart-based psychiatric group around Wolfgang and Ursula Huber. Yet many of the student groups that later provided members for the terrorist organizations were more or less satellites of the SDS by the end

2. 'So wurde sie zur Brandstiftung', *Abendzeitung*, 28 October 1968, p. 5.

3. 'Zuchthaus für Brandstifter', *Der Abend*, 1 November 1968, file Alles außer Kommune, Aktenbestand des Sozialistischen Anwaltskollektivs, HIfS.

4. Meinhof, U.M., 'Warenhausbrandstiftung', *Konkret*, 4 November 1968, p. 5.

5. 'Gudrun Ensslin und Andreas Baader gegen eine Brandstiftung zu', *Die Welt*, 22 October 1968, file Alles außer Kommune, Aktenbestand des Sozialistischen Anwaltskollektivs, HIfS.

of the decade.[6] The debate on violence and illegality that suffused the whole of the far left by 1968, and which centred on the SDS, therefore fed directly into the rhetoric and motivations of the terrorist organizations, especially the RAF: Ensslin and Baader had been in Frankfurt to attend the SDS conference at the time of the arson attack in April 1968. By late 1968 the SDS was split between various factions warring over violence, the role of women, the use of anti-authoritarian and traditionalist tactics, or even the pursuit of success in parliamentary elections. As Bernd Rabehl said, 'the anti-authoritarian revolt destroys its own organization', and on 21 March 1970 the national organization liquidated itself at a conference in Frankfurt, although some local groups remained in existence.[7]

With the Left in a state of flux, it took some time for the terrorist organizations to coalesce into meaningful replacements for the SDS leadership. Baader, Ensslin and their associates were only released, pending their appeal, in June 1969, at which point they began to pursue the kind of contacts that would make a more organized campaign of violence possible. Even at this stage, however, the ad hoc nature of the move toward violence should not be underestimated: Baader and Ensslin do not seem to have conceived of a long-term plan for creating a co-ordinated terrorist organization until much later. Instead they seem to have been motivated by a desire to find out what was possible in pushing the boundaries of tolerance. In the meantime the levels of violence escalated continuously, notably in Berlin, where the Summer of 1969 was marked by a particularly fierce campaign against the deportation of *Bundeswehr* deserters back to West Germany. Within days of a demonstration on the Kurfürstendamm in which widespread damage had been done, a wave of fire-bomb and terrorist attacks began in Berlin that was to last for several years. The Berlin State Administrator for Justice estimated in 1972 that between July 1969 and May 1972 there were 115 terrorist attacks in Berlin alone, including 49 arson and 16 bomb attacks.[8]

From this point onward the development of the RAF, and of the other terrorist groups, was rapid and full of incident. In February 1970 Baader and Ensslin's appeal against their convictions failed and they went underground. The following month the SDS ceased to exist and just a few days

6. Bund Freiheit der Wissenschaft, *Hochschule und Terrorismus: Pressekonferenz, Bonn, September 1977*, file Originale Dokumentation, Bewaffneter Kampf, RAF, Ulrike Meinhof, H.M. Schleyer, Hungerstreik, Diverses, APOusB, lists many of the student affiliations of members of different terrorist organizations.

7. 'Studenten: SDS', *Der Spiegel*, 25 November 1968, p. 56. For the demise of the SDS see Fichter and Lönnendonker, *Kleine Geschichte des SDS*, p. 143.

8. 'Berlin: 115 Terror-Anschläge seit Juli 1969', *Bild*, 31 May 1972, p. 1.

later, on 4 April, Baader was arrested in Berlin. On 14 May Ulrike Meinhof, who had by now committed herself to the small group, was able to use her status as a journalist to gain an interview with Baader at the FU Berlin. In a daring escape, during which a member of staff was shot and seriously injured, Baader was whisked away and Meinhof began her life underground, pursued by the police for attempted murder. A few days later the group, referring to itself as a *Rote Armee* for the first time, made their first public announcement in the anarchist newspaper *Agit 883*, in vitriolic, hate-filled language. The influence of the rising tide of violence was clear: 'did the pigs, who shot first, believe we would allow ourselves to be shot down peacefully as animals to the slaughter?' they asked, adding, 'whoever doesn't fight dies'. Confirmation that they were taking the phrases of the 1968 Vietnam Conference seriously came with the announcement '"Vietnam is the Spain of our Generation", we said in 1968 . . . Berlin is an outpost of American imperialism. Our enemy, and the enemy of the Japanese and Vietnamese people, the enemy of all blacks in the USA, the enemy of workers in Berlin – the enemy is American imperialism'.[9]

The following month, on 15 June 1970, *Der Spiegel* published a statement by Meinhof, explaining the motivation for the Baader escape. In a long and rambling text often divorced from political realities, and typical of the tedious theorizing mixed with simplistic conclusions that ran throughout RAF literature, Meinhof only partially succeeded in clarifying their position. Their aims, which boiled down to bringing about 'the revolution' necessitated armed struggle because 'the revolution will not happen unless revolutionaries arm themselves'. In a particularly chilling passage Meinhof said

> naturally the cops are pigs. We say the type in uniform is a pig, he is no human, and so we have a problem with him. That means, we have nothing to say to him, and it is completely wrong to speak with him, and naturally he can be shot at.[10]

After training by the Popular Front for the Liberation of Palestine (PFLP) in Jordan, on 29 September they carried out a number of bank robberies in Berlin. These provided the financial means for them to launch a sustained campaign, although on 8 October they suffered a serious setback

9. 'Die Rote Armee aufbauen!', *Agit 883*, 22 May 1970, p. 2. The slogan 'Vietnam is the Spain of our Generation' was used regularly in the literature advertising the 1968 International Vietnam Conference, such as the flyer *Aufruf zur Internationalen Vietnamkonferenz*, Berlin file 00127, BfZS. This uses the phrase as its first sentence, and is signed by Horst Mahler and Ulrike Meinhof.

10. '"Natürlich kann geschossen werden": Ulrike Meinhof über die Baader-Aktion', *Der Spiegel*, 15 June 1970, p. 74.

when members Horst Mahler, Ingrid Schubert, Brigitte Asdonk and Monika Berberich were arrested in Berlin.

The violence intensified in the New Year. On 10 February 1971 police in Frankfurt attempted to arrest RAF members Manfred Grashof and Astrid Proll, who tried 'to shoot themselves free and flee with many shots'.[11] A massive nationwide search operation for 'a thirty-head armed group' was launched by the Federal Criminal Office (*Bundeskriminalamt* or BKA) the next day.[12] A few days later the RAF was named as 'Germany's public enemy number 1' by Federal Interior Minister Hans-Dietrich Genscher, and this was followed in April by Federal Judge Ludwig Martin's declaration that the Baader-Meinhof Gang was an illegal organization.[13] The police search operation took some time to get results, but on 6 May Astrid Proll was captured in Hamburg carrying a pistol and false identification papers. In Berlin the trial of Mahler and his associates on terrorist charges was reaching its climax, accompanied by riots for several days. Tear gas and batons were used against rioters shouting 'hands off Mahler' who threw stones at the police on the Kurfürstendamm on 17 May.[14] On 21 May, however, Georgens and Schubert were found guilty of attempted murder and the illegal possession of firearms in connection with Baader's escape. They were sentenced to four and six years in prison respectively. Mahler was found not guilty of assisting the escape and was released from custody, although he soon faced further charges and a new trial.

The RAF campaign suffered its first fatality, and gained it first martyr, on 15 May 1971 when 20-year-old Petra Schelm was shot dead while resisting arrest in Hamburg. In a statement in July the RAF compared Schelm's death to the Ohnesorg and Dutschke shootings. They claimed 'on 15 July 1971 Petra Schelm was murdered. That is an organized crime by the pigs!' and promised 'revenge for Petra'.[15] More deaths and injuries were to follow: on the night of 22 to 23 October, a Hamburg policeman, Norbert Schmid, was shot and killed while trying to arrest a man and two women, probably Margrit Schiller, Irmgard Möller and Gerhard Möller. Of course, the police were becoming aware that they were not dealing

11. 'Großfahndung nach Mitgleidern der Gruppe Baader und Mahler', *Tagesspiegel*, 12 February 1971, p. 1. The quotation is from the police statement on the events.

12. 'Bisher 13 Mitgleider der Gruppe um Baader und Mahler verhaftet', *Tagesspiegel*, 13 February 1971, p. 1.

13. 'Bonner Geheimpolizei jagt Staatsfeind Nr. 1: Die Baader-Bande', *Welt am Sonntag*, 15 February 1971, p. 1 and 'Generalbundesanwalt nennt Baader-Meinhof-Gruppe kriminell', *Die Welt*, 21 April 1971, p. 1.

14. 'Drei Nächte lang Krawall der "Schwarzen Zellen"', *Tagesspiegel*, 18 May 1971, p. 8.

15. *Rache für Petra!*, Originale Dokumentation, file 'Bewaffneter Kampf, RAF, Erklärungen', APOusB.

simply with one group, and the *Bewegung 2. Juni*, which was slowly coalescing into a distinct organization, grabbed the headlines next. On 4 December plain-clothes members of the political police (*Abteilung I*, Kurras' former unit) investigating the terrorists shot and killed Georg von Rauch during a stop-and-search operation in Berlin. Immediately the press, the Left, and the parliamentary authorities asked whether there was a shoot-to-kill policy in operation. Contradictory circumstantial, eyewitness, and forensic evidence added to the air of conspiracy surrounding the case, and *Der Spiegel* soon despaired that the events were becoming 'more mysterious from week to week'.[16] The *Tagesspiegel* even produced an eleven-point list of queries about the case, including speculation that von Rauch was the victim of the security services, and questions about the nature and trustworthiness of the police investigation.[17] Only in May 1972 was it established that the police had shot in self-defence and that von Rauch was a leading figure in the new *Bewegung 2. Juni*.[18] Perhaps more than any other previous event, the affair introduced concerns beyond the far left that the state might be undermining democracy in its determination to defeat the terrorists.

Heinrich Böll aired such views in particularly controversial manner in January 1972. Writing in *Der Spiegel*, Böll attacked inflammatory headlines in *Bild*, accusing it of inciting 'lynch justice', and charged that for politicians to give interviews to the newspaper was 'no longer cryptofascist, no longer fascistoid, that is naked fascism'.[19] In a famous passage he described the RAF campaign as 'a war of 6 against 60,000,000' and called for understanding and inclusion of the RAF in the political process, just as Adenauer had included former Nazis among his advisers. As a parting shot he asked 'does your free democratic constitutional order present itself as so infallible that no one may place it in question?' The article provoked outrage: in a systematic response to Böll's view, for instance, Diether Posser (SPD), Minister for Federal Affairs in North Rhein West phalia, opposed every one of Böll's points, and wondered whether Böll had actually identified himself with the Group and its actions.[20] It was a common conclusion,

16. 'Feuer eröffnet', *Der Spiegel*, 27 December 1971, p. 55. 'Geschwärzte Hände', *Der Spiegel*, 10 January 1972, p. 61.
17. 'Katalog offener Fragen zum Fall Georg von Rauch', *Tagesspiegel*, 13 January 1972, p. 10.
18. See 'Ergebnis des Garäuschgutachters: Erster Schuß aus 9-mm Pistole', *Tagesspiegel*, 30 May 1972, p. 10 and 'Es wird geschossen, schnell, Mensch', *Der Spiegel*, 27 December 1971, p. 56.
19. Böll, H., 'Will Ulrike Gnade oder freies Geleit?', *Der Spiegel*, 10 January 1972, pp. 54-57.
20. Posser, D., 'Diese Praxis ist verheerend', *Der Spiegel*, 24 January 1972, pp. 40-1.

and henceforth Böll was marked as an RAF sympathizer by a wide cross-section of the press and public.

Indeed, far from prompting reflection and caution by the state authorities, Böll's article came just a month before the government introduced anti-terrorist measures of unprecedented scope that brought fundamental assumptions about German democracy into question. In February 1971 Chancellor Brandt had told the Federal Cabinet that the harshest policies available to a constitutional state would be used against both Left and right-wing radicalism.[21] To this end the Federal government took a number of steps to unify the campaign against the terrorists, including the appointment of Horst Herold as head of the *Bundeskriminalamt* in Wiesbaden. Herold was given massively increased funds and resources to approach the task in a scientific manner, including the creation of national computer filing systems for the first time, raising the spectre of 'Big Brother'-style data storage and unaccountable surveillance techniques.[22] Police roadblocks and checks on identification papers had already been intensified. On 24 January 1972 Baader sent a letter to the German Press Agency in Munich in which he mocked 'the "security powers", the safety groups, police, BND, constitutional guardians, Federal justices, "Der Spiegel", the Springer Press, you all know nothing'. Crucially 'the tactical line' for the RAF was 'the development of the propaganda of the urban guerrilla in the still legal revolutionary organizations and the construction of a broad logistical base in all sections of the people'. He warned 'the struggle has only just begun'.[23] Just four days later Willy Brandt announced an agreement with the *Länder* Minister Presidents that those who had supported organizations that sought to undermine the constitution would be barred from government posts. This effectively removed teachers, civil servants, lawyers, and so on, who had any record of membership in radical organizations and parties. The new law, known variously as the *Extremistenbeschluß* or the *Radikalenerlaß* was extended in May 1975, when the Federal Court decreed that members of organizations opposed to the rule of law should be banned from joining the police, whether the organization was banned or not.[24] The law was notoriously divisive and difficult to

21. 'Bundeskanzler für Härte gegen Extremisten von rechts und links', *Die Welt*, 18 February 1971, p. 2.

22. Schenk, D., *Der Chef* is an exhaustive account of Herold's activities.

23. Quoted in 'Baader droht: Volkskrieg in Deutschland', *Bild*, 25 January 1972, p. 1.

24. Brandt has argued that the new law was an attempt to prove to the German public that his *Ostpolitik* did not mean a desire to introduce Communism in West Germany. Brandt, W., *My Life in Politics*, pp. 276–7. 'Auf dem Weg zur Gesinnungsschüffelei', *Der Spiegel*, 8 December 1975, pp. 28–9 gives some details of the application of the law and the opposition to it.

enforce: it resulted in only 430 sackings from the hundreds of thousands of people in government employment and by the end of the decade most *Länder* had abandoned it as unworkable, although the Saar did not cease to apply it until 1985. Yet it was at odds with constitutional guarantees of freedom of speech and belief and bore a startling resemblance to laws passed by the Nazis for the suppression of critical debate.

The law was indicative of widespread confusion about how to deal with the terrorist threat. Although President Heinemann perhaps naively appealed to the RAF to 'end the struggle of violence' and saw, like Böll, the possibility for a peaceful solution, Brandt took the opposite view. For him 'free democracy may not be misunderstood as a feeble state'.[25] In the press, while the Springer titles were stridently supportive, an article in the *Frankfurter Rundschau*, entitled 'never again Weimar' was representative of a more thoughtful response. This talked of an 'old German illness' in which the state assisted the enemies of democracy in destroying that democracy. In this instance 'the Baader-Meinhof Group are not endangering the state, but police actions and public demonization give new life to a latent fascism' because Germans wanted 'either perfect democracy or perfect order or nothing at all'.[26] The article accurately summarizes the dilemma facing the German government, and the extreme answers it provoked, with little room for middle ground. Once again, there was scant evidence of 'measured judgement' or 'repressive tolerance'. For the RAF, then, the new law was a sign that their campaign of trying to alter the state, or trying to instil fear, was working.

Predictably, the violence continued. On 2 March RAF member Thomas Weisbecker was killed in a shoot-out with police in Augsburg. Carmen Roll was arrested. When police caught up with Manfred Grashof in Hamburg next day, Grashof, thinking the police were operating a 'shoot to kill' policy, opened fire and shot Hans Eckhardt, the head of the Hamburg State Protection Section of the Criminal Police. Grashof, who was himself shot, had fired expanding bullets, which had been illegal under the Geneva Convention since the nineteenth century. One had hit Eckhardt's chest, another his stomach, causing massive damage to his internal organs; he died nearly three weeks later, on 22 March. The campaign then entered a new stage, involving bomb attacks for the first time and marking a change of direction for the RAF, in which they struck first. On 11 May, just a few days before the anniversary of Schelm's death, the *Kommando Petra Schelm* detonated two bombs at a US military base in Frankfurt, killing an

---

25. "Stellt euch den Gerichten", *Der Spiegel*, 7 February 1972, p. 19–20.

26. Ziegler, G., 'Nie wieder Weimar', *Frankfurter Rundschau*, 5 February 1972, file Originale Dokumentation RAF 1972, APOusB.

officer and injuring 13 others. A press statement by the RAF a few days later claimed the bomb was in reaction to President Nixon's decision the previous month to launch a renewed bombing campaign against Hanoi and Haiphong. They demanded an end to the bombing and the immediate withdrawal of American troops from Vietnam, saying 'West Germany and West Berlin should no longer be a safe hinterland for the eradication strategy in Vietnam'.[27] The day after the Frankfurt bombing the *Kommando Thomas Weisbecker* set off a bomb in the Police Headquarters in Augsburg, injuring five officers, and later the same day another bomb went off in the car park of the *Land* Criminal Offices in Munich. The bomb was so large that 60 cars were destroyed. The RAF insisted Weisbecker had been 'murdered' by a police 'execution commando' and claimed their bombs were part of the 'fight against the SS practices of the police'.[28]

The next bomb blew up Federal Judge Wolfgang Buddenberg's car at the Federal Court building in Karlsruhe on 15 May. Buddenberg had not been in the car, but his wife was seriously injured, the car park was badly damaged, and 40 cars were destroyed. The RAF accused Buddenberg of putting imprisoned terrorists in permanent isolation and ordering that Carmen Roll be given narcotics to make her talk. He was charged with 'attempted murder' for taking Grashof out of hospital and placing him in a prison cell. In a moment replete with irony, the RAF even argued that the justice system was in breach of the Geneva Convention of Human Rights and the Charter of the United Nations on the imprisonment of political prisoners.[29] The *Kommando 2. Juni*, under Meinhof's leadership, was the next to strike, this time in Hamburg on 19 May. A massive bomb attack on the Springer building left 17 people injured, destroyed everything within 100 square metres, and was heard 2 kilometres away from the city centre.[30] The RAF statement, written by Meinhof, ingenuously demanded that the Springer newspapers 'put an end to the anti-communist hate against the New Left, against the solidarity actions of the working classes such as strikes, against the communist parties here and in other countries'.[31] The bombings reached their climax on 24 May when an

27. *Presseerklärung der Roten Armee Fraktion (RAF)*, dated 14 May 1972, file Originale Dokumentation, Bewaffneter Kampf, RAF Erklärungen, APOusB.

28. RAF statement dated 16 May 1972, file Originale Dokumentation, Bewaffneter Kampf, RAF Erklärungen, APOusB.

29. RAF Statement dated 20 May 1972, file Originale Dokumentation, Bewaffneter Kampf, RAF Erklärungen, APOusB.

30. Stäcker, D., 'Sprengstoffanschlag aus Springer-Haus', *Frankfurter Rundschau*, 20 May 1972, p. 1.

31. Statement by *Kommando 2. Juni*, file Originale Dokumentation, Bewaffneter Kampf, RAF Erklärungen, APOusB.

explosion at a US military base in Heidelberg killed three American soldiers and injured five others.

Fear and panic was the understandable popular response. The press presented the bombings as attacks on press freedom, on democracy, and on Germany's American Allies, as well as confirmation of their long-held fears about the far left. Axel Springer called it 'the devil's seeds from the Left radicals, that are now bearing fruit. Our newspapers have warned in vain of precisely this for years.'[32] The Munich Police Chief demanded that a one million DM reward be issued for the capture of the terrorists, and the Federal government discussed plans to ban all anarchist organizations.[33] The risk of another explosion, anywhere and at any time, clearly had an effect upon the public: Stuttgart's streets were empty on 2 June after an anonymous bomb threat to mark the fifth anniversary of Ohnesorg's death. The *Frankfurter Rundschau* described the terrorists as standing 'outside any discussion', but repeated its fears that 'human life is not only at risk. Our free constitutional state is threatened' and reiterated concerns that the greatest threat came from the desire for a stronger state reaction to the terrorists. 'The worst' it insisted, 'would be to lose nerve now'.[34] Such fears were added to by three government alterations to the Basic Law on 22 June that created a unified national law on weapons, put border security in the hands of the *Länder*, and allowed for arrest on suspicion that known terrorists would repeat their actions.

At the end of the month the police across Germany launched the largest search operation in the history of the *Bundesrepublik* in an attempt to capture the leaders of the RAF within a week. Axel Springer offered a reward of 250,000 DM for their arrest, taking the total reward to 440,000 DM.[35] The search achieved an early success when, after a tip-off, the police caught up with Baader, Raspe and Holger Meins in a house in Frankfurt on 1 June. After a shoot-out that included the deployment of an armoured car the RAF members were finally arrested, Baader having been shot in the leg by a police marksman. A week later Gudrun Ensslin was arrested in a shop on the fashionable Jungfernstieg in Hamburg, and on 15 June Meinhof, along with Gerhard Möller, were arrested in Hanover. In Meinhof's apartment police found an arsenal of pistols, hand-grenades, a machine pistol,

32. Nitschke, E. and Schütte, E., 'Axel Springer: wir haben gewarnt', *Die Welt*, 23 May 1972, p. 3.

33. Körner, H. and Gallmeister, I., 'Baader-Meinhof: Eine Million Belohnung', *Bild*, 24 May 1972, p. 1, and 'Bonn erwägt Verbot anarchistischer Organisationen', *Die Welt*, 27 May 1972, p. 1.

34. 'Doppelte Gefahr', *Frankfurter Rundschau*, 26 May 1972, p. 3.

35. 'Bundesweite Größfahndung nach Mitgliedern anarchistischer Gruppen', *Tagesspiegel*, 1 June 1972, p. 1.

ammunition that included expanding bullets and a 4.5 kg bomb. This spectacular success for the police was followed in July by the arrest in Tübingen of Hans-Peter Konieczny, who was persuaded to entrap fellow RAF members Klaus Jünschke and Irmgard Möller.

In parallel with these developments, the RAF's links with international terrorism, usually related to the Palestinian struggle against Israel, gave an instructive insight into its worldview, particularly its attitudes to democracy and capitalism. The aeroplane hijackings, assassinations, bombings, and so on that afflicted Europe from the late 1960s onward provided a focus for terrorist groups in numerous countries, and in May 1972 RAF representatives met with Palestinian and Japanese terrorists to agree on some co-ordination in their actions. This meeting resulted in an agreement that 'some of the groups would help or "represent" each other in attacks within their own territories'.[36] On 5 September the Palestinian Group 'Black September' attacked the Israeli team at the Munich Olympics, killing two and taking nine hostages. They demanded the release of Baader and Meinhof as well as 234 Palestinians in Israeli custody, and began a siege at the Olympic village that ended with them being transported to the airport, where they were ambushed by the police. The operation was badly bungled and the ensuing shoot-out left 11 hostages, a police officer and five terrorists dead. Only three terrorists were arrested. This disastrous outcome showed to the world how unprepared the *Bundesrepublik* was for dealing with such situations, and led to the creation of a more systematic and professional response to terrorism, including the formation of the crack anti-terrorist special forces group *Grenzschutz Gruppe 9* (Border Security Group 9 or GSG 9).

Although there is no evidence that the RAF provided concrete support for the Palestinian attack, the leadership did express its full solidarity for Black September in another long and rambling statement. Rather than producing a critique of Israeli policy the RAF went a step further in identifying Israel as part of an international capitalist conspiracy. Referring to the 'complicity of Israeli/West German imperialism' and 'Israel's Nazi-fascism', the RAF argued erroneously that the German police had never had any intention of negotiating.[37] Above all they felt 'that their enemy is not only Israel, the enemy is imperialism, that not only Israel is bloodthirsty, not only the USA in regard to Vietnam, but the whole imperialism against liberation movements'.[38] Although the document was not

36. Reeve, S., *One Day in September*, p. 45.

37. From 'Die Aktion des "Schwarzen September" in München: Zur Strategie des antiimperialistischen Kampfes, November 1972', quoted in *Rote Armee Fraktion: Texte und Materialien*, p. 159 and pp. 172–3.

38. Ibid., p. 173.

informed by racial arguments, and was not a polemic against Judaism, the identification of Israel as part of an international conspiracy had clear parallels with the paranoia that informed Nazi anti-Semitism. In a period full of ironies this is perhaps one of the greatest: a group that presented itself as anti-Nazi had tied itself in so many theoretical knots that it was espousing a view that bore a striking resemblance to the theories it claimed to reject.

While the RAF regrouped, the captured leadership continued their campaign against the state from their prison cells. At first Baader, Ensslin et al., were separated and kept in solitary confinement in prisons across Germany, while a new prison facility was constructed for their trial at Stammheim near Stuttgart. Once again the authorities, in their desire to prevent escapes, presented the RAF with weapons in the propaganda war: permanent solitary confinement, censored mail, CCTV surveillance, and so on, were viewed by the RAF, and even by many who opposed them, as infringements of their human rights.[39] The RAF had little regard for the human rights, or right to a fair trial, of those they had arbitrarily killed. Yet they had not been convicted of any terrorist crimes and could claim with some justification that the government was ignoring legal rights that stood at the heart of the constitution. From 17 January to 12 February 1973, forty of the imprisoned RAF members held the first of a series of hunger strikes against their conditions. The strike, which lasted for two months, gained them international publicity and sympathy, and again brought the democratic credentials of the *Bundesrepublik* into question. Another hunger strike was begun by eighty imprisoned terrorists on 8 May, during the course of which the authorities used force-feeding for the first time. The RAF accused the authorities of resurrecting the 'methods of the recent past' in order 'openly to terrorize a section of the proletariat' with the prospect of 'Treblinka, Maidanek, Sobibor' so that they could break 'the resistance of the great majority of the people against exploitation'.[40] The hunger strike had no effect, however, and came to an end on 29 June 1973.

Despite the best efforts of the second-generation RAF members to form themselves into an effective force, the focus of the RAF campaign remained with those in prison. In February 1974 police conducted mass searches across Frankfurt and Berlin and captured 15 RAF members, destroying

39. After his visit to the RAF leaders in Stammheim on 4 December 1974, Jean-Paul Sartre argued that 'this group endangers the Left. They are bad for the Left', but he still expressed concern at the conditions in which they were kept, and noted the negative effects of the hunger strikes and the isolation on Baader's mental and physical health. See Aust, *Der Baader-Meinhof Komplex*, pp. 317–18.

40. From 'Hungerstreikerklärung vom 8. Mai 1973', quoted in *Rote Armee Fraktion: Texte und Materialien*, pp. 187–8.

whole cells in one fell swoop. In August, while the active RAF members regrouped and reassessed their position, Meinhof was transferred to Berlin to stand trial for her part in the freeing of Baader in 1970. Horst Mahler, whose original not guilty verdict had been quashed by the Federal High Court was also accused. He had been given a sentence of 12 years after a trial in February 1973 on charges of bank robbery and founding an illegal organization, i.e., the RAF. At the end of November 1974 they were both found guilty, with Meinhof sentenced to 8 years in prison for attempted murder, and Mahler to 14 years. During the trial, on 13 September 1974, forty imprisoned members of the RAF began another hunger strike against 'dehumanization through social isolation', the use of constant television surveillance, 'attempted murder through withdrawal of water during hunger strikes', as well as attempts to carry out psychological studies, often with the forced administration of narcotics.[41] Holger Meins died on hunger strike on 9 November, although the RAF claimed his doctors had decided to feed him only 400 calories a day once he had lost consciousness, effectively sentencing him to death.[42] The hunger strike was not brought to an end until 5 February 1975, although after 145 days it had gained almost nothing for the terrorists.

By this stage the long and tortuous process of bringing the RAF leaders to trial had also begun. In October 1974 Federal Prosecutor Siegfried Buback, who had served under the Nazis and had been one of the state prosecutors involved in the Spiegel Affair in 1962, brought charges of murder and the formation of a criminal association against Baader, Ensslin, Meinhof, Meins and Raspe.[43] The authorities further added to concerns about human rights infringements when the *Bundestag* passed the so-called 'Baader-Meinhof Law' at the end of December, allowing judges to bar defence lawyers from courts if they were suspected of participating in, or aiding, the crime under investigation. This new law also made it possible to bar joint defences, and to allow court hearings to continue even if the defendants made themselves incapable of attending.[44] The trial, which started on 21 May 1975, dragged on for years, and it is impossible to give details here of the day-to-day difficulties of the case.[45] The defendants

41. *Unserer Hungerstreikerklärung*, file Originale Dokumentation, Bewaffneter kampf, RAF Erklärungen, APOusB.

42. *Erklärung anläßlich des Todes von Holger Meins*, file Originale Dokumentation, Bewaffneter Kampf, RAF, Ulrike Meinhof, H.M. Schleyer, Hungerstreik, Diverses, APOusB.

43. Aust, *Der Baader-Meinhof Komplex*, p. 301.

44. Ibid., pp. 322–3.

45. A detailed pro-RAF account is given in Bakker Schut, P.H., *Stammheim*.

refused to cooperate with what they saw as a political show trial in a court that represented the interests of a fascist regime. Their behaviour in court was undoubtedly provocative and unrepentant, and generally succeeded in prompting some form of authoritarian punitive response. The machinations of the court also provided them with evidence of state interference in the justice system: the presiding judge, Theodor Prinzing, had to resign in January 1977 after allegations of collusion with the state prosecutors.[46] Once again, the biases against those who questioned the post-war settlement were laid bare, as was the threat to democracy from a state determined to defeat the terrorists.

The start of the trial was immediately preceded by a renewed terrorist campaign, this time involving a multiplicity of groups, whether the RAF, SPK, *Schwarze Hilfe*, *Bewegung 2. Juni* or a host of others, presenting the police with a hydra-like problem. The *Bewegung 2. Juni* showed their capabilities on 10 November 1974, the day after Meins's death, when they shot and killed Günter von Drenkmann, the President of the Berlin Supreme Court, during an abortive attempt to kidnap him.[47] They were more successful on 27 February 1975 when they kidnapped the Berlin CDU leader and Mayoral candidate Peter Lorenz. This was the first time in the history of the *Bundesrepublik* that a politician had been the victim of a kidnapping. A day later the terrorists released a photograph of Lorenz, along with a demand for the release of six imprisoned colleagues, including Horst Mahler.[48] Heinrich Albertz, the hate figure for the protesters of the late 1960s who had by this stage recanted his earlier position, was requested by the *Bewegung 2. Juni* (named, of course, after the events that cost Albertz his political career) to act as an intermediary.[49] Mahler decided to stay behind, but the five remaining terrorists along with Albertz were flown to Aden on 3 March, and Lorenz was released unharmed two days later. The Lorenz case shows particularly well how the terrorists failed to gain public support. In the aftermath of the kidnapping 61 per cent of people asked in a survey by *Der Spiegel* said it was wrong to hand over terrorist prisoners in exchange for kidnapped politicians, and 53 per cent felt the same when ordinary people had been kidnapped. Despite the findings of

46. Aust, *Der Baader Meinhof Komplex*, pp. 437–8.

47. Ibid., pp. 305–6.

48. 'Entführer wollen Mahler befreien', *Frankfurter Rundschau*, 1 March 1975, p. 1 includes the photograph of Lorenz holding a sign saying 'Peter Lorenz – prisoner of the Bewegung 2. Juni'.

49. Schuster, *Heinrich Albertz*, p. 278. Albertz told *Der Spiegel* that 'I was the guarantee that we would not all be shot like hares' and that he had shaken hands with the terrorists when he left them, something unthinkable for him in 1967. See 'Kein First-Class-Gefühl', *Der Spiegel*, 10 March 1975, p. 16.

a survey just before the Lorenz kidnapping that less than half of the population supported the death penalty, in the *Der Spiegel* survey 57 per cent said that the death sentence was the best method of dealing with the terrorists.[50] This bucked a consistent trend toward public opposition to capital punishment and was the only instance of a rise in support for the death sentence up to this time.

The state response toward renewed RAF activities exemplified a new ruthlessness in dealing with terrorists that was often at odds with the self-proclaimed objective of defending democracy. On 24 April 1975 the RAF *Kommando Holger Meins* took 11 hostages at the German Embassy in Stockholm in an attempt to get core RAF members released from prison. They killed two members of staff, and after the German government refused to meet their demands they accidentally detonated a bomb that destroyed much of the building, killed one of the terrorists, Ulrich Wessel, and injured the five others. The Ambassador, Dieter Stoecker, was among the casualties. Siegfried Hausner, who had taken part in the attack, was flown to prison in Germany despite the seriousness of his injuries, and died in Stammheim prison on 5 May, leaving the German government open to accusations of inhumane treatment.[51] This was followed in September by a massive bomb explosion at Hamburg railway station, in which 11 people were injured. Although the press unanimously blamed the RAF, the imprisoned RAF leaders distanced themselves from the bombing.[52] The year's bloody events came to a close with an attack on the OPEC headquarters in Vienna on 21 December under the leadership of Carlos 'the Jackal' and including two of the terrorists released as a result of the Lorenz kidnapping, Hans-Joachim Klein and Gabriele Kröcher Tiedemann. Two security guards and an OPEC representative were killed, and 10 OPEC ministers, along with 25 others, were kidnapped. They were only released the next day after the terrorists were flown to Algiers.[53]

---

50. 'Mehrheit für harten Kurs', *Der Spiegel*, 10 March 1975, p. 22.

51. The *Komitee gegen Folter an politischen Gefangenen in der BRD* claimed Genscher had insisted on Hausner being transported to prison in Germany despite protestations from doctors in Sweden, and that he was the victim, like von Rauch and Meins, of a state campaign to murder 'revolutionaries'. See *Siegfried Hausner vom Staatschutz ermordet*, file Originale Dokumentation, Bewaffneter Kampf, RAF, Ulrike Meinhof, H.M. Schleyer, Hungerstreik, Diverses, APOusB.

52. 'Erklärung zum Bombenanschlag in Hamburger Hauptbahnhof', quoted in *Rote Armee Fraktion, Texte und Materialien*, pp. 196–8. The RAF argued that the bombing was 'reactionary' because the 'actions of the urban guerrilla are never directed against the people'.

53. See Vocke, H., 'Hinter dem Wiener Terrorakt stehen die arabische Linke und Moskau', *Frankfurter Allgemeine Zeitung*, 24 December 1975, file Lorenz 20.2–26.12 Akte 2, Aktenbestand des Sozialistischen Anwaltskollektivs, HIfS.

Attention then returned to the RAF trial at Stammheim. The simmering tensions between Meinhof and Ensslin boiled over on 4 May 1976 when Ensslin distanced the RAF leadership from the 1972 bombing of the Springer building in Hamburg. This was the first public split in their solidarity, and indicated Ensslin had succeeded in isolating Meinhof from the rest of the leadership.[54] Just five days later Meinhof was found hanging dead in her cell in mysterious circumstances that prompted a flood of conspiracy theories. Numerous aspects of the story presented by the authorities were problematic, inconsistent or contradictory, prompting suspicions that Meinhof had been murdered.[55] Even if she had committed suicide, it was still possible for sympathizers to argue that she had been driven to take her life by the terrifying prospect of indefinite isolation in prison.[56] The response from the international terrorist community was swift. On 27 June the PFLP and others, including two RAF members, hijacked an Air France airbus on its way from Tel Aviv to Paris. It was flown to the airport at Entebbe in Uganda where the non-Jewish passengers were released and the terrorists put forth their demands that 53 imprisoned terrorists around the world be released, including six RAF prisoners. The authorities refused to cooperate and the impasse continued until 4 July when Israeli Special Forces stormed the aeroplane, killing seven of the hijackers. Among the 53 hostages, 31 were killed in the firefight.[57] In direct response to the Entebbe events, Hans-Dietrich Genscher proposed the creation of a Convention against Hijacking to the UN General Assembly in September. This was finally adopted in December, with signatories promising not to meet the demands of hijackers and to seek to bring them to justice. Genscher, who had negotiated with the Palestinian terrorists at the Munich Olympics and had been scarred by the spectacular failure of the rescue operation, was able to apply the new Convention all too soon as the terrorist campaign reached a crescendo in 1977.

54. Aust, *Der Baader-Meinhof Komplex*, pp. 388–90. The file Originale Dokumentation, Bewaffneter Kampf, 2. Juni, Bücher, Broschuren, Zeitschriften, APOusB includes photocopies of letters between Meinhof and Ensslin from 1973 to 1976, in which the rivalry between the two women worsens into open and petty abuse. Meinhof's mental health deteriorates noticeably. See also Krebs, M., *Ulrike Meinhof*.

55. *Rache für Ulrike: Ulrike ist ermordet worden!*, file Originale Dokumentation, Bewaffneter Kampf, RAF, Ulrike Meinhof, H. M. Schleyer, Hungerstreik, Diverses, APOusB says the state was presenting murder as suicide in order to silence criticism from the Left.

56. *Mord*, file Originale Dokumentation, Bewaffneter Kampf, RAF, Ulrike Meinhof, H.M. Schleyer, Hungerstreik, Diverses, APOusB. This document, dated 13 May 1976, argues that solitary confinement was responsible for Meinhof's state of mind when she killed herself, and that she was therefore murdered by the state.

57. See 'Das Geiseldrama: "Professionell, eingeübt"', *Der Spiegel*, 5 July 1976, pp. 84–8.

RAF actions once again centred on the plight of those in prison. Yet another hunger strike was begun on 29 March, with the RAF prisoners this time demanding to be treated according to the Geneva Convention for Prisoners of War.[58] This would have meant a radical change in their conditions, and the criminal proceedings against them would necessarily be terminated, which the state authorities could not countenance. The strike was bolstered on 7 April when the RAF *Kommando Ulrike Meinhof* assassinated Siegfried Buback and two of his colleagues in Karlsruhe.[59] His assassination did not prevent the announcement, on 28 April, that Baader, Ensslin and Raspe had been found guilty of murder and sentenced to life imprisonment, making the hunger strike moribund, and prompting its abandonment on 30 April. The release of the RAF leadership had already been the subject of two previous kidnappings, but the prospect of long-term isolation gave a new sense of urgency to the actions of the active RAF membership. In July the RAF attempted to kidnap Jürgen Ponto, the head of the Dresdner Bank, at his home near Frankfurt, but it was bungled and Ponto was murdered.[60] Shortly afterward the RAF leadership began another hunger strike, but this was called off on 2 September, just three days before the final RAF attempt to gain their release.

Hans-Martin Schleyer, the head of the Employer's Association and of the Federal Union of German Industry, was kidnapped in Cologne by the RAF *Kommando Siegfried Hausner* on 5 September 1977. The four people travelling in his car at the time were shot and killed.[61] It was only on 13 October that the RAF released a photograph of Schleyer, showing that he was still alive. They demanded the release of 11 RAF prisoners, and on the same day their ultimatum was reinforced when Palestinian terrorists hijacked a Lufthansa jet. Of course, by this stage the position of the Federal authorities was clear: no negotiations with terrorists and no concessions. Unlike with Munich in 1972 the authorities were now in a position to deal forcefully and ruthlessly with the terrorists, having established clear procedures, command structures, information systems, lines of communications and, above all, effective special forces. In Mogadishu airport in Somalia on 17 October, GSG 9 units under Ulrich Wegener, who had witnessed the Munich Massacre, stormed the hijacked jet, killed three

---

58. 'Tief in der Tinte', *Der Spiegel*, 11. April 1977, pp. 31–2 and 'Hungerstreikerklärung vom 29. März 1977, quoted in *Rote Armee Fraktion: Texte und Materialien*, pp. 265–7.

59. Peters, B., *RAF*, pp. 220–7 is a detailed account.

60. Ibid., pp. 227–32.

61. Aust, *Der Baader-Meinhof Komplex*, pp. 483–7 is an excellent account of the kidnapping. *Rote Armee Fraktion: Texte und Materialien*, pp. 270–3 reprints the RAF press releases covering the period of the kidnapping.

of the terrorists, injured a fourth, and released all 86 hostages. When the news filtered back to Stammheim prison, Baader, Raspe and Ensslin committed suicide. Irmgard Möller was discovered severely injured in her cell and later challenged the official version of collective suicide. The same day, 18 October, the RAF executed Schleyer and dumped his body in the back of a car, which was discovered in Mülhausen the following day.[62] It is difficult to overestimate the impact of these climactic events on German society.[63] The fear, horror and outrage generated by the continuous terrorist threats and attacks, culminating in the violence of September and October 1977, was such that these few months are now commonly referred to by the shorthand term of the *Deutsche Herbst* (German Autumn). This was effectively the end of the terrorist campaign launched by Baader in 1968: RAF bombings and assassinations continued throughout the 1980s and 1990s, but they never again achieved the scale and frequency of the campaign in the 1970s.

The terrorist attacks were brutal, counter-productive, and patently unsuccessful in provoking a revolution. The view of West German democracy presented by the terrorists had little resonance for the majority of the population, for whom the Federal Republic still represented the best hope of stability, peace, and a renewed place for Germany in the wider world. This does not mean that responses to the terrorists were universally disapproving, however. A survey carried out by the Institut für Demoskopie Allensbach in March 1971 found that an incredible 82 per cent of people had heard of the RAF, even at this early stage of the terrorist campaign. Among all age groups disapproval of the terrorists was found to be high: 51 per cent of 16-to-29-year-olds, and 59 per cent of 45-to-59-year-olds regarded them as 'criminals'. Yet 25 per cent of people between 16 and 29 years of age described them as 'political fighters', compared to 18 per cent for the total population. Moreover, 10 per cent of people in this age group said they would provide shelter for members of the RAF being pursued by the police, compared to just 5 per cent of the population as a whole.[64] While such results could be taken to indicate deep-seated disapproval of the Federal Republic in a minority of the population, the disparity between the numbers who viewed the terrorists as freedom fighters and those willing to help them does not suggest unqualified approval. Rather a minority of West Germans, particularly among the young, felt alienated

62. The *Kommando Siegfried Hausner* announced they had ended Schleyer's 'despicable and corrupt existence'. See *Rote Armee Fraktion: Texte und Materialien*, p. 273.

63. "Deutsche können stark und menschlich sein", *Der Spiegel*, 24 October 1977, pp. 4–9 gives some indication of the outpouring of anguish over these events.

64. Noelle-Neumann, *The Germans*, p. 151.

from the Federal Republic, or at least critical toward the attitudes informing state and public responses to terrorism. This could be identified as a
dangerous threat to democracy, or alternatively as a symptom of the
extreme reactions of the state that in itself helped to keep state policies in
check. In contrast to the possibilities for largely uninhibited government
actions during the Nazi period, or the widespread apathy to politics that
marked the immediate post-war years, by the 1970s at least some press,
public and political opinion sought to challenge the extreme responses of
state institutions, whether as a result of approval of the terrorist campaign,
or fears over the threat to West German democracy represented by both
terrorism and the response to it. In this sense it is notable that the *Extremistenbeschluß* was largely unenforceable in the democratic context of the
Federal Republic, while events such as the von Rauch shooting prompted
a storm of disapproval from across the political spectrum that helped to
set limits upon the actions of the state. The state and popular responses to
the terrorist campaign were nevertheless a low point for West German
democracy at a time when attitudes to other aspects of daily life were
becoming more tolerant. The terrorist campaign in West Germany was
particularly ruthless and violent, even in comparison with events in other
Western countries, and this, along with the Nazi past, and the fears prompted by the cold war, help to explain the extreme state policies and public
attitudes toward terrorism. Above all, though, it underlines the immaturity
of West German democracy just a few decades after its creation, and the
fact that both the state and the wider population were still negotiating an
understanding of the meaning of democracy, and of the checks and
balances necessary for its preservation. Fears of a repetition of the mistakes of the past made a sense of proportion difficult to maintain, and state
authorities, along with the public and the press, were still learning the
value of measured judgement.

The Women's Movement

The story of the women's movement that developed in the late 1960s gets to the heart of the conflict over the legacy of the 1960s. Dealing as it did with women's equality in law and in the workplace, sexual liberation, contraception, abortion reform, child-care, women's expectations, their role within the family and society, as well as their relationships with men, it tackled moral dilemmas, entrenched attitudes and privileges head on. For some it was perhaps the most enduring and valuable legacy of both the protest movements and the new freedoms in daily life made possible in the 1960s. For others, both men and women, it meant the destruction of cherished values and a concomitant confusion about acceptable behaviour. For those who feel that women's emancipation still has some way to go, there are others who feel it has already gone too far down the road of stifling political correctness and destructive social disintegration. For the Right, the 1960s in general, and the women's movement in particular, is to blame for a rise in divorce rates and in the number of single parents that has destroyed the family as a social unit. The changes rested, though, on the freedoms and choices made possible by post-war economic prosperity, necessarily making any resistance to change an attack on symptoms rather than on causes. The resulting tension, between sex and the family as significant for national survival and social cohesion that made state interference essential, contrasting with an emphasis on the private sphere and personal decision-making, played a central role in the formation of the women's movement.

This new movement was the latest in a long line of campaigns on women's issues, but because of its basis in unprecedentedly extensive social change its influence was considerably more far-reaching than that of earlier movements. Struggles for abortion reform and birth control can be traced back to the Weimar and Nazi periods; demands for voting rights and parliamentary representation pre-dated the First World War. In the immediate post-Second World War period, with so many men dead or prisoners of war, women outnumbered men by seven million: in 1950 every second woman from 20 to 30 years of age was unmarried.[1] Married women had unprecedented control within the family, and both married and single women, without male financial support, were forced to seek paid employment. Eva Kolinsky views these women as 'trailblazers of change' because 'the conventional taboos about what women can or cannot do were increasingly out of step with the realities of women's activities'.[2] Nevertheless from the early 1950s women's traditional roles within the family were reaffirmed with state measures to encourage large families that presented the family as the cornerstone of West German life. Robert G. Moeller's exhaustive account of state attitudes to the family in the 1940s and 1950s makes it clear that the successive Adenauer administrations took a conservative Christian view of the family in which paternal authority was supreme. CDU declarations even applied Nazi terminology by insisting 'the family is the fundament of the social organization [*sic*] of life. Its living space (*Lebensraum*) is holy.'[3] Klaus-Jörg Ruhl, in his history of women in the post-war period, quotes a number of documents from the late 1940s through to the 1960s that convey the prevailing conservative attitudes to women. The 1948 statement by the Ackermann Congregation appears to be typical of the many contemporary paeans to domestication: 'as wife she is made the "helper of the man", who is subordinate to his authority as father of the house. As mother she is appointed to propagate the human race . . . as maiden she represents the personal dignity of humanity, that is independent of anyone's regulation.'[4] It may seem a grotesque caricature in hindsight, but for conservatives of the 1940s and 1950s the ideal woman seems to have been a housewife with a large family, who was obediently servile to her husband. She would be passive, romantic, innocently non-sexual, dependent and above all perfectly contented with this situation as the true expression of femininity. The ambitious career woman was, according to this model, an abomination.

The importance of preserving West German women's role was central to Adenauer's decision to create a Ministry of Family Affairs, under a Minister with Cabinet status, after the September 1953 election victory. The first incumbent of the office, Franz-Josef Wuermeling, was a conservative Christian for whom paternal authority within the family was the

1. Kolinsky, E., *Women in West Germany*, pp. 25 and 79. The figure for the number of women refers to 1946.

2. Ibid., p. 80.

3. Moeller, *Protecting Motherhood*, p. 65. See also Nave-Herz, R., *Wandel und Kontinuität der Familie in der Bundesrepublik Deutschland*.

4. 'Die Rolle der Frau aus der Sicht der Ackermann-Gemeinde, Mai 1948' quoted in Ruhl, K-J., (ed.), *Frauen in der Nachkriegszeit*, p. 111.

natural order. According to Moeller he 'explicitly denounced any conception of women's equality that might shake "the Christian foundations of the family authority exercised by the father" and pronounced his post to be a "defensive position" against any misunderstandings of equality'.[5] Article 3 of the Basic Law explicitly recognized equality between the sexes, and for the CDU there was no contradiction between defending female equality and asserting paternal authority within the family. On the contrary, the family was identified as a key battleground against the communist East, where traditional values were being undermined by collectivism and the destruction of the family as a social unit. Defending paternalism benignly ensured the protection of traditional female roles, as well as encouraging the population growth deemed necessary to defend the West German 'national spirit' from communist hordes.[6] For the CDU 'the choices were simple – between "freedom, human dignity [and] Christian-occidental thinking of mankind," and the "spirit of darkness and slavery," the "anti-Christian spirit"; "between good and evil, between life and destruction"'.[7] In another of the documents reproduced in Ruhl's invaluable collection, Klaus Mörsdorf, writing in 1952, asserted forcefully that 'unity and order of the family will be secured through a double hierarchy: the authority of the parents over the children and the primary place of the father'.[8] There is much here that smacks of thrashing around for excuses to maintain a hegemonic authority that was under threat, but it would be a mistake to interpret fears of the catastrophic social consequences of women's equality as purely disingenuous manipulation. They seem to have been genuinely held by both men and women.

Policy decisions that aimed to preserve the family, with the domesticated and obedient woman at its heart, ensued. The Basic Law, and particularly its provisions guaranteeing women's equality with men, was incompatible with the Civil Code of 1900, especially the latter's emphasis on paternal authority. Recognizing the difficulty of creating laws that resolved this conflict, the Parliamentary Council gave the *Bundestag* until 1 April 1953 to pass new laws on marriage and parenting, with the proviso that failure to meet the deadline would bring the provisions of the Basic

5. Moeller, *Protecting Motherhood*, p. 102.

6. Poiger, 'Rock n' Roll', discusses the ways in which female teenagers, especially *Halbstarke*, were seen as communist or fascist subversives, undermining traditional wholesome ideals of femininity.

7. Moeller, *Protecting Motherhood*, p. 104.

8. 'Klaus Mörsdorf über die hierarchische Struktur von Ehe und Familie, 1952', quoted in Ruhl, *Frauen in der Nachkriegszeit*, p. 116.

Law into effect, making incompatible laws null and void. After years of wrangling, the deadline came and went, with the CDU maintaining its stance that paternalism within the family was essential for 'order' and that this did not contradict women's right to equality. Once the deadline had been passed the right to decide on family law devolved onto the legal system, making for a chaotic situation in which different courts handed down contradictory rulings.[9] In May 1957 the *Bundestag* voted for a new family law that again upheld patriarchal authority within the family, and this came into effect in July 1958. A year later, however, the Federal Constitutional Court declared that maintaining paternal authority in law was not consistent with the guarantees of equality included in the Basic Law which, it decided, should mean equal authority.

Although it had lost the battle over equality, by this stage the Adenauer government had already introduced a number of policies designed to strengthen the family. In 1952 a *Mutterschutgesetz* (Law for the Protection of Mothers) was passed, giving maternity leave for pregnant women, and protection for working mothers against unscrupulous employers. It would be a mistake to see this as a victory for women's rights: the new law was framed above all to protect children from the unnatural demands of working mothers. In turn, women were to be protected from employers who threatened the fulfilment of their roles as mothers.[10] The November 1954 decision to introduce *Kindergeld* (child money) was perhaps of even greater importance for the family. Starting on 1 January 1955 the state made payments of 25 DM per month to workers with families with three or more children. The unemployed, divorced mothers or those receiving widow's pensions were not eligible for the payments, meaning those with the greatest need received no help, but then this was not the aim of the law: the women with large families who qualified for state assistance were unlikely to be working mothers. It was not possible to maintain this contradictory and flagrantly biased stance for long and in December 1955 the law was altered to allow payments to unemployed parents. In July 1957 *Kindergeld* was increased to 30 DM, followed by another increase to 40 DM in May 1959. Finally, in June 1961 *Kindergeld* was reformed to allow 25 DM per month to parents with an annual income lower than 7,200 DM for each child after and including their second child, making it a more equitable and inclusive system that would help those most in need. The CDU emphasized its family policies in elections throughout the Adenauer era, clearly feeling not only that this was a key issue for the

9. Moeller, *Protecting Motherhood*, p. 190.
10. Ibid., p. 160.

electorate, but that in introducing 'a legal and social order that is one of the most protective of the family' it had made popular decisions.[11]

To a great extent they were correct: campaigns for women's rights all but disappeared and women's predominantly domestic responsibilities remained largely unchallenged and unchanged throughout the 1960s. Statistics about the number of women in work vary, but all point to only a slight increase. Post-war family policy and the attitudes that informed them were successful in keeping women at home, with Moeller stating that 29.2 per cent of married women were in employment in 1933, dropping to 25 per cent in 1950, only for it to rise to 32 per cent in 1961.[12] Ute Frevert quotes similar data, with 30.1 per cent of married women in work in 1933, 26.4 per cent in 1950, and 36.5 per cent in 1961.[13] Even the most optimistic figures indicate that in 1965 39 per cent of the workforce were women, and when they are examined more closely, these statistics expose further inequalities.[14] Among wage earners 51 per cent of men were skilled workers, compared to just 6 per cent of women, and while a mere 13 per cent of men were unskilled workers, 48 per cent of women met this description. This situation was repeated among salaried workers, with 22 per cent of men in managerial positions, alongside only 3 per cent of women. Nearly two-thirds (61 per cent) of female salaried workers were in 'subordinate' posts, although they were accompanied by only 28 per cent of men, the greatest numbers of whom, 45 per cent, were in 'supervisory' positions. In July 1968 Ulrike Meinhof gave her endorsement for a new women's movement in an article in *Konkret* in which she lamented the wide discrepancies in income between men and women. Citing 3.54 DM as the lowest male hourly wage rates in 1964, she argued that the highest wages available to women workers in the same year only reached 3.17 DM. She asked 'why despite enjoying the guarantee of equal rights in the Basic Law women still don't have emancipation [*sic*]'.[15] The answer lay in traditional views on 'femininity' and the role of women: a survey conducted in 1964 found that 75 per cent of men and 72 per cent of women believed women's place was in the home.[16]

11. 'Aus einer Broschüre über die Familienpolitik der CDU. Mai 1961', quoted in Ruhl, *Frauen der Nachkriegszeit*, p. 146. Cramer, A., *Zur Lage der Familie und der Familienpolitik in der Bundesrepublik Deutschland* gives a highly detailed theoretical discussion of family policy from a Marxist perspective, emphasizing state policy as a tool of social control.

12. Moeller, *Protecting Motherhood*, p. 217.

13. Frevert, U., *Women in German Society*, p. 333.

14. 'Gesellschaft: Frauenarbeit', *Der Spiegel*, 14 April 1965, p. 56.

15. Meinhof, U. M., 'Frauenkram', *Konkret*, July 1968, pp. 24–5.

16. Quoted in Frevert, *Women in German Society*, p. 287.

In many other respects, though, women's position in society had been transformed. Throughout the 1960s, of course, West Germany experienced profound social changes, including a liberalization of attitudes to sex. Traditional conceptions of femininity and women's social role clashed with the new expectations of the sexual revolution. The sexual revolution was certainly not without its contradictions: both the deeply conservative Springer press and the far-left magazine *Konkret* used ever greater amounts of nudity to increase their sales as the decade progressed. While the authoritarian Right represented by the Springer empire could make use of right-libertarian notions of freedom of expression to defend the use of nudity, the Left presented the challenge to sexual mores as a revolutionary development. *Konkret* appears to have made a concerted effort in the mid-1960s to present itself as a left-wing German version of *Playboy* by championing the freedoms of the sexual revolution, most notably through its conspicuous use of female nudity.[17] Nudity in the media, predatory sexual behaviour by men, sexual permissiveness of the kind preached by *Kommune I*, and so on, could be (and were) seen as liberating.

In the Spring and Summer of 1968 *Konkret* ran a series of articles on 'Sex and Revolution' by senior SDS member Reimut Reiche that are worth looking at in detail because of its attempt to outline the revolutionary perspective on the sexual revolution. The first article began 'what has sex to do with politics? Everything, says the New Left, the pupils of Marcuse and Dutschke.' For the Left 'regulation of sexual desire and feelings of guilt' were methods of oppression used by ruling classes to keep workers in check.[18] Although questioning the effectiveness of sexual liberation as a tool for class struggle, Reiche did argue that the limited availability of the contraceptive pill, as well as the attitude of Springer titles like the teen magazine *Twen*, were deliberate attempts by 'rulers' to maintain control over sexuality.[19] In the third article in the series, Reiche even began by calling the Springer press a 'manipulation instrument for social conformity' by encouraging women to comply with norms of attractiveness

17. *Konkret*, November 1962, pp. 20–1 features the magazine's first article on *Playboy* and further articles followed this over subsequent months. After several years of printing photographs with partial nudity, *Konkret* used a nude on its front cover for the first time in October 1964. From this point onward the amount of nudity rapidly increased, as did the number of articles on sex, with a particular emphasis on teenage sex. *Konkret*, July 1965, p. 17 even included an advertisement for *Playboy*, and in the October 1965 edition an article on *Playboy*, pp. 6–9 was the feature article dominating the cover. *Playboy* was first published in December 1953.

18. Reiche, R., 'Sex und Revolution', *Konkret*, April 1968, p. 10.

19. Ibid., p. 12.

and to restrict themselves to 'narcissistic' jobs such as modelling.[20] For Reiche the supposed liberalism toward sex expressed in the Springer titles was informed by a desire to impose limits, with sex before marriage at best being a preparation for married life, and sex itself being presented as a form of titillating consumption by men.[21] For many on the Left, then, even members of the SDS for whom the pacifist phrase 'make love, not war' was anathema, the sexual revolution was an important challenge to imposed, restrictive norms of behaviour. It is notable, though, that this debate was dominated by men, many of whom do not seem to have shared Reiche's sensitivities about the portrayal of women. In this sense it is notable that the anarchist newsletter *Agit 883*, while supportive of the violent aims of the RAF, was also overflowing with aggressive, and often misogynist, sexual imagery.

The ambiguities in the situation, particularly the difficulty of drawing the line between liberation, empowerment and exploitation, was already causing problems. In December 1967 Rudi Dutschke had insisted 'today's form of senselessness is the unconscious form. Take James Bond films. Here the woman is totally the object of men, a sadistic object.'[22] A feature article in *Der Spiegel* a year later made it clear that sexual imagery had come to dominate magazines, television, film, theatre and advertising, and that articles on sex had become almost an obsession for the overwhelmingly male editorial staff of magazines like *Jasmin*, *Twen*, *Es*, and *Quick*. *Der Spiegel* observed how 'the APO magazine "Konkret" fills it's cover page with 120 square centimetres of female flesh ("How women really love") and 15 square centimetres of Dutschke'.[23] It could be argued that the media were merely representing changes in attitudes to sex, that they exemplified these changes, or that they contributed to them, but it can hardly be said that women were in control of their own bodies or of the liberalization of attitudes to sex in the 1960s. Media images of women were overwhelmingly aimed at a male audience or confirmed women's traditional roles. Limited access to contraception, and a concomitant fear of pregnancy or of the risks of illegal abortions, was combined with an ongoing double standard toward women's sexuality and confusion over what constituted 'femininity', including contradictory demands between domestic life and the work place.

In many respects the emergent women's movement of the late 1960s was a negotiation of the meaning of the sexual revolution and post-war

20. Reiche, R., 'Sex bei Axel Springer: Sex und Revolution III', *Konkret*, p. 36.
21. Ibid., pp. 38–9.
22. Dutschke, R., "Überall wird entkleidet", *Der Spiegel*, 11 December 1967, p. 62.
23. 'Gesellschaft: Sex', *Der Spiegel*, 18 November 1968, p. 46.

prosperity for and by German women. Hermann Korte argues that the changes in sexual attitudes of the 1960s were informed by assumptions that men and women had the same sexual appetites and that the differences between the sexes were superficial. For Korte the women's movement represented an attempt to reassert women's differences. In this sense, aspects of the women's movement can be seen as an attempt by women to wrest control of their bodies and decision-making from the domination of men and the state.[24] In this situation, then, the women's movement was able to gain, from a cross-section of West German women, widespread support far beyond the restrictions of revolutionary politics.

The origins of the women's movement are to be found within revolutionary politics because inequality of treatment and opportunity played an unmistakable and contradictory part in the protest campaigns of the 1960s. In an article on female protesters entitled 'the brides of the revolution', the *Abendzeitung* in May 1968 took the opportunity to publish numerous photographs of young women, describing the 'barricade hot stuff' as 'especially pretty'.[25] Similar attitudes appear to have been held by the majority of male protesters, and few women attained senior positions within any of the protest campaigns or organizations. It is notable that men dominate the protests discussed in the chapters of the current volume. Although numerous eyewitness statements by women have been quoted, none of the speeches, declarations and articles are by women, with the exception of those by Ulrike Meinhof during her tenure at *Konkret*. Rudi Dutschke seems to have been unusual in arguing 'woman is not only for the pleasure of men'.[26]

On 20 May 1968, female activists discontented with this situation created an *Aktionsrat zur Befreiung der Frauen* (Action Committee for the Liberation of Women) in Berlin.[27] Women at the *Republikanischer Club* had been active on women's issues for several months, and had launched a campaign for the improvement of Berlin's kindergartens in March.[28] They had rapidly become dispersed into different discussion groups, however, and the new *Aktionsrat* was partially a reaction to this atomization. Although its founders were insistent that they were 'not the "women's working group of the *Republikanischer Club*" or the "SDS Women's

24. Korte, H., *Eine Gesellschaft im Aufbruch*, pp. 100–2.

25. 'Die Bräute der Revolution', *Abendzeitung*, 31 May 1968, p. 29.

26. '"Überall wird entkleidet": Dutschke über Ehe, Liebe und Sex', *Der Spiegel*, 11 December 1967, p. 62.

27. *Aktionsrat zur Befreiung der Frauen, Rundbrief, Berlin, den 20. Mai 1968*, Originale Dokumentation, file Frau Träger 221, APOusB.

28. *Protokol vom 27.3.68*, Originale Dokumentation, file Frau Träger 221, APOusB.

Section"', the situation within the SDS was a key factor in the formation of the *Aktionsrat*, and its members contributed in no small measure to the SDS's disintegration.[29] Anna Pam, an SDS member and one of the founders of the *Aktionsrat*, recalls

> at the time we weren't thinking of setting up a separate women's movement, but to make the SDS and the movement deal with issues of direct concern to women ... It began with a rather aggressive rebellion of SDS women against the male patterns of leadership. We also felt uneasy about the theories of sexual liberation, without being able to pinpoint it concretely. And finally, we were angry about the behaviour of the men in the movement – today you'd say their male chauvinism. The last was so obvious that we immediately got a large following of women.[30]

In September the *Aktionsrat* placed their grievances before the SDS Delegates Conference in Frankfurt. In a resolution drawn up in advance they expressed their frustration that 'reflection on the problems of personal development' had been 'made taboo' by the SDS, to the extent that attempts by female members to discuss them were constantly obstructed. They presented a class-based interpretation of family relations 'with the man as bourgeois and the woman as proletarian – lord and vassal' that 'implied the objective function of men as class enemies'. They insisted 'the denial of [the existence of] the leader principle in the SDS is just grotesque'. They wanted recognition that the private sphere had to be altered as a revolutionary act if the transformation of society, and especially the rejection of bourgeois capitalist assumptions, was to be achieved. Even at this early stage the role of men in the women's movement was being debated and the *Aktionsrat* came to the conclusion that they could only challenge the 'patriarchal society' on their own. They acknowledged that 'that is not isolation bound by the illusion that one can emancipate oneself independently from men' but they contended that as a first step they needed to articulate their own needs.[31] Helke Sander told the assembly that most women were non-political 'because until now politics has been one-sidedly defined and their needs have not been covered'. She responded to

29. While carrying out research at the Archiv 'APO und soziale Bewegungen' in February 2000 I was lucky enough to strike up a conversation with Heide Berndt, a former SDS member who had been active in Frankfurt in the 1960s and 1970s. She proudly informed me that 'the women destroyed SDS'. I am grateful to Heide Berndt for sharing her insights into this and other areas of SDS history with me.

30. Quoted in Fraser, *1968*, p. 269.

31. *Resolution für die 23. O. DK des SDS Vorgelegt vom Aktionsrat zur Befreiung der Frauen Berlin*, Originale Dokumentation, file Frau Träger 221, APOusB.

abuse from the men in the audience by telling them women were 'resolved not to take your oppression . . . without a fight any more'. She accused them of 'arrogance' and asked 'why do you speak here of class struggle and at home of orgasm problems? Isn't that a theme for the SDS?'[32] The laughter and insults Sander received reduced her to tears, which one of her colleagues Sigrid Rüger responded to by throwing tomatoes at Hans-Jürgen Krahl.[33] The conference had to be abandoned amid chaos.

Within a short time SDS women's groups had been established across the country. On 12 October the newly established Frankfurt group of the *Aktionsrat* disrupted a ceremony at Frankfurt's Paulskirche to mark the fiftieth anniversary of women's right to vote. Placards saying 'where is the emancipation of manhood?' and 'equal rights – conformity to a pre-existing power system' were carried by a small group who then used physical force in an attempt to wrestle the microphone from the Mayor, who told them 'a minority cannot terrorize us'.[34] A few days later the Berlin branch published the first manifesto of the *Aktionsrat*. In this they presented themselves first and foremost as a 'political group' in the 'anti-authoritarian camp'. They were concerned with the 'problems of the oppression of women in our society' but were not a 'bourgeois emanc-ipation movement' since they rejected every form of reformism for failing to bring the 'socio-economic basis' of capitalist society into question. Instead they felt emancipation could only be achieved through 'a socio-economic revolution'. They reiterated their belief that the men in the SDS were currently incapable of helping their struggle or the formulation of their position, and so they resolved upon a temporary isolation.[35] Even at this early stage, then, many of the issues that would exercise the women's movement for years to come were being raised: the involvement of men, attitudes to the sexual revolution, the nature of women's work, male attempts at vilification, and the pursuit of revolution or reform.

When the SDS Delegates Conference reassembled in Hanover in November, feelings were running high on the issue of women's position

32. *Helke Sander (Aktionsrat zur Befreiung der Frauen)*, Originale Dokumentation, file Frau Träger 221, APOusB is the original typewritten speech. Extracts are reprinted in Helke Sander 'Der SDS – ein aufgeblasener konterrevolutionärer Hefeteig', *Konkret*, 7 October 1968, p. 6.

33. Fraser, *1968*, pp. 269–70 includes a useful but frustratingly brief account. Nave-Herz, R., *Die Geschichte der Frauenbewegung in Deutschland*, pp. 68–9 also gives some useful details.

34. 'Mädchen-Demonstration zum Frauen-Wahlrecht', *Frankfurter Rundschau*, 14 October 1968, p. 11.

35. *Selbstverständnis des Aktionsrats zur Befreiung der Frauen*, dated 16 October 1968, Originale Dokumentation, file Frau Träger 221, APOusB.

within the organization. An 'emancipation flyer' in the *FU Spiegel* by SDS women attending the Conference accused SDS men of being 'dickless' and said that when women opened their mouths, men tried to 'stuff it' with 'socialist constraints, socialist children, love, socialist dismissal, pompousness, potent socialist lecherousness, socialist intellectual pathos, socialist counselling, revolutionary pawing, sexual rational arguments, social orgasms, socialist emancipation drivel'. Such male attempts to reinforce traditional gender roles and views of what constituted 'femininity' stretched to accusations of 'penis envy' and 'hysteria'.[36] At the Conference the *Aktionsrat* was reinforced by the many new women's groups and successfully used anti-authoritarian provocation tactics to disrupt the proceedings. The *Aktionsrat* had exposed strong frustrations that had remained hidden for some time and the Conference was marked by bitter exchanges: the Frankfurt group even threatened 'castrations'.[37] The hostility specifically included sectarian interpretations of the role of revolutionary politics: in an article following the Conference, one disgusted male delegate reiterated Marx's views on the position of Jews in nineteenth-century Germany. Quoting Marx, he replaced the word 'Jew' with 'women', saying 'no one in Germany is politically emancipated. We are not free ourselves. How should we liberate you? You women are egoists, if you demand a special emancipation for yourselves.'[38] Shortly after the Conference, on 12 December 1968, eight female supporters of SDS member Ursula Seppel went topless during her trial in Hamburg. Seppel was accused of breach of the peace during a previous trial and attended the court wearing nothing under a see-through blouse. Accusing the judge of bias, her supporters sang a 'ballad of the asexual judge' and were dragged from the court by police officers. In a rare display of measured judgement the judge refused to charge them with contempt of court and acquitted Seppel of the charges against her.[39] Again APO women had made the link between personal and political emancipation.

36. 'Emanzipationsflugblatt des "SDS-Weiberrates" zur SDS-Delegiertenkonferenz in Hannover', *FU Spiegel*, November and December 1968, Originale Dokumentation, file Frau Träger 221, APOusB.

37. Quoted in 'Unser Thema: Emanzipation', *Nobis*, December 1968, p. 2, AFAS. This is also quoted in Brügge, P., 'Die Rosa Zeiten sind vorbei', *Der Spiegel*, 25 November 1968, p. 60. This is a report on the Conference that discusses the role of the female delegates, including accounts of the debates and insults. See Linhoff, U, *Die Neue Frauenbewegung*, pp. 42–3 for a full reprint of the *Aktionsrat* resolution to the Conference.

38. 'Unser Thema: Emanzipation'.

39. "Und wir zeigen unsere Brüste für jeden", *Der Spiegel*, 16 December 1968, p. 24. The article 'Striptease auf der Anklagebank: Die Nackten und die Roben', *Konkret Extra*, 30 December 1968, p. 7 quotes the women attacking the 'terrorism of the law and the police'.

This was given perhaps its most sustained expression in the late 1960s by a campaign to improve child-care provisions. Starting in Spring 1968 the women's groups at the *Republikanischer Club*, and then the *Aktionsrat*, established a system of *Kinderläden* (children's shops) as day nurseries across Berlin. By October 1968 seven nurseries had been established, with immediate plans in place for the creation of a further five, and just before Christmas 1968 the West Berlin Senator for Family, Youth and Sport, Horst Korber, announced state funding for the *Kinderläden*.[40] It was not a universally popular decision: echoing earlier debates on higher education, one angry citizen wrote to the *Berliner Morgenpost* that education should not be politicized in such schools and that the state was establishing the circumstances for future intolerance. He continued 'from the radical revolutionary children's shops, radical revolutionary schools, universities and other institutions will follow'.[41] His fears were without foundation: although similar state-funded nurseries were quickly established across the country, representing one of the most tangible and lasting success stories of the APO, the revolutionary views of groups like the *Aktionsrat* had only limited appeal to the wider population. When the *Aktionsrat* called a 'strike' among nursery workers in Berlin for 10 June 1969 in the hope of persuading the Berlin Senate to increase spending on nurseries, they manifestly failed to gain anything more than token support.[42] Nevertheless, the women's movement continued to gain strength because it addressed issues that affected women across the political spectrum.

Perhaps no campaign better reflects this, and the fundamental social changes that gave the women's movement its base of support, than the struggle over abortion reform and contraception. The campaign had a long history: paragraph 218 of the 1900 Civil Code banned abortions and although attempts at reform reached a peak in the Weimar period, an amendment in 1926 allowed only for medically necessary abortions. In the Nazi period the limited moves toward the provision of birth-control and family-planning advice under Weimar were overturned as socialistic and inconsistent with the need for rapid population growth to secure the future of the *Volk*. Such views, informed by an acceptance that the state had a right and a duty to interfere in family planning, continued in the post-war

40. Helke Sander, *Übersicht über schon bestehende oder in Entstehende begriffene Kinderläden*, dated 15 October 1968, Originale Dokumentation, file Frau Träger 221, APOusB and 'Senatsgeld für APO-Kinder', *Frankfurter Rundschau*, Weihnachten 1968, p. 4.

41. 'Zuviel Toleranz', *Berliner Morgenpost*, 26 January 1969, p. 2.

42. *Warum kein Streik?*, Originale Dokumentation, file Frau Träger 221, APOusB discusses the failure of the strike.

period with the CDU's identification of the family as a weapon against communism. Most Weimar family planners had fled the Nazis, and the absence of this corrective to the overwhelmingly pro-Nazi stance of the medical profession meant that any moves to revive a movement for birth control were quickly stifled by stigmatization as communist subversion. Atina Grossman has noted that Hans Harmsen, who became head of the German Association for Marriage and Family, or *Pro Familia*, in 1950, had actively assisted the Nazis in the forced sterilization of the mentally disabled. Under his direction *Pro Familia*, which directed birth control policy, was dominated by the need for 'prevention of abortion' and the promotion of the 'will to a child'.[43] It was not until the late 1960s, then, that a reinvigorated campaign for birth-control and abortion reform was able to gain widespread popular support amid a gradual acceptance that sex was a matter for private discretion and less inflexible codes of conduct.

The liberalization of attitudes to sex may have been made possible by the changes in expectations resulting from economic prosperity, but it would be a mistake to overestimate the role of contraception and abortion. These were available, and economic prosperity made them more accessible to a wider cross-section of society, but in many ways their availability lagged behind the pace of change rather than reflecting or even driving it. In 1968 only 4 per cent of West German women were being prescribed the contraceptive pill, and prevailing medical opinion still insisted that only married women should take it, although other forms of contraceptive were becoming more widely available and accepted.[44] This restrictive view was further reinforced in July 1968 with the promulgation of Pope Paul VI's Encyclical *Humanae Vitae*, banning Roman Catholics from using artificial methods of contraception. Eva Kolinsky notes that 'well into the Sixties, one in three first marriages was a *Muß-Ehe*, i.e., entered into to legalize the birth of a child' although this declined later when contraception became more widely available.[45]

Attitudes to sex had changed and although abortion remained illegal *Konkret* estimated that there were a million illegal abortions a year in West Germany by the mid-1960s.[46] *Konkret* also argued that numerous doctors were performing illegal abortions without regulation, with devastating consequences, and repeated the gory details of botched abortions carried out by amateurs whom women had turned to in desperation. Among others

43. Grossman, *Reforming Sex*, p. 211.
44. *Konkret*, July 1968, p. 31.
45. Kolinsky, *Women in West Germany*, pp. 80–1.
46. 'Abtreibung in Deutschland', *Konkret*, June 1964, pp. 7–10. This article launched *Konkret*'s campaign for abortion and birth-control reform.

it quoted the example of Waltraud A, an 18-year-old who was six months pregnant when a doctor performed an abortion on her, resulting in massive loss of blood, followed by her death the next day.[47] In August 1968 *Der Spiegel* published results of a survey that showed every ninth female student with sexual experience had undergone an abortion and half of all students who had become pregnant reported having had an illegal abortion. The author of the report concluded that these students saw abortion as a form of birth control despite the risks involved in unregulated abortions.[48] Information on sex, contraception and abortion was not widely available and *Konkret*'s campaign, begun in 1964, was a rare instance of activism on these issues in the mid-1960s. The fact remained, however, that attitudes to sex had changed, that more people than ever before were experiencing sex before marriage, that women's expectations were changing, and that the positions held by the state and the medical profession had lagged behind.

It would be misleading to argue that by 1971, when the campaign for abortion reform began in earnest, women's groups had moved beyond university campuses or limited community actions such as the *Kinderläden*. The demonstrations that took place for International Women's Day on 6 March 1971, for instance, were restricted to small gatherings in major cities. Activists nevertheless seized the opportunity presented by the Brandt administration's decision to review the abortion laws in light of the fact that strict enforcement had not taken place for several years. On 2 June 1971, following the example of a similar action in France, the magazine *Stern* published the names and photographs of 374 women who admitted they had had abortions and who demanded the immediate repeal of paragraph 218.[49] Within weeks the Federal Justice Minister, Gerhard Jahn, had received lists containing 90,000 signatures, along with 3,000 letters, from women demanding abortion reform.[50] The nature of the campaign that followed necessarily appealed to women across society: the slogan *Mein Bauch gehört mir* or 'my belly belongs to me' exemplified a fundamental shift in attitudes, in which the demands of the state for an expanding population to meet national needs were superseded by personal considerations, particularly lifestyle choices over sex, marriage and

47. '§ 218 oder Baby-Pille für Alle', *Konkret*, August 1964, p. 8.
48. 'Studenten: Sex-Report', *Der Spiegel*, 26 August 1968, p. 48.
49. Quoted in Frevert, *Women in German Society*, p. 294. The French protest in the magazine *Nouvel Observateur* took place in April 1971 and involved 343 prominent women who demanded abortion reform. Unlike for the *Stern* article, only a few of them admitted to having undergone abortions. See Marwick, *The Sixties*, p. 703.
50. Quoted in Hervé, F., (ed.), *Geschichte der deutschen Frauenbewegung*, p. 162.

childbirth. It further reflected opposition to the fact that women could become pregnant accidentally and yet doctors, politicians and judges, most of whom were male, could enforce a law that forbade an abortion or put them in a position where they would have to risk their lives in an illegal abortion. For the first time women united in a common cause irrespective of age and social background: 71 per cent of women in 1971 favoured legal abortion and by 1973 this had risen to 83 per cent.[51]

Besides demonstrations and disrupting official discussions on the reform of the abortion law, women from across West Germany came together in March 1972 for the first *Bundesfrauenkongreß* (Federal Women's Congress) in Frankfurt. Over a two-day period the Congress discussed a wide variety of issues, including abortion reform, equal pay and maternity leave, in line with the various concerns of the many organizations taking part.[52] The role of revolutionary politics should not be ignored, with groups like the *Spartacus Kommunistische Jugendorganisation* (Spartacus Communist Youth Organization) attempting to subordinate the campaign against paragraph 218 to 'the revolutionary struggle of the working class' by railing against 'petit bourgeois feminism'.[53] The fact remains that revolutionary politics, with all its sectarianism, theoretical abstraction, and frequent displays of intolerance, did not have the mass appeal necessary for a successful campaign. The far left continued as the key motivating element in the development of the women's movement in the 1970s, particularly the formation of theoretical models, and in provocative acts of protest, but the abortion-reform campaign was so successful in attracting wide-ranging support because of the broad appeal of the issues involved. By 1975, 20 million women in West Germany considered themselves feminists and 20,000 actively took part in feminist political activity.[54]

After its review of the abortion laws, in May 1973 the Brandt administration held the first of a series of *Bundestag* readings of measures to reform paragraph 218. The proposals allowed for abortions within the first three months of pregnancy (the *Fristenmodell* or 'time limit model'),

51. Frevert, *Women in German Society*, p. 294.

52. *Programm*, file Originale Dokumentation, 12.12. Soz. Frauen 68–72, APOusB. This is a copy of the programme of the Congress, although details of the subjects discussed are not included. This file includes documents from various groups including *Brot und Rosen*, *Weg mit dem § 218*, the *Komitee gegen § 218* and *Aktion 218*.

53. *Der Kampf gegen den Paragraphen 218 organisieren!*, file Originale Dokumentation, 12.12. Soz. Frauen 68–72, APOusB. This is an open letter to Congress covering several pages.

54. 'Frau '75: "Grosse Erotische Mutter"', *Der Spiegel*, 30 June 1975, p. 30.

which would be reliant upon medical advice. This was energetically opposed by the CDU who felt abortions should only be allowed on ethical, medical and, significantly, eugenic grounds. The readings were accompanied by demonstrations, street theatre, tribunals and petitions around the country: in June 1973, 5,000 women held a demonstration in the centre of Bonn.[55] On 26 April 1974 the *Bundestag* narrowly passed the law in its third reading by 247 votes to 233, and it scraped through a vote in the CDU/CSU-dominated *Bundesrat* the following month, finally becoming law in June. On 21 June, the day of its announcement, the Federal Constitutional Court, prompted by complaints from the CDU and CSU *Land* governments in Bavaria and Baden-Württemberg, as well as from the *Bundestag* CDU/CSU faction, suspended the law pending investigations into its compatibility with the constitution. In February 1975, amid massive country-wide protests by women's groups, the Constitutional Court decided by 6 to 2 that the law was incompatible with provisions in the Basic Law giving the state the responsibility for preserving life that had been introduced in response to Nazi policies, notably forced sterilization. The Court did say, however, that while a new law was prepared doctors performing abortions should not be prosecuted. In September the SPD/FDP coalition government announced a new bill, giving the right to free abortions within the first three months of pregnancy on medical, ethical and social grounds, and in criminal cases such as rape. This was far from abortion on demand, and women seeking abortions had to go through counselling sessions in advance. The law was passed in February 1976 and came into effect in May, although Ute Frevert has argued that many doctors, particularly those in Catholic areas, refused to perform the operation.[56]

Many inequalities undoubtedly remained. In 1975, 53 per cent of West German women felt their equal rights remained 'still on paper' and had yet to be translated into daily life.[57] In political parties, only 15 per cent of FDP members were women, with the CDU and SPD only slightly better, at 17 per cent and 19 per cent respectively.[58] Fewer than half a million men between the ages of 20 and 40 had a net income of 300 to 600 DM compared to more than a million women, and around two million men earned 1,000 to 1,200 DM, while less than half a million women had a similar income. Only 5.8 per cent of *Bundestag* members were women.[59]

55. Hervé, *Geschichte der deutschen Frauenbewegung*, p. 162.

56. Frevert, *Women in German Society*, p. 295.

57. 'Frau '75: "Grosse Erotische Mutter"', *Der Spiegel*, 30 June 1975, p. 30.

58. Ibid., p. 39

59. Ibid., p. 36.

These statistics should not detract from the fact that much had been achieved. I can do no better than quoting Eva Kolinksy's assessment: for her,

> the study of women in West Germany also charts the pace of change towards a democratic society: the displacement of pre-democratic legacies by democratic political behaviour, or, to pick up Böll's impatient metaphor, the transformation of women from *Stimmvieh* [voting cattle] to citizens for whom democracy matters and who matter to democracy.[60]

With contraception, growing financial independence, and a world view that looked beyond a role as mother and wife, women were increasingly free to make choices about their lifestyles, career, and so on. Perhaps nowhere was this more striking than in the rise in the number of single mothers. In 1966 only 45 out of every 1,000 babies were born to an unmarried mother. By 1975 it had already risen to 54 in every 1,000, and by 1976 it was 61. For some this was the result of divorce or widowhood, for others of a mistake, but for a growing number it was as a definite choice.[61] One single mother told *Der Spiegel*, 'better an unmarried mother than an unlucky wife'. Another expressed her belief that 'every marriage destroys the positive tensions between two people'. Looking at the number of unhappy marriages she had encountered she concluded 'rather twelve unmarried children than one married'.[62] The emphasis was on individual choice rather than on social responsibility or conformity with tradition. Not everyone saw this as necessarily a good thing: in 1972 the Springer magazine *Jasmin* led an article with the headline 'mother without a man: a life without a chance', and in 1974 *Die Zeit* asked 'a child and no man: disgrace?'[63] Single mothers have been particular sources of indignation for conservatives, who vilified them as indicators of social dysfunction and disintegration, although for many women the choice to follow this path would not have been possible without the economic prosperity of the post-war period.

---

60. Kolinsky, *Women in West Germany*, p. 4.
61. 'Lieber zwölf Kinder als einmal heiraten', *Der Spiegel*, 5 September 1977, p. 84.
62. Quoted ibid., p. 92.
63. Quoted ibid., p. 84.

Conclusion

One of Adenauer's biographers, Ronald Irving, has argued that at the start of Adenauer's regime, 'most West Germans were only just beginning to get used to liberal democracy: they accepted its outward symbols such as elections, but were suspicious of its participative side'. Along with Adenauer they also 'retained many of the attitudes of a bourgeois German of the Wilhelmine Empire', particularly deference.[1] By the 1970s this was no longer the case, and the events outlined in this book played a central role in the creation of a democratic political environment, in which ordinary people were willing to criticize government policy and participate in political activity.

Such developments were by no means unopposed, as has been demonstrated, and protest activity in the 1960s and 1970s was frequently identified as incompatible with, and a threat to, West German democracy. Conflicts over the meaning of 'democracy' were at the heart of the 1960s protests and these battles were, for all sides, informed by a constant awareness of the catastrophic consequences that had resulted from the failure of democracy in Germany in the past. The disproportionate overreaction to protests and eventually to terrorism was the response of an immature democracy, still in the process of establishing the acceptable norms of democratic behaviour, negotiating the application of the checks and balances that help to preserve democracy. Added to this were attitudes toward democracy, government, political involvement and authority that were inherited from the Nazi period, and that were distorted by the cold war. These attitudes were often incompatible with the demands of democratic government, and frequently placed a priority upon consensus, preventing a Nazi revival, and countering perceived threats to the freedoms, peace and prosperity created by the Federal Republic, at the expense of tolerance, critical debate and multiplicity of opinion. The protest movements of the 1960s were crucially important agents in the maturation process for this West German democracy, forcing extreme responses from government bodies, the press, and the public that in turn forced open, if bitter, public debate that helped

---

1. Irving, *Adenauer*, p. 155.

to establish the boundaries of democracy. Above all the protests both represented and further encouraged a greater participation in political life by ordinary citizens, a desire to hold politicians and government agencies to account, and a belief that deferring to those in authority amounted to an abrogation of individual moral responsibility that in itself placed democracy under threat and repeated past mistakes.

The change in attitudes toward politics and democratic participation is clear. Surveys carried out by the Institut für Demoskopie Allensbach found that in 1952 only 11 per cent of women said they were interested in politics, but that this had jumped to 27 per cent by 1969, and to 36 per cent by 1977. Those who said they were not interested in politics at all fell from 50 per cent to 17 per cent over the same period, with those saying they were 'not very' interested in politics, but who nevertheless maintained at least some interest, rising from 39 to 47 per cent.[2] These remarkable findings were reflected in an increase in popular political activity, with the number of demonstrations rising from 1,300 to 5,000 per year from 1970 to 1982.[3] Moreover, there was a qualitative change in political activity, and this may represent the APO's most enduring legacy. The anti-nuclear campaign of the late 1950s and early 1960s had initiated a process of political organization, outside the confines of party politics or the labour movement, with the establishment of local and national co-ordinating committees. This was developed further throughout the 1960s, whether within organizations such as the SDS, or around campaigns on issues such as the *Notstandsgesetze*. In the 1970s, with the far left in sectarian disarray, the extra-parliamentary example set in the 1960s was continued by the multiplicity of *Bürgerinitiativen* (Citizens' Initiative) groups that sprang up all over Germany, usually to campaign on single, local issues.

Interestingly, Diane L. Parness has approached the formation of *Bürgerinitiativen* from a different angle. She argues that in the early 1970s the SPD, having first ignored the APO and then attacked it without success, attempted to neutralize the existence of a political alternative that was further to its left in the political spectrum by integrating former APO supporters into the SPD membership. In contrast to traditional SPD members who were expected to toe the party line, 'these experienced demonstrators had no intention of stifling dissent in return for the benefits of party membership, and the SPD was soon forced to grapple with very serious problems of internal unrest'. The SPD, for its part, came to the realization that APO activists were seeking to infiltrate and reform the Party from

2. Noelle-Neumann, *The Germans*, p. 151.
3. Quoted in Watts, M.W. et al., *Contemporary German Youth and Their Elders*, p. 101.

within rather than desiring integration, and the Party went on the defensive once more. The message to former APO activists was that the SPD was unwilling to address their concerns, forcing them to pursue solutions outside the party political system yet again. According to Parness, this included national, regional and local issues, since 'the great bulwark of SPD strength, the party organization at the Land and local levels, no longer seemed to respond to popular needs and aspirations', resulting in the creation of *Bürgerinitiativen* and eventually the formation of the Green Party.[4] Parness also presents a further interpretation, noting that for Uwe Thaysen

> no direct link can be established between the SPD's abandonment of socialist principles [at Bad Godesberg] and the appearance of Buergerinitiativen in the Federal Republic. Instead, the chief impetus for the appearance of Buerger-initiativen should be attributed not so much to the loss of a truly socialist position in the West German party system as to the betrayed expectations aroused by the social-liberal coalition's reform program.[5]

Each of these interpretations has something to recommend it, but for the purposes of the analysis here it is notable that the APO, and the social changes and rising expectations of which it was a part, were essential to the formation of *Bürgerinitiativen* in the 1970s. This was despite, or perhaps because of, the fact that *Bürgerinitiativen* were not usually wedded to Marxist theoretical models, and often represented an uneasy alliance of disparate political viewpoints, including conservative, often anti-industrialist viewpoints, those with narrow and purely local concerns, as well as supporters of the radical Left, who identified the *Bürgerinitiativen*, and later the Green Party, as gateways for a critique of capitalism and West German democracy.

Indeed the Green Party, created in 1980, is a descendant of the 1960s APO. Eva Kolinsky's analysis of the Green Party adds to Parness's perspective by emphasizing the challenge to German politics represented by the 1960s protests, and which was inherited by the Greens. In Kolinsky's view 'the affinity between participatory culture and protest must not be overlooked. Centred on a segment of young and educated West Germans, protest which had been blunted by consensus politics since the 1950s, has obtained a new lease of political life'. She identifies the 1960s student movements as the first in a series of new social movements that challenged this consensus, arguing

4. Parness, *The SPD*, p. 4.
5. Ibid., p. 99.

Protest has inspired the Green Party as much as the intent to compete in elections and become a voice for new issues in parliaments. At the heart of the policy intent and electoral appeal of the Greens lies a sting against the styles, practices and conventions of West German parties and parliamentary politics. They set out at once to challenge the consensual, non-partisan climate generated by the *Volksparteien*, and also become part of it through elections and parliaments. Green politics have been confrontational, yet tempered by their integration into parliamentary processes. As a political force, the party is both radical and conventional.[6]

Despite proclaiming itself an 'anti-party party' the Green Party won its first seats in the *Bundestag* in 1983 and went on to establish itself as a party of government in the *Länder*.

With the SPD unable to countenance the existence of a political force to its left, cooperation with the Greens has taken place out of necessity at local, *Land*, and national levels, culminating in the SPD-Green Coalition government in 1998 under Chancellor Gerhard Schröder. This situation was not arrived at without considerable soul-searching because, as Charles Lees summarizes

> at the Federal level the Greens remained an outsider party and the idea of their participating in national government alarmed the political establishment. It also alarmed many of their own supporters, who preferred the purity of perpetual opposition to the compromise and horse-trading of government.

The opportunity for participation in national government, possibly the only chance the '68ers' who dominated the leadership were likely to get, proved to be too great, as did the chance 'to demonstrate to their own supporters that not only was the "Long March through the Länder" over, but that it had been worth it'.[7] Of course, it must be acknowledged that the Green Party is not, and has never been, simply a '68er' party: Joschka Fischer, the first Green Foreign Minister and a former SDS activist, is accompanied in the Cabinet by his Green colleague, Jürgen Trittin, who was only 14 years old in 1968. Strained relationships exist within the party between former '68ers' and those for whom such a designation is anathema, and warring factions have existed between Right and Left interpretations of environmental politics, as well as between the priorities of the leadership and grass-roots membership, since the evolution of the environmental campaign in the 1970s.[8] Moreover, former '68ers' are also

6 Kolinsky, E. (ed.), *The Greens in West Germany*, p. 2.

7. Lees, C., *The Red-Green Coalition in Germany*, pp. 1 and 23.

8. For a description of these early conflicts see Hülsberg, W., *The German Greens*, pp. 76–96.

prominent in the SPD: former APO lawyer Otto Schily has turned from poacher to gamekeeper by becoming Federal Interior Minister, while on the other hand Gerhard Schröder took part in no protests and, while acknowledging the importance of the period in forming his political worldview, he steadfastly refuses to consider himself a '68er'.[9] Ostensibly, then, the 'long march through the institutions' by APO supporters proposed by Rudi Dutschke, that aimed to bring an end to bourgeois capitalist 'manipulation', has gained its most significant victories in the Greens and in the Schröder cabinet.[10] Alternatively, it could be said that this is the ultimate expression of the integration of former APO protesters into a political system that simply adapted to them rather than being adapted by them.

In many respects, though, this is to miss the point that the political legacy of the APO has not simply rested in the continued activity of its original adherents, but that above all it has changed the political landscape by encouraging political participation both beyond and within the political parties by all sections of society, and at local and national levels. The protest campaigns of the 1960s therefore won important and lasting victories in making dissent and critical debate acceptable. Governments from the 1950s to the 1970s consistently committed themselves to the defence of 'democracy', but were remarkably poor at identifying genuine threats, of balancing the defence of democracy against undermining it themselves, and of using measured judgement to diffuse tensions. All too often state authorities and popular opinion failed to understand democracy as an organic system, preferring to see it as synonymous with the *Bundesrepublik* as the only viable chance for stability and prosperity. In cases of even minor dissent the risk of a return to the Nazi and Weimar experiences was evoked. The 1960s protests, and the social changes of the 1960s in general, forced a reassessment of this position. Attempts to impose conformity and integration simply created further alienation and indignation. State authorities have been forced to modify previously rigid positions, making possible the tolerance, and even the defence, of protest and dissent that is essential to democratic government for and by 'the people'.

Of course, these changes in political activity and in attitudes took place within the context of profound social changes in the 1960s and 1970s in which previous norms, traditions, and expectations were challenged or even rejected. It has been maintained throughout this book that the protests

9. Leinemann, J., 'Am Ende des langen Marsches', *Der Spiegel*, 16 June 1997, p. 119.
10. The idea seems to have been given its first popular expression in 'Studenten: Dutschke: Der lange Marsch', *Der Spiegel*, 11 December 1967, pp. 52–73.

both originated in, and contributed to these changes, encouraging a reassessment of political and generational relationships, in which old forms of authority and deference were undermined, the interference of the state in personal decisions became increasingly unacceptable, and tolerance of personal-lifestyle choices and varied opinions were largely accepted as essential to strong democracy. It should not be forgotten that ordinary people drove social change in the post-war period, by seizing the opportunities presented by unprecedented wealth and in the process creating a liberal, tolerant society. Ralph Inglehart has pointed to a liberalization of values in the post-war period throughout the Western world, and statistical evidence specific to West Germany confirms his thesis.[11] Survey data suggests, for instance, that 74 per cent of high school children in 1950 favoured capital punishment, compared with just 6 per cent in 1980.[12] Although conservative governments have tried to dictate attitudes to sex, the family, and so on, through social policy, the economic power wielded by ordinary people has enabled them to make individual choices in the private sphere.

A new 'informality' of social codes is one of the most striking aspects of the post-1960s period, and these changes in attitudes are particularly striking between generations. In the 1950s less than 10 per cent of women, and just over 20 per cent of men, had already had their first sexual experience by the age of sixteen. In the 1980s this had risen to 60 per cent for both sexes, leading Watts et al. to conclude that 'social expectations are no longer a reason for young people to refrain from sexual experience'.[13] In 1949, 83 per cent of men aged between 20 and 30 and 91 per cent of women in the same age group stated that the institution of marriage was 'necessary', as opposed to the 3 per cent of men and 2 per cent of women who felt it was 'antiquated'. In 1978 only 40 per cent of 20-to-30-year-old men, and 42 per cent of women in this age range, felt marriage was necessary, and those who felt it was 'antiquated' had risen to 26 per cent of young men and 28 per cent of young women.[14] In 1953, 28 per cent of married men and 33 per cent of married women still believed that it was necessary for 'husband and wife always to be of the same opinion in everything'. By 1979 only 11 per cent of married men and 12 per cent of married women still supported this viewpoint. On cohabitation by unmarried couples, 86 per cent of 16-to-29-year-olds said in 1976 that they

11. Inglehart, R., *The Silent Revolution*.
12. Quoted in Watts et al., *Contemporary German Youth*, p. 100.
13. Ibid., pp. 29–30.
14. Noelle-Neumann, *The Germans*, p. 26.

'wouldn't mind' this, and only 7 per cent felt it was 'going too far'. This contrasted with 44 per cent of those people who were 60 and over who felt it was going too far, and the same percentage who 'wouldn't mind'. The issue of couples living together and having a child while remaining unmarried provoked even more extreme differences in attitudes between generations, with 83 per cent of people in the 19-to-29 age range saying in 1976 that they did not object to this, compared with just 34 per cent of people aged 60 or over who would tolerate this, and 52 per cent who described it as 'going too far'.[15] Eva Kolinsky quotes statistics indicating that in 1966 two in three people aged between 10 and 19 would never disobey their parents. By 1976, just ten years later, nearly the same proportion said they *would* disobey their parents.[16] According to Watts et al. the desire to be 'stricter, more consistent and tougher' with one's own children fell from 24 per cent among 18-to-22-year-olds in 1950 to a mere 5 per cent of 15-to-24-year-olds in 1984.[17] In place of an emphasis on 'children's unconditional obedience' or 'leniency and goodness versus severity of [the parental] educator' in the 1950s, by the 1980s parenting stressed the 'purely human rather than education relationship' and the 'child as personal partner of the adult'.[18] These are general trends, but the move away from the traditional 'seen and not heard' attitude toward children in the 1950s toward a more equitable exchange of views between parents and children was a direct consequence of the reassessment of attitudes regarding authority that took place in the 1960s. Clearly, divisions between the generations were particularly stark in West Germany.

Such divisions were, of course, particularly profound in reference to the Nazi past, and on this, too, the protests encouraged a reassessment, not just of the Nazi period but also of the influence of former Nazis upon postwar West Germany. The 1960s protests certainly cannot be credited with initiating debate on the Nazi past, which was already taking place in the late 1940s. Yet until the 1960s, presentation of the Nazi period in West Germany all too often presented Germans as victims of Nazism and portrayed former Nazis as the targets of Allied persecution in denazification programmes. As Atina Grossmann has observed 'at least until the 1960s, every act of compensation and memorialization toward Jewish victims of Nazism was carefully balanced by recognition of German suffering'.[19]

---

15. Ibid., pp. 247–9.
16. Kolinsky, *Women in West Germany*, p. 90.
17. Watts, et al., *Contemporary German Youth*, pp. 129–30.
18. Ibid., pp. 130–2.
19. Grossmann, A., 'The "Goldhagen Effect": Memory, Repetition, and Responsibility in the New Germany', in G. Eley (ed.), *The 'Goldhagen Effect'*, p. 95.

The demands of reconciliation and reconstruction precluded an intense and uninhibited public debate on the host of issues raised by the period, not least the details of the Holocaust, and it was the 1960s protesters who first challenged this consensus. The protest campaigns are certainly understood in these terms: a millennium review of the twentieth century by the *Süddeutsche Zeitung* in November 1999, describing 'the German variant' of 1968, used the sub-heading, 'the criminals of the Nazi period caused a generation conflict of a special kind, that pushed ahead the necessary change of a hopeful but stifling society'.[20] Events such as the 1961 Eichmann trial, the start of the Auschwitz trials in 1963, and growing debate among historians, may already have been encouraging a trend toward greater public awareness of the Nazi past, of which the 1960s protests were a part. Subsequent debates such as the *Historikerstreit* in the 1980s, or the storm of controversy surrounding Daniel Goldhagen's book *Hitler's Willing Executioners* in the late 1990s, often had little or no direct relationship to the specific issues raised by the protesters. Yet, crucially, the protests, 'whose forceful challenge to the comforts and conventions of West German society was heavily dependent on an accusatory confront-ation with the older generation's Nazi past', encouraged critical public engagement with the moral issues raised by the Nazi past for the first time.[21] That this engagement was marked by intensely bitter disputes, informed by an ongoing desire for evasion, exculpation, or collective amnesia does not detract from the fact that in the late 1960s 'the framework of a certain safe and ritualized official memory in the Federal Republic was dramatically broken apart' and that the protesters were the key agents in the process at that stage.[22]

Indeed, the 1960s protesters were far from successful in creating a new post-war consensus of public contrition for the Nazi past, whether in the 1960s or in subsequent decades. Grossmann has put forward the thesis that 'the entire chronology of postwar Germany . . . loosely clumped by dec-ades, can be read as a continual oscillation between the drive to forget . . . and the injunction to remember, to commemorate, and to work through questions of guilt and responsibility'.[23] There is certainly plenty of evid-ence to support such a viewpoint. On the one hand it is possible for Geoff Eley to insist that

20. Roth, W., '1968, die deutsche Variant', *Süddeutsche Zeitung*, 24 November 1999, p. M57.

21. Grossmann, 'The "Goldhagen Effect"', p. 99.

22. Eley, G., 'Ordinary Germans, Nazism, and Judeocide', in Eley, *The 'Goldhagen Effect'*, p. 1.

23. Grossmann, 'The "Goldhagen Effect"', pp. 89–90.

the extraordinary popular success of Schindler's List, the remarkable popularity of Victor Klemperer's diaries . . ., and then the massive sales and public adulation of Goldhagen's Hitler's Willing Executioners all suggest that Germany's reading, watching, and museum-going publics accepted the importance of continuing to expose the crimes of Nazism.[24]

On the other hand Goldhagen's thesis has provoked fierce and ongoing disputes, often, but by no means always, informed by a desire to gloss over the complicity of ordinary people in Nazi crimes. Regrettably, the politically charged reactions to Goldhagen's book, often defensive in tone, have sometimes overshadowed genuine concerns about Goldhagen's problematic thesis, methodology, and conclusions. Robert R. Shandley's argument, that 'alongside the continuing success of the Wehrmacht exhibit and of the powerfully moving personal writings of Victor Klemperer, the reception of Hitler's Willing Executioners may well be seen as that which many have demanded from Germany for fifty years, that is, an honest reckoning with their past', may have some basis in truth. Certainly the debate that has raged since the publication of Goldhagen's book shows no signs of abating, although Shandley's assessment is qualified by an acknowledgement of the many defensive responses to Goldhagen.[25] Similarly, the peripatetic Wehrmacht exhibition 'War of Extermination: Crimes of the Wehrmacht, 1941 to 1944' launched by the Hamburger Institut für Sozialforschung in 1995, may have received 550,000 visitors, making it the most popular contemporary exhibition in the history of the Federal Republic. Yet Eley notes that in tackling the contentious issue of Wehrmacht participation in Nazi atrocities, the exhibition also 'drew bitter opposition', so that after receiving threats to her safety the President of the Federal Constitutional Court, Jutta Lumbach, needed special police protection when she opened the exhibition in Karlsruhe in 1997.[26] Claims about the role of the 1960s protests in prompting a debate on the Nazi past, and the subsequent impact of that debate, have to be heavily qualified. Although the protests made the first serious challenge to the post-war consensus on the Nazi period, this was part of a series of developments, and the debates that have taken place since the 1960s have often been informed as much by defensiveness and evasion as by expressions of remorse.

The 1960s, then, was a key period in the development of the Federal Republic toward understanding and acceptance of democracy, and by challenging the consensus on the Nazi period, on attitudes to authority and

24. Eley, 'Ordinary Germans', p. 27.
25. Shandley, R.R. (ed.), *Unwilling Germans?*, p. 28. See also pp. 3–9.
26. Eley, 'Ordinary Germans', p. 28.

the state, and encouraging the abandonment of traditional notions of social duty in favour of personal freedoms, the 1960s protests helped to create a largely tolerant society with a stable and relatively balanced democratic political climate. Of course, the far right remained alive and well, the government showed in its reaction to terrorism that the risk of a return to undemocratic attitudes was all too real, and tolerance of a diverse and un- precedentedly permissive society was certainly greater among the young, meaning that permissiveness was far from the ideal envisaged by the likes of *Kommune I*. Nevertheless, by the 1970s far more West Germans took an interest in politics, far more took part in political debate and activity, and far more expressed an understanding of the need for ordinary people to be watchful for threats to democracy, whether from the state or from elsewhere, than had been the case ever before. Reactions to the Spiegel affair, to the Ohnesorg and Dutschke shootings, and to the *Extremisten- beschluß*, among others all indicate the existence of a democracy in which state authority is viewed critically and in which ordinary people are willing to define the boundaries of acceptable state policy. Above all the liberating influence of relative wealth, which created the necessary conditions for both the protests and the remarkable social changes of the 1960s, helped to ensure post-war political stability and freedom of personal expression. For West Germany, the 1960s were neither the best of times nor the worst of times, whether measured in terms of the events that took place in that decade or of their long-term impact, but it was a crucially important period for the formation of West German democracy and the development of personal freedoms from a previously rigid, conformist, deferential and authoritarian environment.

Bibliography

The available list of titles on the 1960s is vast, and any bibliography of this literature therefore has to be selective. With this in mind, the Secondary titles listed below have been restricted to those that have contributed to the writing of this book, rather than forming a comprehensive survey of the literature on the 1960s.

Archival Sources

Archiv für Alternatives Schrifftum in nordrhein Westfalia, Duisburg
APO newspaper collection

Bundesarchiv Koblenz

Bundesministerium für Jugend und Familie, B 153
Sammlung Wolfgang M. Schwiedzrik zur Studentenbewegung, ZSg 153
Verband Deutscher Studentenschaften (VDS), B 166

Dokumentationstelle für unkonventionelle Literatur, Bibliotek für Zeitgeschichte, Stuttgart

Flugblätter collection: files on Berlin, München, Stuttgart, Tübingen
Broschüren, D1144, D0895, D02212

Hamburger Institut für Sozialforschung

Sammlung APO Press
Sammlung Jürgen Klein
Aktenbestand des Sozialistischen Anwaltskollektivs

Institut für Zeitgeschichte, München

Deutsche Liga für Menschenrechte, ED 707
Rechtshilfe der APO München, ED 713
Sammlung Mehringer, ED 308
Sammlung Schlemper: Sammlung zu Studentenbewegung u. APO
1966-72, ED 328
Sammlung Dr. Werner Röder, ED 387

Landesarchiv Berlin

Senatsverwaltung für Wissenschaft und Forschung, Rep B 014

Archiv 'APO und soziale Bewegungen', Fachbereich Politische Wissenschaft der Freien Universität Berlin (ehem. ZI 6)

Files with the following titles in common:

Originale Dokumentation, Bewaffneter Kampf
RAF/ Presse
Aktionsrat zur Befreiung der Frauen
12.12.Soz. Frauen 68–72
File Frau Träger 221
Originale Dokumentation, 'Rabehl'
Siegeward Lönnendonker, Tilman Fichter and Jochen Staadt,
*Dokumentation FU Berlin, Freie Universität Berlin 1948–1973,
Hochschule im Umbruch* (Unpublished printed collection,
reprinting documents from the archive).

Printed Sources

Newspapers and Periodicals

Der Abend
Abendzeitung
Allgemeine Zeitung, Mainz
Bayerische Rundschau
Berliner Morgenpost
Bild

Bibliography

Bild am Sonntag
BZ
Flensburger Tageblatt
Frankfurter Allgemeine Zeitung
Frankfurter Rundschau
Hamburger Morgenpost
Hanauer Anzeiger
Kölner Stadtanzeiger
Kölnische Rundschau
Konkret
Münchner Merkur
Rheinische Post
Rheinische Rundshau
Spandauer Volksblatt
Der Spiegel
Stuttgarter Zeitung
Süddeutsche Zeitung
Südwestdeutsche Allgemeine Zeitung
Tagesspiegel
Trierische Landeszeitung
Die Welt
Welt am Sonntag
Die Zeit

APO and Student Newspapers

Aachener Prisma
Agit 883
Akut
APO Press: Informationdienst für die Außerparlamentarische
    Opposition
Aspekte: Zeitung für Studenten an der Universität Hamburg
Auditorium
Berliner Extra Blatt
Berliner Extra Dienst
BSZ: Bochumer Studenten Zeitung
Colloquium
Diskus
Extra
Facit

Facts: Zeitung des RCDS
5 vor 12: Freie Studentenzeitung
Freiburger Studenten Zeitung
Forum Academicum: Heidelberger Studentenzeitung
FU Spiegel
Hamburger Extrablatt
Information zur abrüstung
Koop Kooperative: Antiautoritäre Wochenzeitung
Liberale Studenten Zeitung
Linkeck
Links: Sozialistische Zeitung
Love
Marburger Studenten Zeitung
MSZ: Münchner Studenten Zeitung
Nobis: Mainzer Studentzeitung
Oberbaum Blatt: Wochenblatt in Berlin
Peng: Provo Zeitung
Politica
Politikon: Göttinger Studentenzeitschrift für Niedersachsen
Rebell
Rote Presse Korrespondenz
Revolutionärer Weg
Rote Fahne
Rote Skizze
Rotes Forum
Roter Morgen
SDS Info
SDS Korrespondenz
Semester-Spiegel
Skizze: Studentenzeitschrifft an der Universität Kiel
Spartacus
Spots
Stuttgarter Studenten Zeitschrift
SZ: Sozialistische Studenten Zeitung
Was tun

Secondary Sources

Abelhauser, W., *Die Langen Fünfziger Jahre: Wirtschaft und Gesellschaft der Bundesrepublik Deutschland 1949–1966*, Düsseldorf: Schwann, 1987.

Bibliography

Adenauer, K., *Memoirs, 1945–53*, translated from the German by Beate Ruhm von Oppen, London: Weidenfeld & Nicolson, 1966.

Albrecht, W., *Der Sozialistische Deutsche Studentenbund (SDS): vom Parteikonformen Studentenverband zum Repräsentanten der Neuen Linken*, Bonn: Verlag J.H.W. Dietz Nachfolger, 1994.

Allyn, D., *Make Love, Not Wa.: The Sexual Revolution: An Unfettered History*, New York: Routledge, 2001.

Andrews, G., Cockett, R., Hooper, A. and Williams, M. (eds), *New Left, New Right and Beyond: Taking the Sixties Seriously*, London: Macmillan, 1999.

Aust, S., *Der Baader-Meinhof Komplex*, Hamburg: Hoffman and Campe, 1988.

Baier, L., *Die Früchte der Revolte: über die Veränderung der politischen Kultur durch die Studentenbewegung*, Berlin: Wagenbach, 1988.

Bakker Schut, P.H., *Stammheim: Der Prozeß gegen die Rote Armee Fraktion: Die notwendige Korrektur der herrschenden Meinung*, Bonn: Pahl-Rugenstein, 1997.

Bar On, D., *Legacy of Silence: Encounters with Children of the Third Reich*, Cambridge, MA: Harvard University Press, 1989.

Basic Law for the Federal Republic of Germany, Promulgated by the Parliamentary Council on 23 May 1949, As Amended up to and including 29 January 1969, Press and Information Office of the German Federal Government, 1969.

Bauß, G., *Die Studentenbewegung der sechziger Jahre: Handbuch*, Cologne: Pahl-Rugenstein, 1977.

Becker, J., *Hitler's Children: The Story of the Baader-Meinhof Terrorist Gang*, London: Michael Joseph, 1977.

Benz, W. (ed.), *Die Geschichte der Bundesrepublik Deutschland, Band 3: Gesellschaft*, Frankfurt am Main: Fischer Taschenbuch Verlag, 1989.

Benz, W., *Die Gründung der Bundesrepublik: Von der Bizone zum souveränen Staat*, 5th edn, Munich: Deutscher Taschenbuch Verlag, 1999.

Berghahn, V.R., *Modern Germany: Society, Economy and Politics in the Twentieth Century*, Cambridge: Cambridge University Press, 1982.

Berghahn, V.R., *The Americanization of West German Industry 1945–1973*, Leamington Spa: Berg, 1986.

Bergmann, U., Dutschke, R., Lefèvre, W., Rabehl, B., *Rebellion der Studenten oder Die neue Opposition*, Hamburg: Rowohlt, 1968.

Bieling, R., *Die Tränen der Revolution: Die 68er zwanzig Jahre danach*, Berlin: Siedler, 1988.

Bilton, M. and Sim, K., *Four Hours in My Lai*, Harmondsworth: Penguin, 1992.

Bloom, A., *The Closing of the American Mind: How Higher Education has Failed Democracy and Impoverished the Souls of Today's Students*, New York: Simon & Schuster, 1987.

Boutwell, J., *The German Nuclear Dilemma*, Ithaca and London: Cornell University Press, 1990.

Bower, T., *The Pledge Betrayed: America and Britain and the Denazification of Postwar Germany*, Garden City, New York: Doubleday, 1982.

Brandt, W., *People and Politics: the Years 1960–1975*, translated from the German by J. Maxwell Brownjohn, London: Collins, 1978.

Brandt, W., *My Life in Politics*, London: Hamish Hamilton, 1989.

Bude, H., *Bilanz der Nachfolge: Die Bundesrepublik und der Nationalsozialismus*, Frankfurt am Main: Suhrkamp, 1992.

Bude, H., *Das Alten einer Generation: Die Jahrgänge 1938 bis 1948*, Frankfurt am Main: Suhrkamp, 1995.

Bude, H. and Kohli, M. (eds), *Radikalisierte Aufklärung: Studentenbewegung und Soziologie in Berlin 1965 bis 1970*, Munich: Weinheim, 1989.

Bunn, R.F., *German Politics and the Spiegel Affair: A Case Study of the Bonn System*, Baton Rouge: Louisiana State University Press, 1968.

Burns, R. and van der Will, W., *Protest and Democracy in West Germany: Extra-Parliamentary Opposition and the Democratic Agenda*, London: Macmillan, 1988.

Caute, D., *Sixty-Eight: The Year of the Barricades*, London: Hamish Hamilton, 1988.

Chaussy, U., *Die drei Leben des Rudi Dutschke: Eine Biographie*, Berlin: Ch. Links, 1993.

Clay, L.D., *Decision in Germany*, London: William Heinemann, 1950.

Cohn-Bendit, D. and Mohr, R., *1968: Die letzte Revolution, die noch nichts vom Ozonloch wußte*, Berlin: Wagenbach, 1988.

Collier, P. and Horowitz, D., *Destructive Generation: Second Thoughts about the Sixties*, New York: Summit Books, 1989.

Cramer, A., *Zur Lage der Familie und der Familienpolitik in der Bundesrepublik Deutschland*, Opdalen: Leske and Budrich, 1982.

Daniels, R.V., *Year of the Heroic Guerrilla: World Revolution and Counterrevolution in 1968*, Cambridge, MA: Harvard University Press, 1989.

DeGroot, G.J. (ed.), *Student Protest: The Sixties and After*, London: Longman, 1998.

Diefendorf, J.M., Frohn, A. and Rupieper, H.-J. (eds), *American Policy and the Reconstruction of West Germany, 1945–1955*, Cambridge: Cambridge University Press, 1993.

Drummond, G.D., *The German Social Democrats in Opposition, 1949–1960: The Case Against Rearmament*, Norman, OK: University of Oklahoma Press, 1982.

Dutschke, G., *Rudi Dutschke, Wir hatten ein barbarisches schönes Leben: Eine Biographie*, Munich: Knaur, 1996.

Dutschke, R., *Mein langer Marsch: Reden, Schriften und Tagebücher aus zwanzig Jahren*, Gretchen Dutschke-Klotz, Helmut Gollwitzer and Jürgen Miermeister (eds), Hamburg: Rowohlt, 1980.

Eley, G. (ed.), *The 'Goldhagen Effect': History, Memory, Nazism – Facing the German Past*, Ann Arbor: University of Michigan Press, 2000.

Ermarth, M. (ed.), *America and the Shaping of German Society 1945–1955*, Oxford: Berg, 1993.

Fichter, T., *SDS und SPD: Parteilichkeit Jenseits Der Partei*, Opdalen: Westdeutscher Verlag, 1988.

Fichter T. and Lönnendonker, S., *Kleine Geschichte des SDS: Der Sozialistische Deutsche Studentenbund von 1946 bis zur Selbstauflösung*, Berlin: Rotbuch, 1977.

Fink, C., Gassert, P. and Junker, D. (eds), *1968: The World Transformed*, Cambridge: Cambridge University Press, 1998.

Fitzgibbon, C., *Denazification*, London: Michael Joseph, 1969.

François, E., Middell, M., Terray, E. and Wierling, D. (eds), *1968: Ein europäisches Jahr?*, Leipzig: Leipziger Universitäts Verlag, 1997.

Fraser, R. (ed.), *1968: A Student Generation in Revolt: An International Oral History*, New York: Pantheon, 1988.

Frevert, U., *Women in German Society: From Bourgeois Emancipation to Sexual Liberation*, Oxford: Berg, 1989.

Friedan, B., *The Feminine Mystique*, London: Penguin, 1992, first published London: Victor Gollancz, 1963.

Fröhner, R., *Wie Starke sind die Halbstarke? Beruf und Berufsnot, politische, kulturelle und seelische Probleme*, Bielefeld: Maria von Stachelberg Verlag, 1956.

Gassert, P. and Richter, P.A., *1968 in West Germany: A Guide to Sources and Literature of the Extra-Parliamentary Opposition*, Washington, DC: German Historical Institute, 1998.

Gathorne-Hardy, J., *Alfred C. Kinsey: Sex the Measure of All Things: A Biography*, London: Pimlico, 1999, first published London: Chatto & Windus, 1998.

Gilcher-Holtey, I. (ed.), *1968: vom Ereignis zum Gegenstand der Geschichtswissenschaft*, Göttingen: Vandenhoeck & Ruprecht, 1998.

Gitlin, T., *The Whole World is Watching: Mass Media in the Making and Unmaking of the New Left*, Berkeley: University of California Press, 1980.

Glaser, H., *Kleine Kulturgeschichte der Bundesrepublik Deutschland 1945–1989*, Munich: Carl Hanser Verlag, 1991.

Grossman, A., *Reforming Sex: The German Movement for Birth Control and Abortion Reform, 1920–1950*, Oxford: Oxford University Press, 1995.

Grotum, T., *Die Halbstarken: Zur Geschichte einer Jugendkultur der 50er Jahre*, Frankfurt am Main: Campus Verlag, 1994.

Habermas, J., *Toward a Rational Society: Student Protest, Science and Politics*, translated by Jeremy J. Shapiro, London: Heinemann, 1971.

Hahn, H.J., *Education and Society in Germany*, Oxford: Berg, 1998.

Hearnden, A. (ed.), *The British in Germany: Educational Reconstruction after 1945*, London: Hamish Hamilton, 1978.

Heinemann, K.H. and Jaitner, T., *Ein langer Marsch: '68 und die Folgen*, Cologne: Papy Rossa Verlag, 1993.

Herf, J., *Divided Memory: The Nazi Past in the Two Germanys*, Cambridge, MA: Harvard University Press, 1997.

Hermand, J., *Kultur im Wiederaufbau: Die Bundesrepublik Deutschland, 1945–1965*, Munich: Nymphenburger, 1986.

Hermand, J., *Die Kultur der Bundesrepublik Deutschland 1965–1985*, Munich: Nymphenburger, 1988.

Hervé, F. (ed.), *Geschichte der deutschen Frauenbewegung*, Cologne: Papy Rossa, 1995.

Hobsbawm, E., *Age of Extremes: The Short Twentieth Century 1914–1991*, London: Michael Joseph, 1994.

Hoffmann, C., *Stunden Null? Vergangenheitsbewältigung in Deutschland 1945 und 1989*, Bonn and Berlin: Bouvier Verlag, 1992.

Hülsberg, W., *The German Greens: A Social and Political Profile*, London and New York: Verso, 1988.

Humphreys, P.J., *Media and Media Policy in West Germany: Press and Broadcasting since 1945*, Oxford: Berg, 1990.

Inglehart, R., *The Silent Revolution: Changing Values and Changing Political Styles among Western Publics*, Princeton: Princeton University Press, 1977.

Irving, R., *Adenauer*, London: Longman, 2002.

Jahrausch, K.H., *Deutsche Studenten 1800–1970*, Frankfurt am Main: Suhrkamp, 1984.

Jamison, A. and Eyerman, R., *Seeds of the Sixties*, Berkeley: University of California Press, 1994.

Juchler, I., *Die Studentenbewegung in den Vereinigten Staaten und der Bundesrepublik Deutschland der sechziger Jahre: Eine Untersuchung hinsichtlich ihrer Beeinflussung durch Befreiungsbewegungen und theorien aus der Dritten Welt*, Berlin: Dunker and Humbolt, 1996.

Junker, D. (ed.), *Die USA und Deutschland im Zeitalter des Kalten Krieges 1945–1990: Ein Handbuch*, 2 vols, Stuttgart and Munich: Deutsche Verlags-Anstalt, 2001.

Katsiaficas, G., *The Imagination of the New Left: A Global Analysis of 1968*, Boston, MA: South End Press, 1987.

Kiesinger, K.G., *Die Große Koalition 1966–1969: Reden und Erklärungen des Bundeskanzlers*, Dieter Oberndörfer (ed.), Stuttgart: Deutsche Verlags-Anstalt, 1979.

Klarsfeld, B., *Die Geschichte des PG 2633930: Kiesinger*, Darmstadt: Joseph Melzer Verlag, 1969.

Klemperer, V., *I Shall Bear Witness: The Diaries of Victor Klemperer 1933–1941*, translated by Martin Chalmers, London: Phoenix, 1999.

Klemperer, V., *To the Bitter End: The Diaries of Victor Klemperer 1942–1945*, translated by Martin Chalmers, London: Phoenix, 2000.

Kleßmann, C., *Zwei Staaten, eine Nation: Deutsche Geschichte 1955–1970*, Göttingen: Vandenhoeck and Ruprecht, 1988.

Kolinsky, E., *Parties, Opposition and Society in West Germany*, London: Croom Helm, 1984.

Kolinsky, E. (ed.), *The Greens in West Germany: Organisation and Policy Making*, Oxford: Berg, 1989.

Kolinsky, E., *Women in West Germany: Life, Work and Politics*, Oxford: Berg, 1989.

Korte, H., *Eine Gesellschaft im Aufbruch: Die Bundesrepublik in den sechziger Jahren*, Frankfurt am Main: Suhrkamp, 1987.

Kramer, A., *The West German Economy, 1945–1955*, Oxford: Berg, 1991.

Kraushaar, W., *1968: Das Jahr, das alles verändert hat*, Munich: Piper, 1998.

Kraushaar, W., *1968 als Mythos, Chiffre und Zäsur*, Hamburg: Hamburger Edition, 2000.

Kraushaar, W. (ed.), *Frankfurter Schule und Studentenbewegung: von der Flaschenpost zum Molotowcocktail 1946–1995*, Hamburg: Rogner and Bernhard bei zweitausendeins, 1998. Three volumes: *Chronik* (1), *Dokumente* (2), *Aufsätze und Kommentare, Register* (3).

Krebs, M., *Ulrike Meinhof: Ein Leben im Widerspruch*, Reinbek: Rowohlt, 1988.

Küntzel, M., *Bonn and the Bomb: German Politics and the Nuclear Option*, London: Pluto Press, 1995.

Landgrebe, C. and Plath, J. (eds), *'68 und die Folgen: Ein unvollständiges Lexikon*, Berlin: Argon, 1998.

Langguth, G., *Die Protestbewegung: Entwicklung, Niedergang, Renaissance: Die Neue Linke seit 1968*, Cologne: Verlag Wissenschaft und Politik, 1983.

Lebert, S., *My Father's Keeper: The Children of the Nazi Leaders – An Intimate History of Damage and Denial*, London: Little, Brown and Company, 2001.

Lees, C., *The Red-Green Coalition in Germany: Politics, Personalities and Power*, Manchester: Manchester University Press, 2000.

Linhoff, U., *Die Neue Frauenbewegung: USA-Europa seit 1968*, Cologne: Kiepenhauer und Witsch, 1974.

Maase, K., *Bravo Amerika: Erkundigungen zur Jugendkultur der Bundesrepublik in den fünfziger Jahren*, Hamburg: Junius, 1992.

Maier, C.S. (ed.), *The Marshall Plan and Germany: West German Development within the Framework of the European Recovery Program*, Oxford: Berg, 1991.

Major, P., *The Death of the KPD: Communism and Anti-Communism in West Germany, 1945–1956*, Oxford: Clarendon Press, 1997.

Marcuse, H., *One-Dimensional Man: Studies in the Ideology of Advanced Industrial Society*, London: Routledge, 1991, first published 1964.

Markovits, A.S., *The Politics of the West German Trade Unions: Strategies of Class and Interest Representation in Growth and Crisis*, Cambridge: Cambridge University Press, 1986.

Markovits, A.S. and Gorski, P.S., *The German Left: Red, Green and Beyond*, Cambridge: Polity Press, 1993.

Marwick, A., *The Sixties: Cultural Revolution in Britain, France, Italy and the United States, c.1958–c.1974*, Oxford: Oxford University Press, 1998.

Merritt, R.L., *Democracy Imposed: U.S. Occupation Policy and the German Public, 1945–1949*, New Haven: Yale University Press, 1995.

Moeller, R.G., *Protecting Motherhood: Women and the Family in the Politics of Postwar West Germany*, Berkeley, University of California Press, 1993.

Mosler, P., *Was wir wollten, was wir wurden: Studentenrevolte zehn Jahre danach*, Hamburg: Rowohlt, 1977.

Nave-Herz, R., *Wandel und Kontinuität der Familie in der Bundesrepublik Deutschland*, Stuttgart: Ferdinand Enke Verlag, 1988.

Nave-Herz, R., *Die Geschichte der Frauenbewegung in Deutschland*, Hanover: Niedersächsischen Landeszentrale für politische Bildung, 1989.

Negt, O., *Achtundsechzig: Politische Intellektuelle und die Macht*, Göttingen: Steidl, 1995.

Noelle-Neumann, E. (ed.), *The Germans: Public Opinion Polls, 1967–1980*, Westport, Conn.: Greenwood Press, 1981.

Oppen, R.G. von (ed.), *Documents on Germany under Occupation 1945–1954*, London: Royal Institute for Foreign Affairs, 1955.

Otto, K.A., *Die außerparlamentarische Opposition in Quellen und Dokumenten 1960–1970*, Cologne: Pahl-Rugenstein, 1989.

Parness, D.L., *The SPD and the Challenge of Mass Politics: The Dilemma of the German Volkspartei*, Boulder, Colorado: Westview Press, 1991.

Peters, B., *RAF: Terrorismus in Deutschland*, Munich: Knaur, 1993.

Poiger, U.G., 'Rock n'Roll, Female Sexuality, and the Cold War Battle over German Identities', *Journal of Modern History*, 68 (September 1996), pp. 577–616.

Pommerin, R. (ed.), *The American Impact on Postwar Germany*, Oxford: Berghahn Books, 1995.

Preuss-Lausitz, U., *Kriegskinder, Konsumkinder, Krisenkinder*, Weinheim: Beltz Verlag, 1983.

Pritchard, R.M.O., *The End of Elitism? The Democratisation of the West German University System*, Oxford: Berg, 1990.

Prittie, T., *Konrad Adenauer, 1976–1967*, London: Tom Stacey, 1972.

Pulzer, P., *German Politics 1945–1995*, Oxford: Oxford University Press, 1995.

Rabehl, B., *Am Ende der Utopie: Die politische Geschichte der Freien Universität Berlin*, Berlin: Argon, 1988.

Reeve, S., *One Day in September: The Story of the 1972 Munich Olympics Massacre*, London: Faber & Faber, 2000.

Rolke, L., *Protestbewegung in der Bundesrepublik*, Opdalen: Westdeutscher Verlag, 1987.

Rollin, R. (ed.), *The Americanization of the Global Village*, Bowling Green, Ohio: Popular Press, 1989.

Roseman, M., *Generations in Revolt: Youth Revolt and Generation Formation in Germany 1770–1968*, Cambridge: Cambridge University Press, 1995.

Rote Armee Fraktion: Texte und Materialien zur Geschichte der RAF, Berlin: ID-Verlag, 1997.

Ruhl, K.J. (ed.), *Neubeginn und Restoration: Dokumente zur Vorgeschichte der Bundesrepublik Deutschland 1945–1949*, Munich: Deutscher Taschenbuchverlag, 1982.

Ruhl, K.J. (ed.), *Frauen in der Nachkriegszeit, 1945–1963*, Munich: Deutscher Taschenbuchverlag, 1988)

Rupp, H.K., *Außerparlamentarische Opposition in der Ära Adenauer: Der Kampf gegen die Atombewaffnung in den fünfziger Jahren: Eine Studie der innenpolitischen Entwicklung der BRD*, Cologne: Pahl-Rugenstein, 1984.

Ruppert, W. (ed.), *Um 1968: Die Repräsentation der Dinge*, Marburg: Jonas Verlag, 1998.

Schelsky, H., *Die skeptische Generation: Eine Soziologie der deutschen Jugend*, 4th edn, Düsseldorf: Ullstein, 1960.

Schenk, D., *Der Chef: Horst Herold und das BKA*, Munich: Goldmann Verlag, 2000.

Schildt, A., *Moderne Zeiten: Freizeit, massen Medien und 'Zeitgeist' in der Bundesrepublik der 50er Jahre*, Hamburg: Hans Christians Verlag, 1995.

Schildt, A. and Sywottek, A. (eds), *Modernisierung im Wiederaufbau: Die Westdeutsche Gesellschaft der 50er Jahre*, Bonn: Verlag J.H.W. Dietz Nachf, 1993.

Schröder, G., *Wir brauchen eine heile Welt: Politik in und für Deutschland*, Düsseldorf: Econ-Verlag, 1963.

Schuster, J., *Heinrich Albertz: Der Mann, der mehrere Leben lebte: Eine Biographie*, Berlin: Alexander Fest Verlag, 1997.

Seton-Watson, H., *The Imperialist Revolutionaries: Trends in World Communism in the 1960s and 1970s*, Stanford, CA: Hoover Institution Press, Stanford University, 1978.

Shandley, R.R. (ed.), *Unwilling Germans? The Goldhagen Debate*, Minneapolis: University of Minnesota Press, 1998.

Sicharovsky, P., *Born Guilty: Children of Nazi Families*, London: I.B. Tauris, 1988.

Statistisches Bundesamt Wiesbaden (ed.), *Statistisches Jahrbuch für die Bundesrepublik Deutschland, 1953*, Stuttgart-Köln: W. Kohlhammer Verlag, 1953.

Statistisches Bundesamt Wiesbaden (ed.), *Statistisches Jahrbuch für die Bundesrepublik Deutschland, 1960*, Stuttgart and Mainz: W. Kohlhammer Verlag, 1960.

Statistisches Bundesamt Wiesbaden (ed.), *Statistisches Jahrbuch für die Bundesrepublik Deutschland, 1969*, Stuttgart and Mainz: W. Kohlhammer Verlag, 1969.

Stiftung für die Rechte zukünftiger Generationen (ed.), *Die 68er: Warum wir Jungen sie nicht mehr brauchen*, Freiburg: Kore, 1998.

Tent, J., *The Free University of Berlin: A Political History*, Bloomington and Indianapolis: Indiana University Press, 1988.

Teschke, J.P., *Hitler's Legacy: West Germany Confronts the Aftermath of the Third Reich*, New York: Peter Lang, 1999.

Thurnwald, H., *Gegenwartsprobleme Berliner Familien: Eine Soziologische Untersuchung an 498 Familien*, Berlin: Wiedmannsche Verlagbuchhandlung, 1948.

Turner, I.D. (ed.), *Reconstruction in Post-war Germany: British Occupation Policy in the Western Zones, 1945–55*, Oxford: Berg, 1989.

Uesseler, R., *Die 68er: "Macht kaputt, was Euch kaputt macht!": APO, Marx und freie Liebe*, Munich: Wilhelm Heyne Verlag, 1998.

Voigt, L., *Aktivismus und moralischer Rigorismus: Die politische Romantik der 68er Studentenbewegung*, Wiesbaden: Deutscher Universitätz Verlag, 1991.

Wallerstein, I., '1968, Revolution in the World System: Theses and Queries', *Theory and Society*, No. 18, July 1989.

Watts, M.W., Fischer, A., Fuchs, W. and Zinnecker, J., *Contemporary German Youth and their Elders: A Generational Comparison*, New York and London: Greenwood Press, 1989.

Weinreich, M., *Hitler's Professors: The Part of Scholarship in Germany's Crimes Against the Jewish People*, New Haven: Yale University Press, 1999, first published 1946.

Westernhagen, D. von, *Die Kinder der Täter: Das dritte Reich und die Generation danach*, Munich: Kösel, 1987.

Wiesen, S.J., *West German Industry and the Challenge of the Nazi Past, 1945–1955*, Chapel Hill: University of North Carolina Press, 2001.

Williams, C., *Adenauer: Father of the New Germany*, London: Little, Brown and Company, 2000.

Willett, R., *The Americanization of Germany 1945–1949*, London: Routledge, 1989.

Wolfschlag, C.M. (ed.), *Bye-bye '68 . . . Renegaten der Linken APO-Abweichler und allerlei Querdenker berichten*, Graz: Leopold Stocker Verlag, 1998.

Zinnecker, J., *Jugendkultur 1940–1985*, Opdalen: Leske und Budrich, 1989.

Index

Index

Index

Index

Index

Index

Index

Index

Index

Teufel, Fritz
Bewegung 2. Juni and, 191
Dutschke shooting, 173
Flyer trial, 103–4, 183–4, 189–90
FU Berlin, declared *Rektor* of, 139
Gedächtniskirche protest, 189
Kommune I philosophy, 98–9
later career, 191
Pudding Bomben Attentat, 65, 99–100,
186, 188–9
Rathaus Schöneberg go-in, 187
SDS and, 98, 103–4, 187
Schütz disruption, 189
stone-throwing trial, 184–189
protests against, 186, 189
Thadden, Adolf von, 97
Thatcher, Margaret (1925–), 20
Thurnwald, Hilda, 14, 27–28
Titze, Wolfgang, 96
trade unions
protests, 65
collective bargaining, 25
Emergency Laws, 87–92
Ohnesorg shooting, 117
re-armament policy, attitudes to, 33, 35
Vietnam War and, 70
Tschombe, Moise (1919–69)
demonstrations against, 93–4
Tübingen
RAF arrests, 211
University, 196
Turin University, 135
Turner, Ian, 21

Ulbricht, Walter (1893–1973, SED), 76,
76fn20, 80, 114, 148, 170
Ulm, 113
United States of America
cultural influence, 17, 18n25, 159,
161–3, 204, 211–2
protests in, 16, 56, 78, 204
sexual revolution, 101–2
terrorist attacks on, 208–10
see also Vietnam War
universities
former Nazis in, 51–2, 132–34, 143
funding for, 144
staff numbers, 144
student numbers, 144

university reform 8, 16, 49–68 passim,
127–145 passim
Aktion 1. Juli, 54–5
Allied policy, 51–2
Fachidioten issue, 64–5, 129–30, 134
Federal reforms, 142–4
Free University (FU) Berlin, 52–68
see Free University (FU) Berlin
Nazi policy, 50–1
one-third parity, 128, 138, 144
SDS, 56–67, passim, 127–145 passim
social role of universities, 49–51, 85,
129–130
see also universities

Van der Will, Wilfred, 4
Vehof, Udo, 96
Verband Deutscher Studentenschaften
(VDS), 54–5, 63, 116
Vietnam War
campaign against, 69–85 passim,
147–163 passim
Berlin International Vietnam
Conference156–60
FU Berlin, 58, 71, 77–81, 84–5
international campaign, 16–17, 78,
148, 155–160
International News and Research
Institute (INFI), 158
Kommune I, 98–100, 103–4
My Lai massacre, 161–2
peace movement and, 69–71, 75–7,
83, 148
SDS and, 58, 61, 71–4, 76–85
passim, 148–50, 154–61
terrorism and, 162–3, 202–4, 208– 211
United States and, 69, 157, 161
Vietnam – Analyse eines Exempels
conference, Frankfurt 76
Geneva Agreements, 70–1, 73
public opinion and, 69–70
violence, link to, 69, 85, 147, 154–7,
161–3
violence
against protesters, 75, 109–10, 154–5,
159–60
debate about use of, 128, 130–1, 136,
140–2, 147–59, 163, 178–80,
184–91, 196

Index

link to Vietnam, 69, 85, 147, 154–7,
  161–3
police, 16, 32, 40–42, 45, 66, 78–82,
  94–6, 110–123 passim, 132, 138–9,
  141–2, 147–9, 155–7, 170–76
protesters, 73–4, 78, 82–3, 110–11,
  128, 136–8, 142, 152, 154–5, 159,
  167–8, 170–76, 184–93
  see also Dutschke, Rudi
  see also Meinhof, Ulrike
  see also terrorism
Vogel, Hans-Jochen (1926–, SPD), 42

Wallerstein, Immanuel, 16
Washington, DC, 148
Watts, Meredith W, 244–5
Weimar republic
  democracy and, 2, 24
Weisbecker, Thomas
  shooting of, 208
  Kommando Thomas Weisbecker, 209
Wegener, Ulrich, 217–8
Wehrmacht exhibition, 247
Wenke, Hans, 52, 133
Werner, Frank, 194
Werner, Hans-Ulrich, 191–2
Wessel, Ulrich, 215
Westdeutscher Rektorenkonferenz (WRK),
  129
Wetter, Reinhard, 133–4
Wilhelmer, Bernhard, 66
Williams, Charles, 24
Wirtschaftswunder
  see economy
Wolff, Karl-Dietrich

Emergency Laws, 195
International Vietnam conference,
  158
Women
  abortion reform campaign, 221, 232–6
  Aktionsrat zur Befreiung der Frauen
    creation, 228–30
    child care, 228, 232
    SDS and, 228–31
  Bundesfrauenkongreß, 235
  CDU family policy, 222–5
    Basic Law and, 223–4
    Kindergeld, 224
    Ministry of Family Affairs, 222–5
    Mutterschutzgesetz, 224
  contraception, 101, 221, 227, 232–3,
    237
  impact of the Second World War, 13
  income, 225, 236
  revolutionary politics and, 203,
    226–32, 235
  sexual revolution and, 100–2, 226–8
  single mothers, 237
  women's work, attitudes to, 225
  see also sex
Woodstock, 20
Wuermeling, Franz-Josef, 222–3
Würzburg University, 196

Yippies, 99
youth culture
  development, 18–19
  see also Halbstarke

Ziebura, Professor Gilbert, 57